Ethics out of Economics

Many economic problems are also ethical problems: should we value equality? How much should we care about preserving the environment? How should medical resources be divided between saving life and enhancing life? It also turns out that many of the formal techniques of economics can do important work in ethical theory. In particular, utility theory can help analyse the structure of good. *Ethics out of Economics* examines some of the theoretical and practical issues that lie between economics and ethics, and especially aims to show how utility theory can contribute to ethics.

John Broome's work has, unusually, combined sophisticated economic and philosophical expertise, and *Ethics out of Economics* brings together some of his most important essays, augmented with a new introduction. The first group of essays deals with the relation between preference and value, the second with various questions about the formal structure of good, and the concluding section with the value of life. This work is of interest and importance for both economists and philosophers, and shows powerfully how economic methods can contribute to moral philosophy.

JOHN BROOME is Professor of Philosophy at the University of St Andrews and was previously Professor of Economics at the University of Bristol. He edits the journal *Economics and Philosophy*, and has contributed to many books and journals. His publications include *The Microeconomics of Capitalism* (Academic Press, 1984), *Weighing Goods: Equality, Uncertainty and Time* (Blackwell, 1991), and *Counting the Cost of Global Warming* (White Horse Press, 1992).

Ethics out of Economics

John Broome

CAMBRIDGE
UNIVERSITY PRESS

PUBLISHED BY THE PRESS SYNDICATE OF THE UNIVERSITY OF CAMBRIDGE
The Pitt Building, Trumpington Street, Cambridge CB2 1RP, United Kingdom

CAMBRIDGE UNIVERSITY PRESS
The Edinburgh Building, Cambridge CB2 2RU, United Kingdom
   http://www.cup.cam.ac.uk
40 West 20th Street, New York, NY 10011-4211, USA   http://www.cup.org
10 Stamford Road, Oakleigh, Melbourne 3166, Australia

First published 1999

Typeset in Times NR 10/12 pt   [SE]

A catalogue record for this book is available from the British Library

Library of Congress cataloguing in publication data

Broome, John.
     Ethics out of economics / by John Broome.
          p.   cm.
     Includes bibliographical references and index.
     ISBN 0 521 64275 2 (hardback). – ISBN 0 521 64491 7 (paperback)
     1. Economics–Morals and ethical aspects.   I. Title.
     HB72.B758   1999
     330–dc21   98–35992 CIP

ISBN 0 521 64275 2 hardback
ISBN 0 521 64491 7 paperback

Transferred to digital printing 2003

Contents

Preface

One brief paper in this collection dates from long ago, but the rest were all first published in the 1990s. Most of my earlier writings in economics and ethics formed part of the long development of my book *Weighing Goods*, and whatever truth I thought they contained was eventually incorporated into the book. *Weighing Goods* offered an account of the structure of good, but it left many questions unanswered. One is the question of the value of life: the value of extending a person's life and the value of creating a new life. How do these fit into the structure of good? How, too, do incommensurable values fit into this structure? What about the value of future goods? Most of this present book represents my work towards answering these and other questions about the structure of good that I previously left unanswered.

I have always known how useful the techniques of economists can be in ethical theory, but recent years have taught me how important it is to propagate this message amongst philosophers. This book is part of my campaign of propagation. I hope economists will find it useful too, since it deals with practical and theoretical topics that concern them as well as philosophers. Some of the papers collected here were originally published in philosophers' books and journals, others in economists' journals. Inevitably, the economists' papers take for granted some terminology and assumptions that philosophers may find puzzling, and the philosophers' papers may raise some similar puzzles for economists. But I hope these difficulties will not be so severe as to prevent anyone from understanding the arguments, except perhaps in one or two of the more technical papers. I have lightly edited most of the papers, and cut sections out of a few.

I have benefited immensely from the help of my academic friends over the years. Each paper in this volume includes its own acknowledgements, but some people's contributions have been wider, and are insufficiently recorded in the individual papers. The work of Richard Jeffrey, Derek Parfit, and Amartya Sen has had a much greater influence on my writing than is recognized in the separate references. Many other people have given me the stimulus and encouragement that is needed in this rather lonely

territory between economics and philosophy. Indeed, now I think back, I
realize how many good colleagues there have been, and that the territory is
not so lonely at all. I cannot possibly list them all, but I do want to mention
Geoff Brennan, Ruth Chang, David Donaldson, James Griffin, Brad
Hooker, Doug MacLean, Philippe Mongin, Adam Morton, Philip Pettit,
Maurice Salles, John Skorupski, Larry Temkin, and Peter Vallentyne.

I also owe debts of gratitude to several institutions. Nearly all these
papers were written while I was employed at the University of Bristol,
where my colleagues in both the Philosophy and Economics Departments
were generous and tolerant towards my idiosyncratic interests, and patient
with my absences. The same goes for my colleagues in the University of St
Andrews, where I now work. The UK Economic and Social Research
Council financed my work on the value of life for a year; some of the resulting writings appear in this volume. I wrote several of the included papers
while visiting the Centre for Applied Ethics at the University of British
Columbia and the Research School of Social Sciences at the Australian
National University. Finally, I put the volume together while I was a visitor
at the Collegium for Advanced Study in the Social Sciences at the
University of Uppsala. I am very grateful to these institutions for their generous financial support and their kind hospitality.

1 Introduction: ethics out of economics

1.1 Economics and ethics

The traffic between economics and ethics travels in both directions. Each discipline can learn from the other. Economics is partly concerned with assessing the merits of economic arrangements, and with deciding how governments ought to conduct their economic affairs. It makes judgements of right and wrong, good and bad, in economic matters. It needs criteria for making these judgements, and the criteria must come from ethics. On the other hand, economists have developed for their own purposes sophisticated methods of analysis that turn out to be useful in philosophical ethics. They can help not only with questions of practical ethics, but also with fundamental issues in ethical theory.

This book concentrates on just one of the areas where the methods of economics can contribute to ethics. It is about those problems in ethics that require us to balance different interests or concerns against each other. For example, we have to balance the interests of future people against the interests of presently living people, fun in retirement against fun in youth, the wellbeing of the deprived against the wellbeing of the successful or lucky, the value of prolonging people's lives against the value of making people's lives better while they last. Many of these are problems of large-scale or public morality – problems for politics and the institutions of society. Weighing the prolonging of lives against the improving of lives is a pressing issue for the health service, for instance. How should the health service value hip replacements, which improve lives, compared with heart replacements, which prolong them? What importance should it give to palliative care, which does nothing to prolong lives, and may even shorten them? Other questions of weighing are problems for individuals rather than the public. Individual patients and their doctors sometimes have to choose between different treatments for a terminal disease: between treatments that will prolong life and treatments that will make life better while it lasts. All of us wonder whether to give up some of the nice things we eat for the

This chapter is an edited version of my inaugural lecture, delivered at the University of Bristol in February 1995.

1

sake of living longer. In planning our lives, we all have to weigh good things in the future against good things now. Many of us have to weigh our own interests against those of others, such as our parents. Weighing and balancing are regular features of all our lives.

Many practical problems of weighing fall within the domain of both economists and philosophers. Economists are particularly concerned with some of the large-scale problems I mentioned. These are places where the scarcity of resources forces a society to weigh up alternative possible uses for these resources, and economics claims to be the science of scarcity. Indeed, there is no sharp division between economics and ethics in this area. Economists pursuing fundamental issues in welfare economics and philosophers pursuing practical issues in ethics have found themselves working on the same questions: is equality valuable?; how much should we care about the wellbeing of future people?; what value should we assign to preserving nature, or to human life?; and many others. Several of the chapters in this book lie in this borderline territory where practical questions of economics and ethics meet.

Others are concerned with more fundamental, theoretical issues involving weighing. From a theoretical point of view, problems of weighing are best handled within the department of ethics known as the theory of good or the theory of value. This is the department that is concerned, first, with what is good for individual people and, secondly, with what is good in general. Questions of weighing are questions about how different goods – for instance, goods coming at different times in a life or to different people – come together to determine how good a life is overall, or how good a society is. As I put it, they are questions about the structure of good.

The techniques of economics can help with understanding the structure of good. They can help to analyse the value of a life: whether a shorter exciting life is better than a longer boring one, for instance. They can help with the question of whether a more equal society is better than a less equal one, and so on. For its own purposes, economics has developed sophisticated formal theories that are intended to analyse the structure of people's preferences. It happens that these theories can be turned to analysing the structure of good. This is something ethics can take out of economics.

Ideas from economics have influenced the theory of good for a long time. Historically, there has been a long association between economists and utilitarian moral philosophers, and utilitarians have a particular interest in the nature and structure of good. Unfortunately, though, what moral philosophers have recently drawn out of economics in this area has generally been the wrong thing. I said the formal methods of economics can help analyse the structure of good. But when philosophers have adopted something from economics, it has often been the substance rather than the form. Implicit in economics, apart from the formal techniques, there is also a substantive theory of good. Few philosophers have taken over this theory wholeheartedly, but it often makes an appearance in ethical arguments. It is a mistaken theory, though. It is a pity it has penetrated ethics at all. In this introductory chapter, I shall argue that what ethics should take out of economics, at least in the area of the theory of good, is form and not substance. The substance should be left alone. Then I shall mention two examples of the useful formal lessons that ethics can learn from economics.

The arguments in this introduction will be brief, because many of them are taken up in more detail in later chapters.

1.2   The preference-satisfaction theory

What is this substantive theory implicit in economics? It is not a complete theory of good, but only a theory about what is good for a person. It is specifically:

> *Preference-satisfaction theory of good.* One thing A is better for a person than another thing B if and only if the person prefers A to B.

(Actually, this biconditional does not express the preference-satisfaction theory completely. The theory also requires the determination to go from right to left: when a person prefers A to B, that makes it the case that A is better for her than B.)

Before assessing this theory, I must say something about the meanings of the terms 'better for' and 'prefer'. In common usage, the expressions 'good for you' and 'better for you' sometimes carry a narrow connotation of prudence. Exercise is said to be good for you even if you hate it, because it will bring benefits in the future. Having mere fun may not count as good for you in this prudential sense. This sense would rule out the preference-satisfaction theory immediately, because people often prefer things just because they are fun or nice, even though they bring no long-term benefit. But I am using the expressions 'good for' and 'better for' more broadly to include anything that is worth your having. So fun is good for you just because it is good in itself, even if it does not lead to good things in the future. Your psychological makeup including your tastes helps to determine what is good for you in this broader sense, so it gives the preference-satisfaction theory a better chance. If you like kayaking more than mountain climbing – perhaps kayaking thrills you more than mountain climbing – then kayaking is better for you than mountain climbing. This broad sense of 'is better for' means the same as 'is more in your interest' or 'makes you better off'. When I say A is better for a person than B, I mean the person is better off with *A* than with *B*. Having *A* rather than *B* would benefit her; it would improve her wellbeing.

Next the term 'prefers'. Preference is a slippery notion, and I cannot consider all its possible senses. Simply in order to make progress, I shall settle on a definition of 'prefer' that often appears in economics books:[1]

> *Dispositional definition of preference.* 'A person prefers *A* to *B*' means the person would choose *A* rather than *B* if she were to have a choice between *A* and *B*.

This definition will certainly need some fixing. It will do for donkeys, but not for people. Jean Buridan tells us that if you stand a donkey exactly halfway between two equally delicious bales of hay, so that it is perfectly indifferent between them, it cannot decide which way to go. It will hesitate till it dies. But such extreme procrastination has never been seen in a person. When a person has a choice between two options, and she is perfectly indifferent between them, she chooses one or the other. According to this definition, then, she prefers one or the other. But that is not so; she is indifferent. So the definition definitely needs fixing to allow for indifference. This is not an important problem, though; the fixing can certainly be done. So let us adopt the dispositional definition of preference, subject to fixing.

After those explanatory remarks, let us go back to the substance of the preference-satisfaction theory of good. This theory is implicit in much of welfare economics. Welfare economists move, almost without noticing it, between saying a person prefers one thing to another and saying she is better off with the first than with the second. All the same, the preference-satisfaction theory is obviously false, and no one really believes it. It is obviously false because people often make mistakes and act on bad information. I brush my teeth thoroughly twice a day, thereby making it true, according to the dispositional definition, that I prefer brushing my teeth thoroughly to giving them a quick swish over. My reason is that I believe thorough brushing promotes my dental health. However, extraordinarily, my dentist has recently been hinting that I ought not to brush my teeth so thoroughly, because it wears them out. If he is right, thorough brushing, which I prefer to a quick swish, is worse for me than a quick swish.

So anyone who is attracted to the preference-satisfaction theory is really attracted to some more sophisticated version such as:

> *Ideal-preference-satisfaction theory of good.* One thing *A* is better for a person than another *B* if and only if the person would prefer *A* to *B* were she in ideal conditions.

'Ideal conditions' include being well informed, and most people also include being in a rational frame of mind. Undoubtedly, this theory is nearer the truth than the unidealized version. Still, there are many objections to it, too. They have been thoroughly rehearsed by many authors, and I shall not dwell on them here.

I shall not dwell on the faults of the theory, but on its attractions. People, particularly economists, have been drawn to it for various reasons, and some of them are good ones. But the appeal of these reasons has been misdirected. They may give grounds for many of the conclusions welfare economists have drawn from them. For instance, they may give support to economic competition in particular circumstances. But they do not support the preference-satisfaction theory of good. My hope is that, once you see the good reasons that lead elsewhere, you will no longer be attracted by this theory.

1.3   Liberalism versus a theory of good

The good reasons I am thinking of are liberal ones. Economists are typically liberal, and typically they believe people should be left alone to manage their own lives. They should make their own choices about private things, and society should be democratically organized to put into effect the people's choices about public things. These are nice ideas, but they do not lead to the preference-satisfaction theory of good. They lead to conclusions about the structure of society, and what should happen in society, not to any theory of good. I want to draw out this point by means of an example.[2]

A river runs through a fertile valley. Over the years, the forests upstream have been cleared and the dikes containing the river have been built higher and higher. By now, everyone knows that within the next few years the Great Flood will come. The river will breach the dikes. It may go left and destroy one side of the valley, bringing ruin to the farmers there. Or it may go right, and ruin the farmers on that side. (There are equal numbers on each side.) However, the surviving farmers will be relieved of competition from their colleagues, and grow rich. The government is wondering whether to do some expensive engineering works that will definitely prevent the flood. If it does these works, the farmers will be taxed to pay for them. Is it better to do them or not?

If the works are done, all the farmers in the valley will continue to live in modest prosperity, paying the tax for the engineering. If the works are not done, half the farmers will be ruined, but the remainder will rise to luxury, spared from competition and paying no tax. So the choice is between, on the one hand, a state of equality where everyone is modestly prosperous and, on the other, a state of inequality where half the people are ruined and the others are rich. The options are shown in table 1.1. Please adjust the

Table 1.1

	River would go left	River would go right		River would go left	River would go right
Left-side farmers	Prosperity	Prosperity	Left-side farmers	Ruin	Great wealth
Right-side farmers	Prosperity	Prosperity	Right-side farmers	Great wealth	Ruin

Build flood-control works   Do not build flood-control works

conditions in your mind till you are sure the first alternative is better than the second. Make the state of ruin as dire and the state of modest prosperity as comfortable as they need to be in order to bring you to this conclusion.

Next imagine the farmers are optimists. They all know there will be a flood and that half the farms will be wiped out. But each one thinks it will probably be the ones on the other side of the valley who will be caught. Each farmer assigns a high probability to her own survival, then. This implies the farmers disagree about probabilities. Left-side farmers think the river will probably go right; right-side farmers think it will probably go left. Still, though they disagree, it does not follow that any of the farmers is irrational or ill informed, and indeed I assume they are not. Which dike the river breaches will depend on a complex conjunction of circumstances. Has the heavy construction in this town weakened the dikes? Is the river too tightly squeezed around that bend? The Great Flood is a one-of-a-kind event, and there is no objectively correct probability of the river's going one way or the other. Since each farmer is an optimist, she started by assigning a high prior probability to her own survival. She has taken account of all the information that has become available, and correctly updated her probabilities by applying Bayes's Rule. After that, she still assigns a high posterior probability to her own survival.

What are the farmers' preferences about the flood control works? If the works are done, each farmer will live in modest prosperity. She compares that outlook with her expectation of how things will go for her if the works are not done. If they are not, she will end up either ruined or rich. Please assume she is optimistic enough to prefer the risky option of not doing the works. She thinks riches are sufficiently likely and ruin sufficiently unlikely that she has this preference. So every farmer will prefer not to have the works done. Previously, I asked you to adjust your idea of the conditions till you were sure it was better to do the flood control works. So the situation is that the people are unanimously in favour of the worse option. Disagreement about probabilities has led to the result that everyone prefers the option that is worse.

What should happen? Since everyone is against them, I am inclined to think the works should not be done. This is presumably what democracy says; unanimous opinion determines what ought to be done. I insisted that doing the works is better than not doing them, so what ought to be done is the worse of the two alternatives. This may sound odd, but there is no contradiction in it. Indeed, if you believe in democracy, you are inevitably committed to believing, sometimes, that what ought to come about is not the best of the alternatives available. When a public decision is to be made, you will evaluate the options on offer, and form a belief about which is the best. At the same time, you may well believe the majority favours another option, and as a democrat you will therefore believe the other option is the one that should come about. So you will believe that what should come about is not the best option. Therefore, unless it is wrong to support democracy, there cannot be any contradiction in this.

When I described the farmers' unanimous preferences, you might have been tempted to go back and revise your view about the goodness of the options. But now you can see you have no need to do that. The preferences determine what ought to be done, but that is a different matter from what is best.

One thing that certainly cannot be true is that the option of not doing the works is better *for everyone* than doing them. It cannot be true, even though everyone prefers that option. Not doing the works will be better for the left-side farmers only if the river is likely to go right, but if the river is likely to go right, then it would be better for the right-side farmers to do the works.

You might think this argument presumes there is an objective probability that the river goes right. But that is not so; I am taking for granted there is no such thing. The basis of my argument is that any statement about goodness in an uncertain situation like this must be made relative to some probabilities. When I make such a statement, I am committing myself to some probability assessment of my own. I can say it is better for the left-side farmers not to do the works only if, like those farmers, I assign a high probability to the river's going right. I cannot then say it is better for the right-side farmers not to do the works. Even though the right-side farmers assign a low probability to the river's going right, I assign a high probability to it, so I must say it is better for them to do the works.

In practice, people differ in their judgements of the probability of many events, and their preferences will be based on their differing probabilities. But when we assess what is good for people, we must do so relative to some probabilities of our own. Therefore, what is good for people cannot always coincide with their preferences. This is one reason why the preference-satisfaction theory is false.

It constitutes an arcane and rather uninteresting objection to the theory. As I said, my intention was not to produce objections but to try and identify the theory's attraction. The attraction is liberalism and democracy. Correctly understood, however, liberalism and democracy lead to conclusions about what should happen in society, based on people's preferences. They do not imply any theory of good. This example shows we need to separate our account of what is good from our account of what should come about. I think there is a pervasive confusion in economics between what is good and what should come about for other reasons besides good. When an economist favours some economic policy, she needs to decide whether she favours it because it is the best policy, or because it is the liberal or the democratic thing to do.

Why does it matter? Why should economists not simply concern themselves with democratic processes and with preferences, and forget about good and bad altogether? Well, perhaps economics could go that way. It would require some changes in the theoretical structure of welfare economics, but I am not concerned here with what economics should do. I am concerned with what ethics should do. Ethics certainly needs a theory of good, whether economics needs one or not, and all I have said so far is that it should not be tempted to adopt the preference-satisfaction theory from economists. That is a bad theory.

1.4   The formal techniques

But it should adopt some of the formal techniques of economics. Economic theory provides formal structures that correspond closely to the structure of good, and can be used to analyse the structure of good. I am thinking of the core theory of economics: 'preference theory' it is sometimes called, or 'consumer theory', or 'utility theory', or 'expected utility theory'. It is a theory that was originally designed as an account of the structure of a person's preferences. The basic primitive notion of the theory is a preference, which is a two-place relation

>*Preference relation.* The person prefers __ to __.

The blanks are to be filled by things the person has preferences about: the objects of her preferences. The theory makes a number of assumptions – axioms – about the form of this relation. For instance, it assumes it is transitive:

>*Transitivity.* If the person prefers A to B and prefers B to C, she prefers A to C.

The axioms provide the basis for many useful theorems about the structure of preferences. In more elaborate branches of the theory, the objects of preference are assumed to have some structure of their own. For instance, the theory accommodates uncertainty by taking the objects of preference to be 'prospects'. A prospect is a sort of portfolio of possible outcomes; it will lead to different outcomes depending on how the uncertainty resolves itself. This gives the basis for more complex axioms and more informative conclusions.

Formally, the theory is nothing more than the axioms and theorems. It can be reinterpreted by substituting in place of preference any other relation that happens to satisfy the axioms. Take these two relations:

> *Betterness relation for a person.* __ is better for the person than __.
> *General betterness relation.* __ is better than __.

I think each of these betterness relations satisfies the axioms fairly well, though not perfectly. Each probably satisfies them better than people's preferences do in practice. So, provided we are careful, the whole of utility theory is available to provide an analysis of the structure of betterness.

What use is that? I think ethics has a lot to gain from formal analysis. I am going to give two examples of formal features of the structure of good, which it is important for ethics to recognize and understand. These are things that can be learnt from economics.

1.5   Think comparatively

The first is very basic: betterness, like preference, is a *relation*. It relates two things together: one thing is better than another. It is a matter of the comparative value of things. Since economists deal so regularly in preferences, they think naturally in comparative terms, and, when they come to think of good, they will naturally ask not what is good, but what is better than what. Philosophers seem not to have this same instinct to think comparatively.

For instance, although the preference-satisfaction theory of good has made some inroads into philosophical ethics, philosophers more often discuss the *want*-satisfaction theory:

> *Want-satisfaction theory of good. A* is good for a person if and only if the person wants *A*.

This is really a fragment of the preference-satisfaction theory. It is no more true than the preference-satisfaction theory, but a lot more useless. To see its uselessness, let us suppose for a moment it is true. Imagine you meet a thirsty person. She wants water, she wants Coca-Cola, she wants beer, and she has many other wants too. Suppose you know all her wants in great detail. You know she wants half a pint of water; she wants a pint of water; she wants a litre of beer; she does not want Coke and beer together; and so on. Given all that, what should you give her to drink? A pint of water? A half-pint of Coke? Coke and water together? Just from knowing everything she wants, you cannot tell.

To know what to give her, you need to know her *comparative* wants. You need to know what she wants more than what. You need to know her preferences, that is. Her preferences put all the options in an order: a pint of beer above a pint of water, a half-pint of Coke and half-pint of water above a half-pint of beer, and so on. If you know all her preferences, and if we grant for a moment the preference-satisfaction theory, you know what to give her; you should put her as high up her preference order as you can. But knowing just her wants is not enough.

Similarly, if you know only what is good for a person, even if you know everything that is good for her, that is useless. If you know everything that is good generally, that is useless too. You need to know what is better than what. Comparisons are the data you need for ethics. The lesson is: think comparatively. Economists know this instinctively; philosophers seem not to.

I shall give one example of a philosophical discussion that has been sent off the rails by a failure to think comparatively.[3] One of the principal doctrines of the Epicureans was that it does you no harm to die. Epicurus offers two arguments for this surprising claim. They are both in this quotation, but I am only going to discuss the first. He says:

Become accustomed to the belief that death is nothing to us. For all good and evil consists in sensation, but death is deprivation of sensation . . . So death, the most terrifying of ills, is nothing to us, since so long as we exist death is not with us; but when death comes, then we do not exist. It does not then concern either the living or the dead, since for the former it is not, and the latter are no more.[4]

The first argument is this. The only bad things that can afflict you are sensations. But death gives you no bad sensations because it deprives you of all sensations. So it cannot do you any harm.

This argument depends on the premise that 'all good and evil consists in sensation'; the only things good for you or bad for you are good sensations or bad sensations. This is the theory of good known as 'hedonism'. So one way of answering Epicurus' argument is to deny hedonism. That is what Thomas Nagel does in his article 'Death', the most famous recent discussion of the evil of death. Nagel's aim is to show that death is indeed bad for you, and his answer to Epicurus is to say that hedonism is false.

I agree that hedonism is false. But it has a lot of backers, and indeed there is quite a lot going for it. For instance, it is a better theory than one of its rivals, the preference-satisfaction theory of good. So if Nagel can only answer Epicurus' argument by first denying hedonism, he has a challenging task ahead of him, and many people might end up on Epicurus' side. But actually none of this is necessary. Epicurus and Nagel have both gone off on the wrong track because they have failed to think comparatively.

Let us formulate hedonism more precisely. Here is a noncomparative version of it, which is evidently the one Epicurus had in mind:

> *Noncomparative hedonism. A* is good for a person only if it gives her a good sensation, and bad for her only if it gives her a bad sensation.

No hedonist ought to believe this. Suppose I have won a prize in a lottery, but you steal the prize before it reaches me, so I never even know I won. Then you give me no bad sensations; you simply deprive me of good ones. But what you do is certainly bad for me. Here is a much better version of hedonism:

> *Comparative hedonism. A* is better for a person than *B* if and only if *A* gives the person a greater balance of good sensations over bad sensations than *B* does.

From this comparative version it follows immediately that dying is worse for you than continuing to live, provided your life has a preponderance of good sensations over bad ones. Continuing to live will give you good sensations that death deprives you of. Death is bad for you – worse for you than living – precisely because, as Epicurus says, it is deprivation of sensation. So hedonism, properly formulated, actually implies death is bad for you, rather than the opposite.[5] If Epicurus had been trained as an economist, he would never have offered such a poor argument. From the start, he would have seen hedonism in its comparative form.

Epicurus' second argument is much better and more interesting, but I cannot consider it here. It is a pity that Nagel, in giving himself an unnecessarily hard time over the first argument, gave less attention to the second. That is what happens if you fail to think comparatively.

1.6   The value of life

Thinking comparatively is a only a little formal tip that economics can bequeath to ethics. My next illustration of the value of economic methods calls on much more substantial formal theory out of economics. As I said in section 1.1, the techniques of economics come into their own in ethics when we face questions that involve weighing together different interests or concerns. Economic theory is very good at that sort of thing; to a large extent it is what economics is about.

Suppose we accept that death does harm. The question then arises: how much harm? How much harm does dying do you? To put the very same question another way: what is the benefit of continuing to live? What is the value of your life? If your life is threatened and someone saves it, how much good does she do you? This is a matter of comparing the life you will live if you are saved with the alternative of dying immediately. To answer the question in general, we shall have to assess the value of different sorts of lives, so we shall have to rank different lives according to how good they are. We shall not just have to compare a life with immediate death, but with other lives too. We shall need to compare long lives and short ones, lives of different qualities, lives that go up and down, and lives that are constant. I have shown some in figure 1.1. Lives like these must be ranked according to their goodness. The vertical axis in each mini-figure represents how well the life is going at different times: the person's wellbeing at each time. I recognize there are many problems over the measurement of wellbeing at each time, and here I shall ignore them.

Assessing the value of different lives is an immediately practical problem in ethics. In making our own plans, all of us need to compare the values of different sorts of lives that we might lead. At times this need becomes particularly acute. I have mentioned the question that may face a patient with a terminal disease of whether to choose aggressive or palliative treatment: a longer life with some pain or a shorter life without.

At another level, the health service in allocating its resources is choosing between different sorts of lives for different people. The value of these lives is by no means the only thing it should be concerned with. It must also deal fairly between people.[6] If there is a choice between saving one person's life or another person's, it may well be unfair to make that choice solely on the basis of which person will have the better life if she is saved. But the value of life is certainly one thing the health service needs to consider. Not surprisingly, health economists have done a lot of work on it.

From a theoretical point of view, the problem is this. In my figures I have shown lives of various different lengths and qualities. Presumably the goodness of each life is determined by how long the life is and how well it goes at each time. But precisely how is the goodness of the life determined by these things? This is an matter of *aggregation*, of putting together wellbeing at different times to make an overall valuation. One obvious idea is simply to add up across time, so the goodness of a life is the total of how good it is at all times the person is alive. In figure 1.1, this total is the area under the graph of wellbeing. This idea is embodied in the use of quality-adjusted life years or 'qalys', which many health economists favour as a measure of the value of a life.[7] But it is by no means the only possibility. Some people suggest that different times in a life should be weighted differently. For

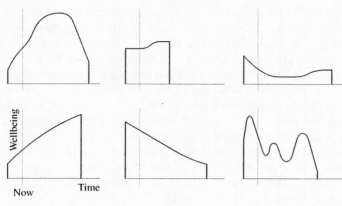

Figure 1.1

instance, some economists give less weight to times later in a life: they discount later qalys compared with earlier ones. We can still call a discounted scheme 'additive', because we add across time, having first put different weights on wellbeing at different times. But the value of a life might not be determined in an additive way at all. For instance, perhaps one consideration that makes for a good life is that it does not go downhill, particularly at the end, or perhaps it should have one really good period even if most of it is humdrum. There are so many possibilities.

Clearly, a great deal of ethical analysis has to go into investigating the value of lives. And in aggregation problems like this, economics excels. Additivity, in particular, is very well understood by economists. They know just what implies additivity and what additivity implies. As it happens, additivity across the times in a life is logically equivalent to a condition called 'strong separability' between different times.[8] Strong separability means that the value assigned to any particular stretch of a life is independent of what happens at other times. If this is so, then the value of the life is additive, but otherwise it is not. For instance, suppose you think it is important for a person to have a good time in her twenties if her childhood was unhappy, but if she had a happy childhood the twenties do not matter so much. The value you assign to events in her twenties is not independent of what happens at another time, then. You do not believe in strong separability, and you cannot think that the value of life is additive across time.

Is wellbeing at different times strongly separable or not? I am inclined to think not. But there are interesting metaphysical arguments that suggest it is. They have to do with the nature of a person. Some people think a person is nothing more than a temporal sequence of person-moments. There is me-now, me-tomorrow, me-next-week, me-last-year, and these are all separate entities. They combine together to make up me, as a sort of collage. Oddly enough, many economists hold this collage theory of personhood; they speak of a person as a sequence of 'selves'.[9] If this is the truth about people, then it might provide an argument for strong separability of wellbeing across time. Or it might not; I am leaving this argument here. I mentioned it only to hint at the fascinating interaction there can be between formal theorems of economics, which establish the link between additivity and separability, and purely philosophical arguments in metaphysics, all combining to produce conclusions in ethics.[10]

It is clear, I think, that moral philosophy can learn from economics. But to do that, it must cast off the substantive ethical theory implicit in economics: the preference-satisfaction theory. It should take the formal theory and treat it as a theory of betterness, not of preferences.

1.7   Outline of the volume

The writings reprinted in this volume develop the themes opened up in this introduction. They fall roughly into three groups, which I have gathered into the three parts of the volume. Part I contains those that look at the relation between preferences and value from various points of view. Part II deals with several specific aspects of the structure of goodness, and Part III with one further specific aspect: the value of human life.

'Utility' in part I complains about the word 'utility'. Economists use this word to denote both a person's good and also a formal representation of a person's preferences. The ambiguity may have lured some economists into adopting the preference-satisfaction theory of good unwittingly – or so this chapter suggests.

'Extended preferences' deals with a specific problem encountered by the preference-satisfaction theory. We often need to weigh one person's good against another's. How can that be done consistently with the theory? This chapter argues it cannot, despite the contrary arguments of some economists.

'Discounting the future' differs from most of the chapters in the volume in that it chiefly aims to explain a particular piece of economic theory for the benefit of philosophers. Economists and philosophers have sometimes clashed over the question of whether future goods should be valued less than present goods. I believe a lot of the disagreement is the result of a misunderstanding, which this chapter tries to clear up. The chapter belongs in this part of the volume because it also sets a limit to the economists' approach to discounting. Economists should not rely as much as they do on people's preferences, because preferences do not accurately reflect the balance of good between the present and the future.

I hope that 'Can a Humean be moderate?' illustrates how a formal theory from economics can illuminate a controversial issue in ethical theory. It examines the 'instrumentalist' idea that reason can tell us what means are appropriate to our ends, but that our ends themselves are not subject to assessment by reason. This chapter uses decision theory to state this idea precisely, and to show it cannot be sustained.

Part II begins with a mathematical chapter, 'Bolker–Jeffrey expected utility theory and axiomatic utilitarianism'. Support for utilitarianism has recently come from the methods of decision theory. This is one of the contributions economics can offer ethics. The main source is the work of John Harsanyi. This chapter reproduces Harsanyi's proof in the context of Bolker–Jeffrey decision theory – a version of decision theory that is more general and more familiar to philosophers than the one Harsanyi relied on. Of course, the conclusions of this proof need to be interpreted carefully before they can give support to utilitarianism; mathematics alone cannot establish conclusions in ethics. But I have not attempted the work of interpretation in this chapter; that is in my book *Weighing Goods*. This chapter also aims to provide an exposition of the Bolker–Jeffrey theory itself, chiefly for economists.

'Fairness' examines how the notion of fairness fits into the structure of good. Then come two chapters on incommensurable values. The incommensurability of values – when values cannot be precisely weighed against each other – is an important issue in understanding the structure of good. What, precisely, is the structure of the betterness relation when there are incommensurable values? 'Is incommensurability vagueness?' attacks this formal problem. 'Incommensurable values' begins work on the corresponding practical question: how should one act when faced with decisions involving incommensurable values?

'Goodness is reducible to betterness' expands the argument sketched in section 1.5 of this introduction. It could equally have gone into part III instead of part II, because its conclusions are particularly applied to the value of life.

I wrote 'Trying to value a life' twenty-five years ago to protest against the method economists commonly use for setting a value on human life. 'Structured and unstructured valuation' develops the same objection in more theoretical depth, and commends an alternative approach to valuing life. Economists need to value people's lives because economic resources can often be used to save lives. They can be spent on improving roads and building hospitals, for instance. Since life saving has to compete with alternative beneficial ways of using the resources, a value must be set on it. But economists' valuations commonly depend too much on people's crude preferences, unfiltered through theory. I favour a more 'structured' method, which depends on a theoretical analysis of the actual value of a life.

Some economists do actually use a structured method. The use of 'quality-adjusted life years' in health-care is an example. 'Qalys' is an examination of the merits and defects of this particular method.

The final two chapters in the volume pursue the theoretical analysis of the value of life. 'The value of living' sets up the problem formally. It particularly makes the point that the value of life encompasses two issues that are generally treated separately: the value of extending the life of an existing person, and the value of creating a new person. I do not believe the first can be dealt with independently of the second. Accordingly, 'The value of a person' discusses some of the difficulties that make it hard to understand the value of creating life.

Part I

Preference and value

2 'Utility'

2.1 Usefulness

'Utility', in plain English, means *usefulness*. In Australia, a ute is a useful vehicle.

Jeremy Bentham specialized the meaning to a particular sort of usefulness. 'By utility', he said, 'is meant that property in any object, whereby it tends to produce benefit, advantage, pleasure, good, or happiness, (all this in the present case comes to the same thing) or (what comes again to the same thing) to prevent the happening of mischief, pain, evil, or unhappiness to the party whose interest is considered.'[1] The 'Principle of Utility' is the principle that actions are to be judged by their usefulness in this sense: their tendency to produce benefit, advantage, pleasure, good, or happiness. When John Stuart Mill speaks of the 'perfectly just conception of Utility or Happiness, considered as the directive rule of human conduct', he is using 'Utility' as a short name for this principle.[2] 'The Greatest Happiness Principle' was another name for it. People who subscribed to this principle came to be known as utilitarians.

Benthamism entered economics in 1873, with the publication of W. S. Jevons's *Theory of Political Economy*. Jevons quoted Bentham's definition of 'utility' and announced: 'This perfectly expresses the meaning of the term in Economy.'[3]

But after Jevons's time, the meaning of 'utility' in economics shifted. The word came to refer not to the tendency of an object to produce good, but to the good an object produces. By a person's 'utility', economists came to mean not the person's usefulness in promoting good around her, but her own good. 'Utility' came to mean *good*. This meaning has since been overlaid by yet another, which I shall be describing later. But it still persists as one of the current meanings of 'utility'.

I cannot give an authoritative history of the shift in meaning. One difficulty is that the interpretation of an author's intentions is often debatable. For Jevons, 'utility' definitely meant usefulness in Bentham's sense.

From *Economics and Philosophy*, 7 (1991), pp. 1–12.

Alfred Marshall, too, thought of utilities as useful properties of objects. He said, for instance:

As [man's] production of material products is really nothing more than a rearrangement of matter which gives it new utilities; so his consumption of them is nothing more than a disarrangement of matter, which diminishes or destroys its utilities.[4]

But another remark of Marshall's illustrates the difficulty of interpretation:

The *total utility* of a thing to anyone (that is, the total pleasure or other benefit it yields him) increases with every increase of his stock of it, but not as fast as his stock increases.[5]

I believe Marshall still meant usefulness by 'utility' here. His parenthesis means, I think, that the *amount* of usefulness a thing has is equal to the *amount* of pleasure or other benefit it yields. But this remark could also be read – wrongly, I think – as *identifying* utility with pleasure or other benefit. Presumably it is ambiguities like this that allowed the shift of meaning to proceed unnoticed. And as early as 1881, F. Y. Edgeworth was occasionally using 'utility' unambiguously in the shifted sense. He referred to 'that quantity which alone the rational unionist is concerned to increase – the *labourer's utility*'.[6] An employer might be concerned to increase the labourer's usefulness, but not a unionist. Edgeworth meant the labourer's good. But this was not his normal terminology. Where later economists would have used 'utility', Edgeworth (like Jevons) normally used 'pleasure'. I do not think the shifted usage became common till much later.

Till recently it occurred exclusively in economics. I should be surprised to find an occurrence in philosophy from much before 1960. Henry Sidgwick's *Methods of Ethics*, the *locus classicus* of utilitarianism, hardly uses the word 'utility' at all. But it contains this footnote about its meaning:

I should point out that Hume uses 'utility' in a narrower sense than that which Bentham gave it, and one more in accordance with the usage of ordinary language. He distinguishes the 'useful' from the 'immediately agreeable': so that while recognising 'utility' as the main ground of our moral approbation of the more important virtues, he holds that there are other elements of personal merit which we approve because they are 'immediately agreeable', either to the person possessed of them or to others. It appears, however, more convenient to use the word in the wider sense in which it has been current since Bentham.[7]

Sidgwick says Bentham widened the sense of 'utility', whereas I said he narrowed it. I do not wish to quarrel about that. No doubt Sidgwick is right that to be immediately agreeable is not, in ordinary usage, a sort of usefulness. It is also true that some sorts of usefulness, according to ordinary usage, Bentham would not have included under 'utility' (the usefulness of a thumb-screw, for instance). So Bentham widened the meaning in one way and narrowed it in another. But the point is that agreeableness is the tendency of an object to produce pleasure, not pleasure itself. So whether or not agreeableness is included in utility, utility is still a valuable tendency in an object, not a benefit derived from the object. Sidgwick, at this point in the book, is explaining that virtues have utility in that they 'are directly or indirectly productive of pleasure to ourselves or to others'.[8]

Recently, however, some philosophers have begun to adopt the economists' usage. This is unwise. As used by economists, the term 'utility' has become so ambiguous as to cause immense confusion. It should be used less, not more.

2.2 Axiomatic utility theory

The confusion stems from a new meaning that was assigned to the word as axiomatic utility theory developed during the course of the twentieth century.[9] The axiomatic theory sets out from a person's *preferences*. It proves that, provided these preferences conform to some axioms, they can be *represented* by a 'utility function'. The values taken by the function are called 'utilities'. The sense in which the function represents the preferences is this: of any pair of alternatives, the function assigns a greater utility to the one that is preferred. So 'utility' acquired the meaning: *the value of a function that represents a person's preferences*. This is by now the official definition of utility in economics. For brevity, let us say: utility is *that which represents a person's preferences*.

Now, let us ask this: of a pair of alternatives, is the one that a person prefers necessarily the one that is better for her? I mean nothing mysterious by this question. I use the word 'good' and its cognates – bad, better, best, and so on – in exactly the sense they have in ordinary conversation. Mother is using this sense when she tells you it would be good for you to have a few days' rest; an economist when she says inflation is worse for retired people than the unemployed; the politician when she tells you you would be better off dead than red. There is your good and my good: some things are good for you, and some are good for me. Everybody knows what 'good' means, though not many of us can define it. Of course, we endlessly disagree about what things are good and what things are bad. We argue with Mother, the economist, and the politician. One question we might argue over is whether it is necessarily good for a person to have what she prefers. That is the question I am asking now.

Again, then: of a pair of alternatives, is the one that a person prefers necessarily the one that is better for her? According to the official definition of 'utility', it has the greater utility. But a person's utility, as officially defined, has no necessary connection with her good. So nothing in the definition suggests that the preferred alternative is necessarily better for her. However, many economists adopt the official definition of 'utility', whilst at the same time *also* using the word to stand for a person's good. Because an alternative preferred by a person is defined to have a higher utility for her, they take it for granted that it must be better for her. They suppose, then, that a person always prefers what is better for her.

We may call a person who always prefers what is better for herself 'self-interested'. This is using 'self-interested' in a very strong sense.[10] It is saying not only that the person pays no attention to the interests of other people, but also that she always prefers exactly what it is in her own interest. It rules out not only altruism, but also *imprudence*; a person is imprudent if, though concerned only for herself, she sometimes fails to do exactly what is best for herself. Simply by muddling the different meanings of utility', many economists find themselves committed to the view that people are necessarily self-interested in this strong sense.

'The first principle of Economics', said Edgeworth, 'is that every agent is actuated only by self-interest.'[11] That may have been true in Edgeworth's day, but it was one of the achievements of modern utility theory to free economics from such a dubious first principle. The achievement was announced by Lionel Robbins: 'So far as we are concerned', he said, 'our economic subjects can be pure egoists, pure altruists, pure ascetics, pure sensualists or – what is much more likely – bundles of all these impulses.'[12] The first principle of economics is, I take it, utility theory. And modern, axiomatic utility theory makes no assumption that people are self-interested. All it assumes is that people's preferences conform to a number of axioms: roughly, they simply need to be consistent. They can conform to the axioms without being self-interested. Yet the muddle over 'utility' leads many economists to forget this important discovery.

It is certainly not very plausible that people's preferences are always self-interested in the strong sense I described. It is a common opinion that many people – parents for instance – have preferences that are partly altruistic: directed towards the good of others. And it is a common opinion that many people are imprudent: for instance, they prefer to take less exercise than is good for them. If either of these opinions is correct, people's preferences are not self-interested.

It may turn out that common opinion is incorrect. Altruism and imprudence may not exist, and everyone may always prefer what is best for themselves. Utility, defined to represent a person's preferences, may indeed turn out also to represent her good. All this is arguable. One argument, for instance, is that a person's good actually *consists in* the satisfaction of her preferences, so that, of two alternatives, the one she prefers cannot fail to be better for her. But at least the argument needs to be made. It is a substantive question whether or not preferences are necessarily self-interested.

If, though, you use 'utility' to stand for a representation of a person's preferences, and at the same time for the person's good, you cannot even express
the question. You will say: by definition, what a person prefers has more
utility for her, so how can it fail to have more utility for her? The ambiguity is intolerable.

2.3   Expected utility theory

The confusion multiplies when it comes to expected utility theory, the
branch of utility theory that takes account of uncertainty. Modern,
axiomatic expected utility theory imposes axioms on a person's preferences
between uncertain prospects – more axioms than ordinary utility theory
does. Granted these axioms, the theory demonstrates the existence of a
utility function that has two properties. First, the function represents the
preferences, just as before: of two prospects, the preferred one has the
higher utility. And, secondly, the function has the 'expected utility form',
which means that the utility assigned to an uncertain prospect is the
expectation (in probability theory's sense) of the utilities assigned to the
prospect's possible outcomes. Axiomatic expected utility theory, then, is
like ordinary axiomatic utility theory in that it defines utility to represent
preferences. 'Utility' still means that which represents preferences; the
person still maximizes her utility. But since the utility of a prospect is also
its expected utility – the expectation of the utility of its outcomes – we can
also say the person maximizes her expected utility.

It happens that utility defined this way is unique up to increasing linear
transformations. Utility with this degree of uniqueness is often said to be
'cardinal'.

There is good evidence that people in practice do not conform to
expected utility theory; they often violate its axioms.[13] But it can be argued
(though this too is controversial) that fully rational people will conform to
the theory.[14] For the sake of argument, let us take that for granted, and from
now on consider only fully rational people. So we can assume they are
expected utility maximizers. For the sake of argument, too, I now want to
set aside the issue of self-interest I mentioned in section 2.2. So let us consider only people whose preferences happen to be self-interested, in the
strong sense I described.

Take, then, a rational, self-interested person. When there is no uncertainty to worry about, this person prefers, of two alternatives, the one that
is better for her. But what about her preferences between uncertain
prospects? Of two prospects, will she necessarily prefer the one that gives
her a greater *expectation* of good? Will she necessarily maximize her
expected good?

A plausible answer is no, for two reasons. First, for an expectation of good even to exist, good must be an arithmetical quantity.[15] And it is plausible that good is not such a precise notion as that. It makes clear sense to say that one prospect is better or worse than another, so goodness at least constitutes an ordering (though not necessarily a complete one). But it is plausible that there are no precise arithmetical quantities of good.

And, secondly, even if there *are* arithmetical quantities of good, it is plausible that a rational, self-interested person might not maximize the expectation of her good. Suppose a person had a choice between ninety-nine units of good for sure, on the one hand, and, on the other, a gamble at equal odds between no units and two hundred units. The gamble has a higher expectation of good for her. Yet it seems perfectly rational for her to play safe and take the ninety-nine units for sure. She would do this if she was risk-averse about her good. Maximizing the expectation of good implies risk-neutrality about good. And it seems perfectly rational to take some different attitude, such as risk-aversion, to risk about one's good.

This needs some more explanation. Our subject is self-interested. Therefore, of two prospects, we can take it that she will prefer the one that is better for her. But it does not follow that she will prefer the one with the greater *expectation* of good for her. The one that is better for her may actually have a lower expectation of good for her. The example shows this. Though the option of ninety-nine units for sure has a lower expectation of good for her, it may nevertheless be better for her, because it is safe.

To be sure, since we are assuming the person conforms to expected utility theory, she maximizes the expectation of her utility. This means she is risk-neutral about *utility*. But it does not follow that she is risk-neutral about good. Axiomatic expected utility theory does not imply risk-neutrality about good; it does not imply that a rational person maximizes the expectation of her good.

But once again the ambiguity of 'utility' can get in the way of understanding this point. A rational person necessarily maximizes the expectation of utility. For an economist who also uses 'utility' to mean good, this will make it seem as though a rational person necessarily maximizes the expectation of her good. But this is a mistaken deduction.

It may turn out, on further investigation, that actually a rational self-interested person *does* necessarily maximize the expectation of her good. This is a common view that began, I believe, with Daniel Bernoulli.[16] I call it 'Bernoulli's hypothesis'. There are arguments in its favour.[17] But it is not implied by axiomatic expected utility theory. And we certainly need to be able to ask whether or not it is true. If, however, you define utility, on the one hand, so that a person necessarily maximizes the expectation of it, and, on the other, you covertly identify utility with a person's good, then you cannot ask the question.

Let me express the question differently. Our self-interested subject always prefers, of two alternative prospects, the one that is better for her. Since she prefers it, by definition it has a higher utility. So her utility represents her good in the sense that, of any two prospects, the one that is better for her has the higher utility. This means that utility can properly be called an *ordinal* representation of her good. It has this property simply because the person is self-interested. But if she *also* maximizes the expectation of her good, then expected utility theory tells us that utility will represent her good more tightly than this: it will be an increasing linear transform of her good. In that case, it is said to represent her good *cardinally*. So Bernoulli's hypothesis is equivalent to the claim that utility represents good cardinally. Our question can be put this way, then: for a rational self-interested person, does her utility, as defined by expected utility theory, represent her good cardinally? We know already that utility itself is cardinal; it is unique up to increasing linear transformations. But that does not imply it represents good cardinally. The question is: actually, does it?

Put this way, it is a question that has very much interested welfare economists. A cardinal representation of good is very useful thing to have if you are interested in evaluating distributions of income and wealth. It is essential if you are a utilitarian concerned to maximize the total of people's good. It was very much in demand in the early 1950s. At that time, welfare economists had been deprived by the 'ordinalist revolution' of the 1930s of their right both to cardinal representations of good and to interpersonal comparisons of good. This had left them with almost nothing to say about distributions of income and wealth. The advent of expected utility theory in the 1940s appeared to offer them back at least the cardinal representations. So they urgently needed to know whether the offer could be trusted. Could expected utility theory really supply cardinal representations of good?

There was great confusion about the question at the time, fuelled by the ambiguity of 'utility'. The confusion showed up in a translation published by *Econometrica* in 1954 of Bernoulli's seminal article on expected utility theory. Bernoulli said that a rational person would maximize the expectation of her *emolumentum*. (He wrote in Latin.) '*Emolumentum*' means benefit or advantage. So this is a statement of Bernoulli's hypothesis, as I called it: a rational person maximizes her expectation of good. But in *Econometrica*, '*emolumentum*' was translated as 'utility'. This lapse in scholarship prevented readers from seeing the crucial difference between Bernoulli's version of expected utility theory and the axiomatic version. The axiomatic version is not committed to the view that a rational person maximizes the expectation of her good. Bernoulli, on the other hand, was.

A clearsighted article published by Daniel Ellsberg in 1954 ought to have sorted out the muddle. Ellsberg, like me, was concerned about the ambiguity of 'utility'. Of von Neumann and Morgenstern, he says:

> The operations that define their concepts are essentially new, and their results are neither intended nor suited to fill the main functions of the older, more familiar brands of 'cardinal utility'. It is unfortunate that old terms have been retained, for their associations arouse both hopes and antagonisms that have no real roots in the new context.[18]

I am sorry to say, however, that confusion persists, still fuelled by the same ambiguity. It is at work, for instance, in this more recent passage from John Harsanyi:

> To be sure, the vNM utility function[19] of any given individual is estimated from his choice behavior under risk and uncertainty. But this does not mean that his vNM utility function is *merely* an indication of his attitude towards risk taking. Rather, as its name shows, it is a utility function, and more specifically, it is what economists call a cardinal utility function. This means that the primary task of a vNM utility function is *not* to express a given individual's attitude toward risk taking; rather it is to indicate how much utility, i.e. how much subjective importance, he assigns to various goals.[20]

2.4   Sen's usage

We cannot now return 'utility' to its original meaning of usefulness. It is a technical term thoroughly embedded in economics. But at least, as a technical term, we should confine it to one meaning. Which should we choose?

A natural place to look for leadership is the work of Amartya Sen. Let us examine how Sen uses this word 'utility' in his recent work. I shall take as examples his books *The Standard of Living* and *On Ethics and Economics*.

Sen's notion of utility plays an important role in his arguments. A major thesis of *The Standard of Living*, for instance, is that a person's standard of living cannot be identified with her utility. But Sen evidently assumes that his readers understand what he means by 'utility', and does not explain it well. I do not find his meaning obvious, though. Two things are clear. Sen does not mean by 'utility' what axiomatic utility theory means by it.[21] Nor does he mean a person's good; there are things he considers good for a person – for instance, her functionings and capabilities – that he does not include in her utility.

My best understanding of Sen's meaning for 'utility' is: *that which utilitarians believe to constitute good*. His reason for adopting this meaning, I suppose, is this. 'Utility' as a technical term was invented by utilitarians.

So we ought to give it the meaning they give it. And utilitarians intend 'utility' to refer to what they believe to constitute good. So we ought to use it to refer to that too.

But this is a poor reason. First of all, it is false that, generally, utilitarians intend 'utility' to refer to what they believe to constitute good. I said that in section 2.1. Among the classical utilitarian philosophers – Bentham, Mill, Sidgwick – none of them used the term that way. They intended it to refer to the tendency to promote good. Among the classical utilitarian economists – Jevons, Marshall, Edgeworth, Pigou[22] – only Edgeworth occasionally slipped into this usage. Even contemporary utilitarian philosophers rarely use 'utility' that way. Generally, utilitarians refer to those things they believe to constitute good by their specific names: 'pleasure', 'happiness', 'satisfaction', 'wellbeing', 'welfare', and so on.

Secondly, even if we suppose that utilitarians *do* intend 'utility' to refer to what they believe to constitute good, and even if we want to give 'utility' the meaning they give it, we should not use it to refer to the same thing as they do, unless we are utilitarians. (And Sen is not one.) In so far as utilitarians use this word in this way, they *mean* by it simply good. Of course, they intend it to *refer* to what they believe to constitute good. But if we are to give the word the same meaning as they do, we must use it to refer to what *does* constitute good. Only if utilitarians are right will this be just what utilitarians believe to constitute good.

If, then, Sen means by 'utility' that which utilitarians believe to constitute good, he is endowing the word with a new meaning. I believe this meaning may be unique to Sen. It is likely to be a useful one only if it is clear what utilitarians believe to constitute good; only then will its reference be unambiguous. But actually utilitarians are divided over what constitutes good. Some think good consists in good feelings; some in happiness; others in the satisfaction of desires; and so on.

Because of this ambiguity, Sen is constantly forced in these books to mention different 'conceptions of utility' separately: the happiness conception, the desire-satisfaction conception, and so on. His arguments have to deal separately with each. In showing that the standard of living is not the same as utility, for instance, he has to show it for the various conceptions one by one.[23] And, since the conceptions differ radically, each demands a radically different argument. I see, therefore, little point in collecting them together under the one heading of 'utility'. It would be a harmless thing to do if 'utility' were not already damagingly ambiguous. As it is, we can do without yet another meaning for it, and especially one that is itself ambiguous.

So I think Sen's lead points in the wrong direction.[24]

2.5   The best usage

As a meaning for 'utility', we should choose either *that which represents preferences*, on the one hand, or *good* on the other. Which should it be?

Both are economists' meanings. Philosophers have not used either till recently, and neither is well established in philosophy. So the needs of economics should have the first say in deciding between them. In any case, they will.

In economics the official meaning is the first: *that which represents preferences*. This is the meaning given in the major doctrinal texts[25] and the best textbooks.[26] It is defined with great precision, as a technical term should be. Its use is universal in theoretical economics. There is no alternative term. Economics cannot do without it.

'Utility' in this sense need not be confined to a representation of a person's actual preferences. A function can also be called a utility function if it represents the preferences a person would have if she were rational and self-interested. But if she were rational and self-interested, she would prefer, of two alternatives, the one that is better for her. So a function that represents the preferences she would have if she were rational and self-interested also represents, ordinally, her good. An ordinal representation of good can therefore be called a utility function.[27] We might also have a use for a notion of 'social' preferences, suitably interpreted, and social preferences too can be represented by a utility function. All of this is within the scope of the official definition of 'utility'.

Ellsberg thinks it unfortunate that 'utility' acquired this new technical meaning.[28] I disagree. Once divorced from usefulness, the word has no *natural* meaning. So it is ideally suited to perform the services of a technical term.

The second meaning, *good*, is also the property of economists. But it is an underground one. You will not often find it openly acknowledged. There is no classical warrant for it. Because it hides underground, its main effect has been to cause confusion. And – a further sin – it is perfectly redundant. We already have an excellent word with the meaning of good: 'good'.

I therefore propose that this second meaning for 'utility' should be prohibited. 'Utility' should be used only for a representation of preferences.

3   Extended preferences

3.1   Introduction

Many economists have adopted a doctrine known as 'ordinalism'. Ordinalism insists that we can know about people's good only by means of our knowledge of people's preferences. Many ordinalists believe their doctrine implies that we cannot know how one person's good compares with another's. But some have resisted this conclusion; they have argued that we can make interpersonal comparisons of good in a way that is consistent with ordinalism. They think a particular class of preferences can constitute a basis for comparisons between the good of different people. They have in mind people's preferences between very widely defined alternatives, each of which consists of a way of life together with the personal characteristics of a person who lives that life. These are called 'extended preferences'. This chapter reveals a flaw in the argument that extended preferences can be a basis for interpersonal comparisons of good. It shows that interpersonal comparisons really are inconsistent with ordinalism.

Section 3.2 of this chapter explains ordinalism in more detail. Section 3.3 describes the notion of extended preferences, and specifies a condition extended preferences must satisfy if they are to serve the purpose they are meant for: everyone must have the same extended preferences. Section 3.4 quotes an argument of John Harsanyi's that is intended to show everyone will indeed have the same extended preferences. Section 3.5 explains that Harsanyi's argument contains an error.

There is an alternative approach to interpersonal comparisons implicit in some ordinalist writings, including Harsanyi's. This second approach is not usually clearly distinguished from the approach through extended preferences, but actually it does not depend on extended preferences.

From *Preferences*, edited by Christoph Fehige, Georg Meggle, and Ulla Wessels, de Gruyter, 1998, pp. 279–96. Reprinted by permission of Walter de Gruyter & Co. I greatly benefited from discussions and correspondence on the subject of this chapter with John Harsanyi, Susan Hurley, Serge-Christophe Kolm, Brian Skyrms, and, particularly, Hans-Peter Weikard. The research for this chapter was funded by the Economic and Social Research Council under grant R000233334.

Section 3.6 describes it. Section 3.7, however, shows it is inconsistent with ordinalism. Section 3.8 argues that this approach is anyway otiose.

My aim in this chapter is only to prove that interpersonal comparisons of good are inconsistent with ordinalism. What conclusion should we draw? I draw the conclusion that ordinalism must be incorrect, since interpersonal comparisons of good are clearly possible. But in this chapter I shall not try to prove as much as that.

3.2   Ordinalism

I shall take *ordinalism* to be the conjunction of these three claims:

1. *The preference-satisfaction theory of good.* If a person has a high-grade preference for one alternative over another, then it would be better for the person to have the first alternative rather than the second.
2. Given a pair of alternatives, we can (sometimes at least) know whether a person has a high-grade preference for one of them over the other.
3. Our knowledge of people's high-grade preferences is the only way we can come to know anything about how good it would be for a person to have some alternative.

By a 'high-grade preference' I mean a preference that passes some test of quality: it is rational and well informed, or something of that sort. It does not matter for my purposes precisely what the test is, though in section 3.7 I shall mention something it cannot be. Some ordinalists may not insist on any test at all; for them, any preference is high-grade. From now on in this chapter, I shall speak only of high-grade preferences, and the word 'preference' is always to be understood as referring to a high-grade preference.

I am treating ordinalism as a theory about what we can know, and not as a theory about meaning. Many authors take ordinalism to include some verificationist view about meaning: perhaps the view that a statement about people's good has no meaning unless we can know whether or not it is true. But this chapter is not concerned with meaning, and I shall leave verificationism aside.

3.3   Extended preferences and interpersonal comparisons of good

One conclusion that has often been drawn from ordinalism is that we cannot compare one person's good with another's. The argument is this. One person i's preferences will tell us whether one alternative is better for i than another. Another person j's preferences will tell us whether one alternative is better for j than another. But no one's preferences will tell us whether one alternative is better for i than another alternative is for j.

Not all ordinalists have accepted this conclusion. Some have argued that preferences can indeed allow us to compare one person's good with another's. It depends on what sorts of alternatives the preferences are amongst. Preferences amongst cheeses will not do it, but these ordinalists say *extended preferences*, as they call them, will. An extended preference is a preference between *extended alternatives*, and an extended alternative consists of a way of life paired together with particular personal characteristics. For instance, one extended alternative is to live the life of an academic whilst possessing a thirst for knowledge and modest material needs. Another is to live the life of an academic whilst possessing an insatiable desire for wealth. No doubt we have preferences amongst such alternatives; I prefer the first of the two I have just described to the second. These are extended preferences. It has been argued that extended preferences can give us grounds for interpersonal comparisons of good.[1]

How would this work? Suppose I have an extended preference for living person i's life with i's personal characteristics over living j's life with j's personal characteristics. According to the preference-satisfaction theory, it would be better for me to lead i's life with i's personal characteristics than to lead j's life with j's personal characteristics. This suggests that i, living her life, is better off than j, living hers. In this way an extended preference seems to allow a comparison between one person's good and another's. In this case my preference seems to have allowed a comparison between i's good and j's.

This is not a convincing argument without some extra support. The fact that John Broome has an extended preference for i's life and characteristics over j's life and characteristics cannot be sufficient evidence that i is better off than j. What if someone else had the opposite extended preference to mine? Even if i herself has this same extended preference, that would not be sufficient evidence; what if j had the opposite one? Evidently, if extended preferences are to be the basis for interpersonal comparisons of good, the extended preferences of different people must coincide to some extent at least.

Those authors who rely on extended preferences as a basis for interpersonal comparisons of good generally insist that everyone will have the same extended preferences, provided extended alternatives are construed widely enough.[2] We must make sure that our extended alternatives are a full specification of all those features of lives and personal characteristics that anyone can possibly have preferences about. Given that, these authors claim we must all have the same preferences about such very widely extended alternatives.

Why should this be? It certainly seems implausible. I myself prefer to live the life of an academic, with my own academic characteristics, even in the conditions allotted to academics in contemporary Britain, to being a financial analyst with the characteristics of a financial analyst living in the conditions allotted to financial analysts. A financial analyst, with her different values, would no doubt have the opposite preference. So her extended preferences will differ from mine. Both our preferences may well be high-grade: they may be rational, well informed, and so on. The reason I have mine is that an academic has some slight chance of making a worthwhile contribution to knowledge. I recognize that, if I were a financial analyst, with all the characteristics of a financial analyst, I would not then value knowledge as I do now. Nevertheless, I do value knowledge, and that is why I prefer to be an academic. The different values of academics and financial analysts lead us to have different extended preferences. Or so it certainly seems.

Appearances, then, are against the claim that different people must have the same extended preferences. Are there, on the other hand, any arguments in favour of this claim? I know of one. It is based on the causes of preference. It is spelt out in most detail by John Harsanyi in *Rational Behaviour and Bargaining Equilibrium*,[3] but other authors have used it too.[4]

3.4   Harsanyi's causal argument

Harsanyi's argument is difficult to interpret, and I do not want to misrepresent it. To reduce the risk of unfairness, I shall quote almost all of it in this section, before going on to explain and criticize it in section 3.5. Harsanyi says:

If all individuals' personal preferences were identical, then we could ascribe the same utility function U to all individuals and could always make interpersonal utility comparisons in terms of this common utility function U. Moreover, all interpersonal utility comparisons could be reduced to *intra*personal utility comparisons. If we wanted to know whether a given apple would give more utility to Peter (who has just had a heavy meal) than to Paul (who had only a very light meal), we could simply ask whether Peter himself would derive more utility from an apple after a heavy meal or after a light meal.

Of course, in actuality different individuals often have very different personal preferences and very different utility functions. But the possibility of meaningful interpersonal utility comparisons will remain, as long as the different individuals' choice behavior and preferences are at least governed by the *same basic psychological laws*. For in this case each individual's preferences will be determined by the same general causal variables. Thus the differences we can observe between different people's preferences can be predicted, at least in principle, from differences in these causal variables, such as differences in their biological inheritance, in their past life histories, and in their current environmental conditions. This means that if Peter had Paul's biological makeup, had Paul's life history behind him, and were currently subject to Paul's environmental influences, then he would presumably have the *same* personal preferences as Paul has now and would ascribe the *same* utility as Paul does now to each particular situation.

Let P_j again denote individual j's *subjective attitudes* (including his preferences), and let R_j denote a vector consisting of *all objective causal variables* needed to explain these subjective attitudes denoted by P_j. Our discussion suggests that the extended utility function V_i of each individual i should really be written as $V_i = V_i[A_j, R_j]$ rather than $V_i[A_j, P_j]$. Written in this form, the utility function $V_i = V_i[A_j, R_j]$ indicates the utility that individual i would assign to the objective position A_j if the causal variables determining his preferences were R_j. Because the mathematical form of this function is defined by the basic psychological laws governing people's choice behaviour, this function V_i must be the same for all individuals i, so that, for example,

$$V_h[A_j, R_j] = V_i[A_j, R_j]$$

for each pair of individuals h and i. In the special case in which $h = j$, we can write

$$V_i[A_j, R_j] = V_j[A_j, R_j] = U_j(R_j).$$

That is, individual i (or individual h) would have the *same* preferences and would assign the *same* utility to any objective situation A_j as individual j now does, if the causal variables determining his preferences took the same value R_j as do the causal variables determining j's preferences.

In other words, even though the 'ordinary' utility functions U_i and U_j of two individuals i and j may be quite different, their *extended* utility functions V_i and V_j will be identical. This is so because, by the definition of the causal-variables vectors R_i and R_j, all differences between the two functions $U_i(A_i) = V_i[A_i, R_i]$ and $U_j(A_j) = V_j[A_j, R_j]$ must be attributed to differences between the vectors R_i and R_j and not to differences between the mathematical form of the two functions V_i and V_j.

Yet, if the two individuals have the same extended utility function $V_i = V_j = V$, then we are back in a world of identical utility functions. Hence individual i will be able in principle to reduce any *inter*personal utility comparisons that he may wish to make between himself and individual j to an *intra*personal utility comparison between the utilities that he is *in fact* assigning to various situations and the utilities he *would* assign to them *if* the vector of causal variables determining his preferences took the value R_j (which is the value that the vector of these causal variables takes in the case of individual j).

For example, if I want to compare the utility that I would derive from a new car with the utility that a friend would derive from a new sailboat, then I must ask myself what utility I would derive from a sailboat if I had taken up sailing for a regular hobby as my friend has done, and if I could suddenly acquire my friend's expert sailing skill, and so forth.[5]

3.5   The causal determination of extended preferences

Harsanyi's argument relies on the notion of a *utility function*, and cannot be expressed without it. So I need first to explain this notion. If a person has preferences over some range of alternatives, and if these preferences conform to a number of conditions, it is possible to *represent* them by a function U, which is called a utility function. U assigns a value called a *utility* to each of the alternatives. To say U represents the preferences means that U assigns higher utilities to alternatives that are preferred. More precisely: the utility assigned by U to one alternative is at least as great as the utility assigned by U to another if and only if the first alternative is preferred or indifferent to the second. This is how Harsanyi explicitly defines 'utility'.[6] Some of his expressions in the passage I have quoted suggest he may also have in mind another meaning for 'utility', and I shall come to that in section 3.6. But for the moment I shall stick with this one: utility is the value of a function that represents preferences. Harsanyi calls a utility function that represents extended preferences an *extended utility function*, and I shall do the same.

One technical point about utility functions. There is not just one utility function that represents a person's preferences; many do. If a function U represents someone's preferences, then another function U' will also represent her preferences if and only if U' is an *increasing transform* of U. U' is defined to be an increasing transform of U if and only if, for any pair of alternatives A and B, $U'(A) \geq U'(B)$ if and only if $U(A) \geq U(B)$. For instance, if U' is the function U/a, obtained by dividing U by some positive constant a, then U' is an increasing transform of U, and it will represent the same preferences as U.

A person j has preferences about ways of life, which may be represented by a utility function U_j. Different people have different preferences, and i will have preferences represented by a different function U_i. But there is a causal explanation of why each person has the preferences she has. Let R stand for the causal variables that determine the form of a person's preferences (her upbringing, friends, sporting ability, and so on). A person who is subject to causal influences R will have preferences that can be represented by a utility function U_R. Any person subject to the same influences R will have the same preferences, so there is no need to index the function U_R by the name of the person whose utility function it is. This function assigns a utility $U_R(A)$ to ways of life A. An alternative notation is $U(A; R)$. I separate A and R by a semicolon rather than a comma for a reason that will appear.

The function U is a universal function, the same for everybody. It represents the preferences that a person subject to causal influences R will have about ways of life A. It certainly does not represent preferences of any sort, belonging to anybody, about the combination (A, R) of a way of life and causal influences.

I hope this is obvious, but an example may help to make it more so. Suppose people have preferences about opportunities to contribute to knowledge, l, and money, m. Suppose a person's preferences can be represented by a utility function that has this particular form:

$$U_\alpha(l, m) = \alpha \log l + (1-\alpha) \log m.$$

Not everyone has exactly the same preferences, because the parameter α (which lies between 0 and 1) differs from person to person. There is a causal explanation of why a person has the particular value of α she has. Let us suppose her α is determined by the age when she was weaned. In fact, let α be equal to w, the age at which the person is weaned (suppose everyone is weaned before one). A person's utility function $U_w(l, m)$, or in an alternative notation $U(l, m; w)$, is:

$$U(l, m; w) = w \log l + (1-w) \log m.$$

This function represents the preferences that a person weaned at w has about l and m. It does not represent anyone's preferences about w. It may be that no one even has any preferences about when she was weaned. The semicolon separates the objects of preference l and m from the cause of preference w. Objects of preference and causes of preference have quite different roles in the utility function.

There is a formal way of demonstrating this point. Let

$$U_\alpha'(l, m) = \log l + (1/\alpha - 1) \log m.$$

U_α' is obtained by dividing U_α by α, which, as a parameter of the function, is a constant. U_α' is therefore an increasing transform of U_α. So U_α' represents the preferences of a person with parameter α, just as U_α does. But, as a causal matter, α is equal to the person's age of weaning w. So the preferences about l and m of someone weaned at w can be represented by the function

$$U'(l, m; w) = \log l + (1/w - 1) \log m.$$

$U'(l, m; w)$ is an increasing transform of $U(l, m; w)$ if the arguments of the function are taken as l and m. But if l, m, and w are all taken as arguments, then $U'(l, m; w)$ is not an increasing transform of $U(l, m; w)$. Consequently, these two functions cannot represent the same preferences over the three variables l, m, and w together. This shows they are not representing preferences over these three variables at all.

Return to the general case. $U(A; R)$ as I defined it is a universal function, the same for everyone. But it is not a universal utility function representing preferences about A and R together. In the argument I quoted, Harsanyi calls $V_i[A_j, R_j]$, which is my $U(A; R)$ expressed in his notation, an extended utility function. He implies that it represents extended preferences over ways of life A and causal variables R together. But it does not. Harsanyi hoped to exhibit universal extended preferences, the same for everyone. But he fails to do so.

There is a complication. The things that have a causal influence over people's preferences may also be things that people have preferences about. For instance, people have preferences about the friends they have, and their friends influence their preferences. Harsanyi's separation between 'objective position' A and causal variables R is too sharp. I must reformulate my point to take this complication into account.

Let A be a variable that stands for ways of life. Let P stand for personal characteristics. Then (A, P) is an extended alternative as I originally defined it: a way of life lived with particular personal characteristics. People have extended preferences about these extended alternatives. Let us make sure that A and P are defined broadly enough to include anything that anyone has a preference about. (It does not matter what is included in A and what in P, so long as everything comes into one or the other.) A person j has extended preferences about (A, P) that can be represented by an extended utility function $V_j(A, P)$. I have given V_j the index j because as yet we have no reason to think j's extended preferences are necessarily the same as anyone else's.

Now, there are causal variables R that determine people's extended preferences. A person who is subject to causal variables R will have extended preferences $V_R(A, P)$. An alternative notation is $V(A, P; R)$. Since anyone subject to the same causal variables will have the same extended preferences, there is no need to index this function by j. V is a universal function.

Many of the variables in R will be things that people have preferences about. So they will also appear in A or P. Indeed, let us now go back and enlarge A and P to make sure that they include not only anything that anyone has a preference about, but also anything that has any causal influence on people's preferences. (A, P) is now a very comprehensive specification of a life and a person living that life. In $V(A, P; R)$ all the variables contained in R will now also appear in A or P.

Still, R is not redundant as an argument of the function. Although all the variables in R will also appear in A or P, it will be different values of the variables in each case. R contains the values of the causal variables that a person is actually subject to. (A, P), on the other hand, contains the values of the variables that the person contemplates as objects of her preference.

$V(A, P; R)$ is a universal function. But it does not represent universal extended preferences. It does not represent any preferences at all over A, P, and R taken together. It represents preferences over A and P, but many different preferences, one set of preferences for each value of R. So, even after taking account of the complication, we have not found universal extended preferences.

Serge-Christophe Kolm says:

At bottom, all individuals have the same tastes, the same desires. Without doubt, this assertion requires explanation.

If two persons have preferences which appear to differ, there is a reason for this, there is something which makes them different from each other. Let us place this 'something' within *the object of the preferences* which we are considering, thereby removing it from the parameters which determine the structure of these preferences. The preferences of these two persons defined in this way are necessarily identical.

We may carry out this operation in the case of any society: namely, the operation of placing in the object of preferences everything which would cause differences between the preferences of different members of society. An identical preference of all members of this society obtained in this way is called 'a fundamental preference' of the members of this society. It is a property which describes the tastes and needs of the 'representative individual' of this society.

If this society includes all human beings, then that which discerns this common preference is at bottom 'human nature'.[7]

Kolm evidently has an idea like Harsanyi's. The causes of people's preferences may indeed also be objects of their preferences. But by including causes amongst objects of preference, we do not stop them from being causes. We do not remove them from the parameters which determine the structure of people's preferences. They retain their role as causes, and they may cause one person's preferences to be different from another's. My preferences are influenced causally by the life I lead. Since I am an academic, I have preferences that differ from the preferences of a financial analyst. The life I lead is also amongst the objects of my preferences: I prefer the life of an academic to the life of a financial analyst. But simply recognizing that the cause of my preferences is also an object of my preference is not going to make my preferences identical to a financial analyst's. No doubt the financial analyst has the opposite preference to mine. It is just not true that, at bottom, all individuals have the same tastes and desires.

Kolm seems to think that, by treating the causes that act upon me as objects of my preference, I can somehow withdraw myself from their influence. But I cannot escape from my own causal situation.

The causal argument was offered as a demonstration that everyone will have the same extended preferences. It fails.

3.6 The causal determination of good

What, then, is the attraction of the causal argument? Why have so many authors put forward an argument that is so plainly mistaken? I suspect they have confused it with another argument that is not mistaken. They have been looking for grounds for interpersonal comparisons of good. And there is a truth about causation that is germane to interpersonal comparisons of good. It is true, but not germane, that if two people were in the same causal situation they would have the same preferences. It is also true, and germane, that if two people were in the same causal situation, they would be equally well off.

This latter truth might possibly give us a route to interpersonal comparisons of good. It would allow us to move from comparisons of good for a single individual to comparisons of good between individuals. Suppose we are able to determine, for a single person i and for any pair of alternatives A and B, whether A or B is better for i, or whether the two are equally good for her. Suppose, that is to say, we can put all the alternatives in order according to their goodness for i. Now suppose the alternatives we are dealing with are very broadly defined. They are extended alternatives, including both ways of life and personal characteristics, and also including all the causal variables that could have an influence on how well off a person is. One of these alternatives could not possibly be any better or worse for i than it would be for anyone else. Take two of these extended alternatives, E and F. Would E be better for one person, say j, than F would be for a different person, say k? This would be so if and only if E would be better for i than F would be for i. It would be so, that is to say, if and only if E comes higher than F when the alternatives are ordered by their goodness for the single person i. When we order the alternatives by their goodness for i, therefore, we are also producing an interpersonal ordering. Provided our alternatives are defined sufficiently widely, an ordering by goodness for a single person is also an interpersonal ordering. Simply, it is an ordering of the alternatives by their goodness.

If I were a financial analyst living the life of a financial analyst, subject to all the causal influences that determine how well off a financial analyst is, then I should be exactly as well off as anyone else would be if she occupied that position. The same is true for the alternative of being an academic in the causal situation of an academic. Therefore, if it is better for me to live the life of an academic, it would be better for anyone. The life of an academic would, simply, be better.

So, if we can discover an ordering of widely extended alternatives by their goodness for any single person, we can make interpersonal comparisons of good: we can know whether one person is better off than another. This conclusion is only conditional. *If* we can discover an ordering for a single person, we can make interpersonal comparisons. How we can discover an ordering for a single person is another matter, which I shall come back to in sections 3.7 and 3.8.

I suspect this possible route to interpersonal comparisons has been in the minds of several of the economists who have more explicitly followed the route of extended preferences. It is difficult to be sure, because of the ambiguous use of the word 'utility' that is common in economics.[8] I defined 'utility' in section 3.5 as the value of a function that represents preferences. This is the definition most often made explicit. But economists also often speak of a person's 'utility' when they mean the person's good. In his discussion of 'extended sympathy' as a basis for interpersonal comparisons of good, Kenneth Arrow says:

We may suppose that everything which determines an individual's satisfaction is included in the list of goods. Thus, not only the wine but the ability to enjoy and discriminate are included among goods . . . If we use this complete list, then everyone should have the same utility function for what he gets out of the social state.[9]

What does Arrow mean when he says everyone should have the same utility function? If he is thinking of a utility function as representing a person's preferences, he must mean that everyone has the same preferences – in this case the same extended preferences. As I say, that is false. If, on the other hand, he is thinking of a utility function as measuring a person's good, he may mean that each extended alternative is as good for one person as it is for another. As I say, that is true, and leads to a different route to interpersonal comparisons of good. I am inclined to think Arrow means to follow this second route, but I am not perfectly sure.

The ambiguity of 'utility' is acute in Harsanyi's writings. It is the main reason why the argument I quoted in section 3.4 is so hard to interpret. When Harsanyi says 'if Peter had Paul's biological makeup, had Paul's life history behind him, and were currently subject to Paul's environmental influences, then he would presumably have the *same* personal preferences as Paul has now and would ascribe the *same* utility as Paul does now to each particular situation', I think he is probably making two quite different points. The first is that, if Peter had the same biological makeup and so on as Paul, he would have the same preferences as Paul. The second is that if Peter had the same biological makeup and so on as Paul, then any particular situation would be exactly as good for Peter as it would be for Paul.

The first of these points led Harsanyi to the argument that is most explicit in the passage I quoted: the argument that everyone must have the same extended preferences. This argument is mistaken, as I explained in section 3.5. The second point is submerged through most of the passage but surfaces at the end, when Harsanyi wants to compare the benefit a friend would get from a new sailboat with the benefit he himself would get from a new car. He says, 'I must ask myself what utility I would derive from a sailboat if I had taken up sailing for a regular hobby as my friend has done.' Harsanyi plans to ask himself not what preferences he would have if he were in his friend's causal situation, but how well off he would be if he were in his friend's causal situation and had bought a new boat. He knows that if he, Harsanyi, were in his friend's causal situation and had bought a new boat, he would be exactly as well off as his friend would be if he had bought a new boat. So, on this occasion, the route he is taking to interpersonal comparisons is not via extended preferences. He is taking the alternative route I have described in this section.

3.7   Ordinalism and goodness for a person

It is not surprising that this second route to interpersonal comparisons is not made very explicit in the writings of ordinalists. It is inconsistent with ordinalism. The route goes like this. First, we must have extended alternatives ordered by their goodness for one person. We know that an extended alternative is equally as good for one person as it is for any other person. So the ordering for the single person will also be an interpersonal ordering. But how do we find an ordering for the single person to start with? The answer cannot be consistent with ordinalism.

According to ordinalism, we should have to find the single person's ordering through her preferences. The ordering we are interested in is the ordering of extended alternatives by their goodness for the person. We could find it through the person's extended preferences if the preference-satisfaction theory of good (see section 3.2) were true. This theory implies that the ordering of extended alternatives by their goodness for a person coincides with the person's extended preference ordering. But by now I am able to say with confidence that the preference-satisfaction theory is false, at least when applied to extended preferences. If it were true, one person's extended preference ordering would coincide with the ordering of the alternatives by their goodness for the person. That is to say, it would coincide with their ordering by, simply, their goodness. Consequently, it would coincide with *everyone*'s extended preference ordering. So the preference-satisfaction theory implies that everyone has the same extended preferences. But people do not all have the same extended preferences. Therefore, the preference-satisfaction theory is false. It follows that we cannot use a person's extended preferences to find an ordering of extended alternatives by their goodness for that person. We cannot find this ordering in a way consistent with ordinalism.

The argument in the previous paragraph depends on my assertion that people do not all have the same extended preferences. Up to section 3.5, I took seriously the claim that everyone necessarily has the same extended preferences, despite the counterexample of the academic and the financial analyst. But now, after the collapse of the causal argument, I need no longer take this claim seriously. I am happy to use the clear fact that extended preferences differ – for instance, that different people have different preferences between the life of an academic and the life of a financial analyst – as

evidence against the preference-satisfaction theory of good. The preferences of all of us are determined by our causal situation, and, in the world
as it is, our preferences are caused to differ. I come out preferring to be an
academic, and an analyst comes out preferring to be an analyst.

To be sure, the preference-satisfaction theory is concerned only with
high-grade preferences (see section 3.2). If either my preferences or the
analyst's were not high-grade, our differing preferences would not confute
the preference-satisfaction theory. But both our preferences might be high-
grade by any reasonable test. We might have thought long and hard about
the relative merits of the two alternatives, scratching our ears, applying our
best mental powers and using all the information available. The difference
between us is our values: our different causal situations cause us to have
different values. But that is no reason to think one of us irrational or ill
informed.

It might be that one of the alternatives that face us is better than the other
as a matter of objective fact. I doubt it, but suppose it is for a moment. Then
either I or the analyst has got it wrong: one of us prefers an alternative that
is objectively worse. Let it be the analyst. Could we say the analyst's preference fails to be high-grade on that account? Could our test of quality for
preferences be that they must be in line with objective goodness? That
would be inconsistent with the epistemology of ordinalism. It would imply
that we could not know whether a preference between two alternatives was
high-grade unless we first knew which of the alternatives was better.
According to ordinalism, however, we could know nothing about the goodness of any alternative unless we already knew some preferences and knew
that those preferences were high-grade. There is no way to break into this
circle. So, even if one of our preferences is objectively wrong, it cannot
follow that it is not a high-grade preference. A high-grade preference
cannot be defined in such a demanding way.

We have to conclude that the preference-satisfaction theory of good is
false when applied to extended preferences. This is not a serious problem
for ordinalism itself; ordinalists can perfectly well decline to apply ordinalism to the arcane domain of extended preferences. But it does mean that
there is no route to interpersonal comparisons of good that is consistent
with ordinalism. Granted their own assumptions, those ordinalists who
deny the possibility of interpersonal comparisons are right.

3.8   From individual orderings to interpersonal orderings?

In section 3.6, I suggested we might be able to move from a ordering of
extended preferences by their goodness for a single person to an interpersonal ordering. In section 3.7, I explained that this idea is inconsistent with

ordinalism because we could not derive a single person's ordering from preferences. Is there any other way we could find out a single person's ordering, in order to discover an interpersonal one?

What must we do to order extended alternatives by their goodness for a person? The task has two parts. First, we must do some theoretical work in ethics to discover what a person's good consists in. Then we must do some empirical work to see how much of this good is delivered by each particular alternative. The nature of the empirical research we shall need to do depends on what conclusion we have reached at the first stage, in deciding what a person's good consists in.

For instance, suppose we conclude that ethical hedonism is correct, and a person's good consists in having good feelings. Then we shall have to do some psychological research into how good are the feelings that different ways of life produce. One way of proceeding would be to take a subject, put her into various causal situations, and ask her which ones make her feel better or worse. This would give us an ordering of the alternative situations by their goodness for the subject. However, the types of alternative we are interested in are whole lives together with the personal characteristics of the people living them. No experiment would allow us to put one subject into a range of alternative situations of this sort. Instead, our empirical research will require us to compare the feelings of a person living one life with the feelings of a different person living another life, to see which feelings are better. But many people – most ordinalists amongst them – are sceptical about the possibility of comparing the feelings of different people. If they are hedonists, this will lead them to doubt the possibility of interpersonal comparisons of good. However, they might think they can overcome the difficulty by undertaking an imaginary experiment rather than a real one. Instead of causing an actual subject to lead various lives, they would try to imagine themselves leading various lives, and see how they feel when they do. That way, they could find out which lives would be better or worse for themselves: they could order lives by their goodness for themselves. From this personal ordering, they could move to an interpersonal one.

So this is one putative way of finding an order for a person and deriving an interpersonal order from it. But this procedure is dubious for at least two reasons. First, the imaginary experiment itself is dubious. You are supposed to imagine yourself leading a different life from your actual life, with different personal characteristics, and find out how good you feel by observing yourself. However, if the characteristics are much different from your actual characteristics, it would actually be impossible (not just causally impossible, but even metaphysically impossible) for you to have those characteristics, because anyone with those characteristics would not be you. So the situation you are supposed to imagine in this experiment is impossible. Just how you are supposed to conduct this imagined impossible experiment is obscure. Probably the best you could do is imagine a person, not particularly yourself, leading the life and possessing the characteristics you are interested in. You could estimate how good that person would feel. But whatever ordering by goodness you derive from this estimation would not particularly be a personal ordering by goodness for yourself. Yet that is what you are supposed to be finding.

The second reason why the procedure is dubious is that it assumes the dubious doctrine of ethical hedonism. I doubt that hedonism would be the right conclusion to draw from our ethical investigation into what a person's good consists in. I think it is more likely that a person's good consists in a number of more traditional good things: health, having friends, material comfort, varied and interesting experiences, and so on. The most difficult part of our work is likely to be the theoretical job of deciding what these goods are, and how they weigh against each other. After that, we shall come to the empirical investigation into how much of the goods each life delivers to the person who leads that life. But if the goods turn out to be overt things like the ones I mentioned, this may not be so difficult. Hedonists may find the empirical task difficult because they believe the good things in life are feelings, which are often supposed to be covert. But overt goods are more easily detected.

I should like to offer two particular speculations about the conclusions we are likely to come to. I think one conclusion is likely to be that there is no objective fact as to whether the life of an academic is better or worse than the life of a financial analyst. Different goods, such as wealth and opportunities to contribute to knowledge, are surely incommensurable to some extent, from an objective point of view. Consequently, there is room for the analyst and me to have different extended preferences, without either of our preferences being open to objective criticism.

A second conclusion is likely to be that nothing can be gained in our research by starting from the good of an individual and then moving to interpersonal comparisons. The question is simply which lives are better than others, and nothing can be gained by asking first which would be better than others for a particular individual. Indeed, this is a peculiar question in the first place.[10] Since it would not have been possible for me to live a life far different from my actual life, it is peculiar to ask how good such a life would be specifically for me. All we can sensibly ask is, simply, how good the life would be. Interpersonal comparisons are unlikely to be a real problem, because our investigation of good is likely to be interpersonal from the start. Section 3.6 mentioned a possible route to interpersonal comparisons through the goodness of lives for individuals; I am now suggesting that this route is redundant.

4   Discounting the future

4.1   Introduction

Should future goods be discounted? Should benefits that will come in the distant future count for less in our planning than benefits that will come in the present or near future? I am not thinking of the plans made by an individual on her own behalf, but of plans made on behalf of the public as a whole, particularly by governments. Should future goods be discounted by public authorities in their planning?

In cost–benefit analysis and other applications of welfare economics, economists typically do count future goods for less than present goods. To many philosophers this seems a reprehensible practice. How, they ask, can the mere date at which a good occurs make any difference to its value? Discounting seems to these philosophers a device for unjustly promoting our own interests at the expense of our descendants'. On the face of it, then, typical economists and typical philosophers seem to disagree. But actually I think there is more misunderstanding here than disagreement. Some economists do indeed disagree fundamentally with some philosophers, but most economists and most philosophers would be on the same side if they came to understand each other properly. I hope this chapter may contribute to a mutual understanding. My first purpose in this chapter is to try and explain to philosophers what economists are doing when they discount the future, and why they are doing it.

The basic point is very simple. When economists and philosophers think of discounting, they typically think of discounting different things. Economists typically discount the sorts of goods that are bought and sold in markets, which I shall call *commodities*. Philosophers are typically think-

From *Philosophy and Public Affairs*, 23 (1994), pp. 128–56. Reprinted by permission of the Johns Hopkins University Press. Much of this chapter was written while I was a visitor at the Centre for Applied Ethics at the University of British Columbia. I am grateful to Wilfred Beckerman, Doug MacLean, Carol Propper, and Tyler Cowen for taking the trouble to write very helpful comments, and to Jonathan Escott and Stefano Vettorazzi for some useful points. This chapter was written with the support of the Economic and Social Research Council, under grant number R000233334.

ing of a more fundamental good, people's *wellbeing*. There are sound reasons to discount most commodities, and there may well be sound reasons not to discount wellbeing. It is perfectly consistent to discount commodities and not wellbeing.

However, it is also true that economists sometimes go too far in discounting; they discount where they ought not. There is some justice in the complaints of philosophers. A second purpose of this chapter is to say where economists overstep the mark.

Section 4.2 describes the idea of discounting wellbeing, but only in order to distinguish it from the discounting of commodities. I shall not discuss whether wellbeing ought or ought not to be discounted; that is not the subject of this chapter. Sections 4.3–4.5 explain the discounting of commodities and how it fits into the theory of cost–benefit analysis, and they explain what justification there is for it. Sections 4.6–4.8 set limits to the justification.

4.2   The pure method of evaluation

In order to distinguish discounting commodities from discounting wellbeing, I shall start by explaining the idea of discounting wellbeing.

Suppose some public authority has to evaluate various alternative actions it might take. For instance, governments these days face a choice between allowing the emission of greenhouse gases to continue unchecked, or doing something to limit it. Let us ignore the uncertainty that in practice always surrounds the results of an action; let us suppose we know what the results of each alternative action will be. So if a particular action is taken, we know how history will then unfold. Particular people will be born, live for a particular time, and die. Each person who lives will have a particular level of wellbeing at each time in her life. If a different action is taken, history will unfold differently. Figure 4.1 shows schematically two alternative histories. Each half of the figure shows one of them. The horizontal axis shows time and the vertical axis people. A vertical solid line marks the present. For each person who lives, a little graph shows her wellbeing from birth to death. Each half of the figure represents a sort of two-dimensional grid, across which wellbeing is distributed. Time is one dimension and people the other. Different actions distribute wellbeing differently across the grid; indeed they may lead to the existence of different people. Alternative *A* in figure 4.1 represents what will happen if greenhouse gases are not controlled; alternative *B* what will happen if they are. *B* shows people worse off in the near future than they are in *A*, because of the cost of controlling the gases. But in the further future it shows more people living, and it shows them better off and longer lived. (I am not pre-

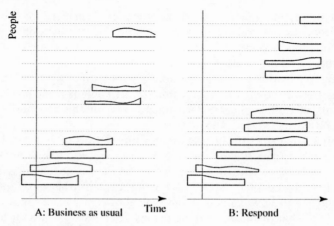

Figure 4.1 Global warning.

dicting that this will definitely be the result of controlling greenhouse gases; the figure is only an illustration.)

An action, then, leads to a particular distribution of wellbeing across the two-dimensional grid of people and times. If alternative actions are open to us, we need to compare one distribution with another in order to decide which action is better. So we need to determine the value of each distribution. Wellbeing distributed across the grid must somehow come together to determine the overall value of the distribution. We need to know how: how is wellbeing *aggregated* across the grid? How is it aggregated across people and across time? Discounting is one part of this question: does wellbeing that comes later in time count for less in the aggregate than wellbeing that comes earlier? If later wellbeing is discounted, I shall call this *pure* discounting. Pure discounting means discounting wellbeing. A pure discount *rate* is the rate at which the value of wellbeing declines as we look forward in time from the present.

Economists often include pure discount rates in their theoretical work, allowing later wellbeing to be counted for less than earlier. But not many economists actually defend pure discounting. Often they include discount rates only for the sake of generality. The rate can always be set to nought, so that later wellbeing is not actually discounted at all. Frank Ramsey, wearing his economist's hat, decried the practice of discounting wellbeing, but nevertheless included discount factors in his work. He says:

It is assumed that we do not discount later enjoyments in comparison with earlier ones, a practice which is ethically indefensible and arises merely from the weakness of imagination; we shall, however, . . . include such a rate of discount in some of our investigations.[1]

So the fact that discount rates appear in their formulae does not show that economists approve of them. Some do, but I think more do not.[2] Most philosophers are opposed to pure discounting, and I think many economists would be on their side; I do not think this is a major point of disagreement. I shall not consider the arguments for and against pure discounting in this chapter. But in order to draw out the contrast with the type of discounting economists do in practice, I shall generally take for granted the majority view that the pure discount rate should be nought: future wellbeing ought not to be discounted.

Theoretical work is one thing. When they come to assessing real projects in practice, such as new roads or plans to control greenhouse gases, economists rarely deal in wellbeing at all. The direct way to evaluate a practical project would be to work out the distribution of wellbeing that would result from it, and then find its overall value by aggregating wellbeing across the two-dimensional grid. I shall call this the *pure* method of evaluation. In practice it would be very difficult. It would require us, first, to work out how well off each person will be at each time in her life, as a result of the project. Even setting uncertainty aside, there are major difficulties in this. To begin with, there may be a fundamental difficulty in principle. In drawing figure 4.1, I took it for granted that the wellbeing of a person at a time is a measurable quantity, which can be compared between people and across times. This assumption is open to serious doubts, which economists know well. Besides, there is in any case the great practical difficulty that information about people's wellbeing is hard to come by. A special problem is that the parts of a modern economy are so tightly interconnected that the effects of any economic action will be propagated to everyone throughout the economy. Remember that any economic project will have to be financed, perhaps by loans or taxes, and that the financing will have its own complex repercussions. It would be impossible in practice to calculate all the effects on everyone.

Working out everyone's wellbeing at every time would only be the beginning of a pure evaluation. We would next have to aggregate all these amounts to arrive at the overall value of a project. To do so, we would need a theory of how this aggregation should be done. This would be an ethical theory, and it would not be easy to arrive at. One component of it would be the question of pure discounting: should future wellbeing be discounted? This alone is hard to settle.

Because of all these difficulties, economists have sensibly looked for a more practical method for evaluating projects. They want a short cut, which cuts through some of the difficulties. In particular, they want to avoid the need for difficult judgements about people's wellbeing and how to aggregate it. It is only a short cut they are after. I think most economists would agree that the pure method would give the right answer if it could be applied.[3] The short cut is not meant to supersede the pure method, but only to arrive at the right answer more easily. Here is the eminent economist Joseph Stiglitz saying as much:

Any project can be viewed as a perturbation of the economy from what it would have been had some other project been undertaken instead. To determine whether the project should be undertaken, we first need to look at the levels of consumption of all commodities by all individuals at all dates under the two different situations. If all individuals are better off with the project than without it, then clearly it should be adopted (if we adopt an individualistic social welfare function). If all individuals are worse off, then clearly it should not be adopted. If some individuals are better off and others are worse off, whether we should adopt it or not depends critically on how we weight the gains and losses of different individuals. Although this is obviously the 'correct' procedure to follow in evaluating projects, it is not a practical one; the problem of benefit–cost analysis is simply whether we can find reasonable shortcuts. In particular, we are presumed to have good information concerning the direct costs and benefits of a project, that is, its inputs and outputs. The question is, is there any simple way of relating the total effects, that is, the total changes in the vectors of consumption, to the direct effects?[4]

Economists have ended up taking a short cut that leads them to deal in commodities rather than wellbeing. It leads them to discount future commodities, but not necessarily future wellbeing.

4.3   The market price method of evaluation

In making an evaluation, the instinct of economists is to draw the information they need from the market. In this section, I shall explain the thinking that supports this instinct at a general level. I shall apply it to discounting in section 4.5.[5]

The market – specifically prices – provides us with information about the values people attach to different commodities. Take the two commodities labour and wine, for instance. Suppose labour is paid £10 per hour, and wine costs £5 per bottle. Each Sunday, in planning your week, you have to decide how much work to do that week, and how much wine to buy. Having decided, you could always change your mind. For instance, you could work one hour more and buy two more bottles of wine, or you could work one hour less and buy two bottles fewer. But suppose you do not make these changes; you are in *equilibrium* – happy with your plans. This shows that two bottles are worth just as much to you as an hour of labour (or – as it appears from your point of view – an hour of *leisure*). More precisely, if your purchases were to *change* by two bottles, given what you are already planning to buy, that would be worth just as much to you as a change of one hour in your leisure time. Economists say two bottles of wine are worth as much to you as one hour of leisure *at the margin*. This expression means that an extra two bottles of wine, added to the bottles you already plan to buy, are worth an extra hour of leisure added to your planned leisure time.

I have explained, then, that the relative price prevailing in the market between wine and leisure must be exactly the same as the relative value to you of the two commodities at the margin. If it were any different, you would change your plans; you would work less and buy less wine, or else you would work more and buy more wine. When you are in equilibrium, the relative price must match the relative value to you.

For the same reason, the relative price of wine and labour must be the same as the relative value at the margin to anyone, and not just to you. But how can the relative value of wine and leisure be the same for everyone? Surely people differ in the values they attach to these things. The answer is that the prices are the same for everyone, and everyone adjusts herself to the prices. Suppose you happen to value two bottles of wine above an hour of leisure. Then you will sign up for more work, earn some more money, and buy some more wine. If you still value two bottles of wine above an hour of leisure, you will sign up for more work still. But eventually, as you work longer and longer hours, the labour will begin to exhaust you, and you will have so much wine that its pleasures begin to pall. The value you attach to wine will fall, and the value you attach to leisure will rise. In saying this, I am assuming that wine and leisure have 'diminishing marginal value' to you: the more of them you have, the less you will value an extra unit. Economists generally make the plausible assumption that commodities have diminishing marginal value, and I am adopting this assumption. You will reach an equilibrium where two bottles of wine are worth one hour of leisure to you, at the margin. That is how your relative values at the margin come to match the relative prices in equilibrium. By the same process, so will everyone else's.

Relative prices, then, measure people's relative values. What do I mean by relative *values*? If a person's aim in life is to maximize her wellbeing, the value to her of a commodity is the wellbeing she derives from it. In that case, prices measure the relative amounts of wellbeing that commodities bring her at the margin. This means they provide data for evaluations of just the sort we are looking for; as I described pure evaluations, the data needed are people's wellbeing, and we are looking for a short cut to a pure evaluation. But suppose a person's aim is not to maximize her wellbeing. In that case, the value to her of a commodity will not be the wellbeing she derives from it. But no matter, many economists would say: people should be free to choose their own aims in life. If they happen not to pursue their own wellbeing, that is their business. When it evaluates a project, a public authority should use the values people attach to commodities, whatever may be the aims that underlie these values.

There is a complication.[6] Many of the things that concern public authorities when they evaluate projects are not bought and sold on the market, so they do not have a price. Examples are public goods such as street lighting and safety equipment installed in nuclear power stations. (Even though they are not marketed, I shall call these 'commodities' in this chapter.) How can we find the value to people of a nonmarketed commodity? We can use the price that people would be *willing to pay* for it if they had to, instead of their actual price. A person might be willing to pay something to have street lighting or safety equipment installed. The amount she is willing to pay for a commodity measures its value to her, compared with the value of other things she buys. It can be used as a measure of value to her in place of market price. People's willingness to pay for a commodity is not as easy to find as a market price, but in practice it can be worked out by various means.

How can prices, or willingness to pay, be used in evaluating a project? A project uses some commodities as inputs and produces others as outputs. Think of one that uses labour as input and produces wine as output. Suppose this project is *profitable* at market prices. That is to say, if prices are £10 for labour and £5 for wine, the project produces more than two bottles of wine as output for every hour of labour used as input. Now, everyone assigns the same value to two bottles as to one hour of labour at the margin. So everyone values the output of this project more than its input. Surely, then, the project is beneficial.

This simple thought is the basis of cost–benefit analysis. To decide whether a project is a good idea (by which I mean it is better to do it than not), first list all the commodities the project will use as inputs and all those it will produce as outputs. Value them all at market prices or, failing that, at people's willingness to pay for them. Call the value of an output a 'benefit' and the value of an input a 'cost'. If benefits exceed the costs valued this way, the project is profitable at market prices. In that case declare it a good idea. I shall call this the *market price method* for evaluating a project.

It seems plausible, but there is a snag. We need to ask how the project is to be operated. Who will supply the inputs and who will get the outputs? One possibility is that the costs are borne by the same people as receive the benefits. In the example, the labour might be done by the people who eventually receive the output of wine. Each of these people might be employed on the project, and paid for her labour in wine. The pay could be more than two bottles per hour, since the project produces more than two per hour. Since each person values two bottles more than one hour of leisure, each would be benefited by the exchange. (Assume each person works only a little time on the project, so that the change is marginal.) All these people would be benefited, and no one would be harmed. Undoubtedly the project operated this way would be a good idea. If it were operated this way, we could sidestep all the theoretical problems of aggregating wellbeing across a grid like figure 4.1. Since the project would make everyone better off, there would be no need to worry about aggregating wellbeing across people and times.

But in practice the benefits of a project often come to people who have not borne the costs, or all of the costs. When a road is built, some people have to suffer the noise it makes, while quite different people benefit. I can fit this possibility into my simple example only by making an exaggerated assumption. Assume the labour is coerced, without pay, and the wine produced is distributed to people who have not done the work. Have we any reason to suppose that the benefit to these people is greater than the cost to the workers? No. We know how each person individually values wine compared with leisure; that information is given us by the market prices. It happens that everyone values two bottles of wine equally with one hour of leisure. But we do not know how one person values wine compared with how another person values leisure; market prices do not convey that information. It may be that the workers value their sacrificed leisure more than the beneficiaries value their extra wine. In general, if some people bear the costs of a project and others get the benefits, we cannot tell from market prices whether the project is a good idea or not.

This is a fundamental difficulty in cost–benefit analysis. So long as a project harms some people and benefits others, valuing commodities by their market prices, or by willingness to pay, is not a reliable way to check whether the project is a good idea. The problem will be most severe if the people who are benefited are much better off or much worse off than the people who are harmed. When a person is in equilibrium, the price in money she pays for a commodity is the value of the commodity to her at the margin, divided by the value of money to her. For a given value of money, the price of a commodity is therefore a measure of the commodity's value to the person. Amongst people who are about equally well off, it is reasonable to assume the value of money to each of them is much the same. So amongst such people, prices may be reasonably good measures of values. On the other hand, money to a poor person is probably worth much more than money to a rich person. Between rich and poor, then, the prices of commodities are not good measures of their values. Of course, economists have ways of coping with this problem, which I shall not go into here.

This chapter is concerned with the distribution of resources between the present and the future. For the sorts of project I am interested in, the people who benefit from a project will often not in practice be the ones who bear the costs; they may well be in different generations. Furthermore, they may not be equally well off, because future generations may be much richer, or much poorer, than us. So one might expect the problem I have mentioned to be particularly acute for projects that cross generations. But actually it is not. The reason is that, in a way, the market price method ignores future generations. Their wellbeing is taken into account by the method only to the extent that it is valued by the present generation. This is a major weakness in the method, which I shall discuss in section 4.7. But it does happen to cancel out the fundamental weakness I have been describing. When the market price method comes to deal with intertemporal questions, it treats them as questions about how the present generation values future commodities compared with present commodities, not as questions about how the values of the present generation compare with the values of future generations. Distribution between rich and poor generations is not really at issue. Consequently, I think it is reasonable to set aside this most fundamental problem with the market price method, and concentrate on difficulties that are specific to discounting. That is what I shall do.

4.4   The present prices of future commodities

Before I can explain how to apply the market price method to discounting, I need to introduce a useful theoretical device: the idea of dated commodities and their prices. Suppose I have £100. I can buy twenty bottles of wine with it at £5 each. Alternatively, I can put it in the bank. After a year I can get the money out, with interest. If the interest rate is 10 per cent I will have £110. If wine has meanwhile gone up to £5.25, I can then buy just about twenty-one bottles of wine. So £100 now will, in effect, buy me twenty-one bottles of wine in a year's time. We can think of wine in one year's time as a commodity on its own, separate from wine now, and its present price is about £4.75 (£100 divided by 21, that is). This is what, in effect, I have to pay now in order to acquire a bottle of wine in a year's time. Since £4.75 is less than £5, the present price of future wine is less than the present price of present wine. In general, a commodity at any date – a *dated commodity* – has a present price. From now on, when I speak of the price of a future commodity, I mean its present price unless I say otherwise. The percentage difference between the present price of a present commodity and the present price of the same commodity next year (I mean, for instance, the 1994 price of the commodity in 1995, not the 1995 price of it) is called the commodity's *own interest rate*. In my example the own interest rate of wine is 5 per cent.

Commodities typically have positive own interest rates. That is to say, future commodities are typically cheaper (in the present) than present commodities. If you have a particular sum of money, you can generally buy more of a future commodity with it than you can of a present commodity, by keeping the money in a bank and earning interest. The only exceptions are commodities whose *current* price (for instance, the 2001 price of the commodity in 2001) increases through time as fast as, or faster than, the rate of interest at the bank. These commodities have own interest rates that are nought or negative.

The relative price of commodities indicates the relative value people place on these commodities. This is true amongst present commodities and also between present commodities and future commodities. In my example, the price of future wine, one year from now, is 5 per cent below the price of present wine. Therefore, once people are in equilibrium – have made their plans, bought the amount of present wine they want, and set aside what they want in order to buy future wine – each person values present wine 5 per cent above future wine, at the margin.

How can this be? Future commodities are generally cheaper than present commodities, which implies that most people value future commodities less than present ones. But why should they? Why should a person value a commodity less just because she will possess it in 2001 rather than 2000?

The answer to this question has two parts. The first part is to explain why future commodities are generally cheaper than present ones anyway. Oddly enough, this has little to do with the values of the people who buy present and future commodities. It has to do with the economy's productive technology, not with its consumption. Technology is, in a particular sense, *fertile*. It is a fact of technology that, to speak roughly, present commodities can be converted into a greater quantity of future commodities, if we choose.[7] Trees grow, for instance. If I fell my forests now, I shall harvest a particular quantity of timber. If I fell them next year, I shall harvest more. Let us say I shall harvest 5 per cent more. The nature of my production process, then, gives me a choice between timber now and 5 per cent more timber next year. This means that, when the economy is in equilibrium, the present price of next year's timber must be 5 per cent below the price of this year's. If it were any higher, I would leave all my harvest to next year, and so would all my landowning colleagues. No timber would be put on the market this year. That would quickly drive up the price of this year's timber till it is 5 per cent above the price of next year's. At that point I would begin harvesting again. Likewise, if this year's timber rose higher than 5 per cent above next year's, the opposite would happen. The economy will be in equilibrium only when the price difference is 5 per cent.

On the scale of a whole economy, things are much the same. Each year, some of the goods produced by the economy are consumed and some are reinvested, and the division between investment and consumption can be varied. If fewer commodities are consumed this year, more can be invested. The result will be more commodities produced next year, and next year's increase will exceed the decrease in consumption this year. Just as timber this year can, in effect, be converted by the production process into a greater quantity of timber next year, commodities in general this year can be converted into a greater quantity of commodities next year. This is what I mean when I say technology is fertile. A consequence is that next year's commodities must be cheaper than this year's. If they were not, producers would increase their investment this year, in effect switching their production to next year's commodities instead of this year's. This will increase the price of this year's commodities relative to next year's, till an equilibrium is reached with future commodities cheaper than present ones. Most commodities will therefore have positive own interest rates. This is a necessary consequence of the fertility of technology.

Not every commodity will have a positive own rate of interest, though; I shall mention exceptions in section 4.6. Nor need it always be true that most commodities will have a positive rate. Our technology may not always be fertile. If, say, runaway global warming damages our productive abilities, or our resources are exhausted, future commodities may become more expensive than present ones. Own rates of interest may become generally negative. Still, with our present fertile technology, they are generally positive.

An economy's fertility may be affected to some extent by the decisions of consumers about saving. Suppose people decide to increase their savings, delaying some of their consumption to the future. In effect, they buy more future commodities in preference to present ones. This could have the effect of raising the prices of future commodities compared with present ones, and so reducing own interest rates. How could this happen? Only by causing a switch in the technical methods employed in the economy, to less fertile methods. Here is a simple example. The change in consumers' behaviour might induce the owners of forests to fell their trees at a more advanced age. But trees grow more slowly as they get older. So the change would cause the fertility of forestry to decline, and the equilibrium own interest rate of timber would be reduced. In ways like this, consumers might influence the fertility of technology. But for reasons I shall not go into here,[8] I think their influence is small. It is a fair approximation to think of fertility, and hence interest rates, as given independently of decisions about saving.

Tyler Cowen and Derek Parfit, on the other hand, stress the influence of savings on interest rates, and suggest it is crucial to the argument about discounting.[9] I think not. But although my approximation is helpful for thinking about the problem, it is not essential for the argument. We are concerned with interest rates established in the market, because these rates indicate the relative values people attach to present and future commodities. The important question is whether or not these rates are generally positive, because a positive rate implies that future commodities have a lower value than present ones. In so far as savings influence interest rates, interest rates in the market will be determined by the mutual interaction of technology on the one hand and consumers' decisions about savings on the other. In present conditions, own interest rates will certainly emerge from this interaction generally positive. That is all that matters.[10]

If interest rates are positive, people attach less value to future commodities than to present ones. The second part of the answer to the question I posed earlier is to explain how this can happen. The explanation is that people must adjust themselves to the prices they face. Suppose next year's wine is as valuable to you as present wine. If it is cheaper than present wine, you will save your money and buy next year's wine rather than this year's. As you do this, and so find yourself with less wine this year, you will find you value this year's wine more, and are less keen on buying yet more future wine. When you are in equilibrium, the relative values you attach to present and future wine at the margin must match their relative prices. Everyone will be in the same position. We shall all adjust our relative values, at the margin, to each commodity's own rate of interest. The process is exactly the same as the one I described in section 4.3 for undated commodities.

This may still be mysterious. Even after adjustment, how can future wine be less valuable to you than present wine? Just because it comes in the future, how can that make it less valuable? I can think of three possible explanations. One is that the benefit you expect to get from wine declines with your advancing years: for any given quantity of wine, you expect to enjoy it less the older you are. I shall ignore this possibility in order to concentrate on the other two explanations, which I think are more important. I shall assume that, at any time in your life, a particular quantity of wine will bring you the same wellbeing as it would at any other time.

The next possibility is illustrated by the indifference curve figure in figure 4.2. I am here assuming your aim is to maximize your own wellbeing. This means, among other things, that you do not discount your own future wellbeing compared with your present wellbeing; both count the same in your present values. Since I have already assumed that a particular quantity of wine brings you the same wellbeing in the future as in the present, your indifference curves must be symmetrical about the 45° line – the dotted line in the figure. Your 'budget line' in the figure shows the options that are available to you, given whatever you have available to spend on wine. Your options are not symmetrical, because future wine is cheaper than present wine. This means the budget line is steeper than 45°. Of all the options available to you on the budget line, you choose the one that puts you on the

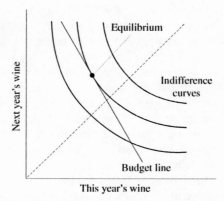

Figure 4.2 Increasing consumption.

highest possible indifference curve. This is where an indifference curve touches the budget line. The figure shows you will buy more future wine than present wine. This is how you end up valuing future wine less at the margin than present wine. All along, I have been assuming wine has a diminishing marginal value: the more of it you have, the less wellbeing an extra bottle will bring you. Since you have more future wine, you value extra bottles of it less.

Wine will presumably have a positive own interest rate throughout your life. Consequently, wine at later dates must always be less valuable to you at the margin than wine at earlier dates. If the explanation I have just given of how this happens is the right one, you must buy progressively more and more wine as your life continues. This point will become important in section 4.8.

The third possible explanation is illustrated in figure 4.3. Here you your-self discount your future wellbeing; you value it less than your present well-being. Let us call this *imprudence* on your part. Imprudence skews your indifference curves towards present wine; the curves are not symmetrical about the 45° line, but steeper than that. Your budget line still has the same slope as before. In equilibrium you must value future wine less than present wine, since its price is less. If you are imprudent that may happen even if you buy the same amounts of present and future wine. That is what the figure shows: the point of tangency between the budget line and the highest indifference curve you can reach lies on the 45° line. This will happen only by coincidence, because your degree of imprudence happens to match the own interest rate of wine. But it certainly can happen.

Figure 4.3 Imprudence.

4.5   Discounting in the market price method

Now back to cost–benefit analysis. In section 4.3, I described how the prices of commodities can be used in cost–benefit analysis. To evaluate a project, list the commodities it uses as inputs and the commodities it produces as outputs, and evaluate them all at their market prices. Since market prices indicate their relative values to people, this seems a good basis for judging whether or not the project is a good idea.

Exactly the same idea extends to projects that have inputs and outputs at different dates. All the inputs and outputs can be evaluated at their market prices. In this case, these are the present prices of dated commodities. They measure the relative values of the dated commodities to people, so they seem a good basis for cost–benefit analysis. Generally, future commodities have lower present prices than present commodities. This process consequently discounts future commodities; it values them less than present commodities. This method provides a basis for discounting, then. The discount is applied to commodities, and not wellbeing.

This is just the market price method of evaluation applied to the present and the future. Its great advantage is that the information it needs comes from the market. I said in section 4.2 that economists were looking for a short cut through the difficulties of the pure method. This is it. There is no need to enquire how much wellbeing each person derives from the project. Nor is there any need to engage in philosophical analysis to work out appropriate discount factors for future wellbeing. The market price method cuts through all that. Its discount factors come from the market like any other prices; they are simply the prices of future commodities compared with present ones. It may well be that future wellbeing ought not to be discounted at all. Even so, the market will value future commodities below present ones. So, if we are going to calculate with commodities at all, future commodities ought to be discounted.

There are, to be sure, some major valid objections to be made to the market price method. I shall come to them soon. But I think it is a mistake to object to the general idea of using this short cut to evaluating projects. In his discussion of discounting in *Reasons and Persons*, Derek Parfit raises several accurate objections to the market price method,[11] but I think he underestimates the method's value. He says:

It may be in several ways more convenient, or elegant, to calculate opportunity costs using a Social Discount Rate. But the conclusions that are established by such calculations could be re-expressed in a temporally neutral way. When describing the effects of future policies, economists could state what future benefits and costs there would be, at different times, in a way that used no discount rate. The arguments that appeal to opportunity costs could be fully stated in these terms. I believe that, on any important questions that we need to decide, this would be a better, because less misleading, description of the alternatives.[12]

Before responding to this remark, let me explain the idea of an 'opportunity cost'. By the opportunity cost of something is meant what we could have instead, if we chose not to have this thing. The opportunity cost of timber today is the timber we could have next year if the trees were not felled today. Because trees grow, this opportunity cost is a greater amount of timber next year. That is why today's timber is more expensive than next year's timber; you have to give up a greater amount of next year's timber to get it. In general, because technology is fertile, the opportunity cost of commodities today is a greater quantity of commodities next year. That is why commodities today are more expensive than commodities next year – why next year's commodities are discounted, that is.

The opportunity costs of commodities are embedded in their prices. A cost–benefit analyst would simply value next year's timber below this year's in her calculations, next year's concrete below this year's, and so on, taking her valuations from market prices. What would Parfit have her do instead? He would have her trace through the economy all the effects on people's wellbeing, at each time in the future, of using timber and concrete at particular dates. He would then have her add up these amounts of wellbeing, without discounting future wellbeing. Parfit, in fact, would like the economist to use the pure method of evaluation, without discounting wellbeing. But this would be a tremendously difficult operation, and normally pointless. The point of using prices is that, in a sense, they encapsulate all that information about the effects on people's wellbeing in an easily manageable and observable form. The market price method is a short cut to the pure method, and it is a hundred times more practical.

In his discussion, Parfit concentrates on difficult cases where a cost–benefit analyst would be wrong to discount a particular future commodity. The existence of a stretch of beautiful countryside is one of his examples of a commodity, and Parfit is right that this one ought not to be discounted. I shall mention these cases in section 4.6. The difficult cases lead Parfit to forget all the mundane cases where the discounting of future commodities is legitimate, and the only practical way of proceeding. Furthermore, as I shall explain in section 4.6, even in these difficult cases the market price method would get the right answer if it was properly applied. This method actually tells us not to discount the future existence of a stretch of beautiful countryside.

Parfit raises a related point. He mentions, as a legitimate reason for valuing future commodities below present ones, that our successors will be better off than us. Being better off, they will derive less wellbeing from extra commodities they receive than we will; this is the law of diminishing marginal value. So it is better, at the margin, for commodities to come to us than to them. However, says Parfit, the reason future commodities are less valuable is not that they exist in the future. It is that they are coming to people who are better off. It is deceptive to say we are discounting for time.[13]

In the theory I have developed so far, I have not yet mentioned our successors. Nevertheless, the situation depicted in figure 4.2 allows me to say something about Parfit's point. That figure shows a person who consumes more wine next year than this year, because next year's wine is cheaper than this year's. Since most commodities are cheaper next year than this, she will consume more of most commodities next year than this. In a sense, she is better off next year than this because she has a greater consumption then. Consequently, the marginal value to her of all these commodities is less next year than this. Her situation mimics within her single life the relation between us and our successors that Parfit talks about. So we can use this example to examine Parfit's point.

Future commodities are discounted compared with present ones: they have a lower present price. Correspondingly, the value to people of future commodities is less than the value of present ones. Is the discount a discount for time? Parfit says no: since future commodities are discounted because people have more future commodities than present ones, it is misleading to say the discount is for time. But I do not think it is misleading. It is commodities we are discounting, not wellbeing. Dated commodities are identified by their dates, and it happens that future commodities are cheaper than present ones. This can reasonably be called a discount for time. What *causes* future commodities to be cheaper than present ones is another matter. Evening phone calls are discounted compared with daytime phone calls. The cause of this discount is that fewer people use the phone in the evening; there is less pressure on the phone company's resources, so that each call costs less to provide. Nevertheless, the discount is for the time you make the call. It is evening calls that the phone company markets at a discount, not calls when few people are using the phone.

As I explained in section 4.4, the fertility of the economy's productive system is the chief cause why future commodities are cheaper. The fact that people, like the person in figure 4.2, end up assigning a lower value to future commodities than present ones is more an effect than a cause. People arrange their affairs so as to consume more in the future, and consequently they end up assigning less value to future commodities at the margin. But even if it were a cause, the discount would still be for time. Commodities are discounted by their own interest rates, and an interest rate is a discount for time.

4.6   Commodities that should not be discounted

I have explained the thinking that underlies the market price method, and said what is right about it. Now I come to what is wrong with it. A lot of sound objections have been raised against it, but I shall mention only three here.[14]

The first objection is not to the theory of the market price method, but to the way the method is applied in practice. I explained that a commodity in the future normally has a lower price than in the present. It is discounted, that is to say, and the appropriate discount is given by its own interest rate. According to the theory, each commodity should be discounted at its own rate. But in practice all commodities are generally lumped together and discounted at the same rate. Normally, they are all discounted at something called the 'real' interest rate, which is a weighted average of the own interest rates of various commodities.

This may be an acceptable approximation for most commodities. Most commodities are produced within the economic system, and most of them have similar own interest rates, determined principally by the fertility of the technology. But some commodities have quite different rates. These include nonreproducible scarce resources, which are not produced at all. I explained in section 4.4 that most present commodities can, in a sense, be converted into a greater quantity of future commodities. That is why future commodities are generally cheaper than present ones. But this is true only of commodities that are produced within the economic system. Scarce resources cannot be converted into a greater quantity of future resources, and they therefore have own interest rates of zero or thereabouts.[15] It follows that they ought not to be discounted, even according to the theory of the market price method. Derek Parfit gives an example: a stretch of beautiful countryside, which might be destroyed to build an airport.[16] The value of this scarce resource will remain the same through time; it will not decline like the value of produced commodities. It ought not to be discounted, and the theory underlying the market price method says it ought not to be discounted.

Parfit mentions another type of commodity that ought not to be discounted. Some industrial plants cause congenital deformities amongst people born in their neighbourhoods. In valuing the plants, cost–benefit analysts often discount deformities that will happen in the distant future; they give them less significance than present ones. But Parfit says that is a mistake. A deformity caused at one time is just as bad as a deformity caused at another. It leads to the same loss of wellbeing, and, since Parfit believes wellbeing ought not to be discounted, he believes deformities ought not to be discounted either.[17]

Let us grant the premise that wellbeing ought not to be discounted. Then I am sure Parfit is right that deformities ought not to be discounted. But this example is theoretically tricky, and more needs to be said about it. Some commodities represent a constant quantity of wellbeing whenever they occur; let us call them constant-wellbeing commodities. Deformities are a negative constant-wellbeing commodity. For theoretical purposes, it is easier to work with positive commodities, so let us work with the converse of deformities: the positive commodity of saving people from deformities. Saving people's lives is plausibly another example of a constant-wellbeing commodity; on average, saving a person's life in one hundred years' time will presumably add just as much wellbeing to the world as saving a person's life now. Granted that wellbeing ought not to be discounted, constant-wellbeing commodities ought not to be discounted.

Some constant-wellbeing commodities are scarce resources, but some are not. Life saving is not, for instance. Life saving is actually a produced commodity. People's lives are saved by care in hospitals, by installing safety devices in factories, by propaganda against smoking, and in many other ways; these are all ways in which the commodity of life saving is produced by the economy. Furthermore, life saving participates in the general fertility of the productive system. It is like timber: a quantity of life saving in the present can be converted into a greater quantity in the future. We can, if we choose, use fewer resources on life saving today, invest them productively, and so have greater resources available next year, which we could use to save more lives next year. Because present timber can be converted into a greater quantity of future timber, future timber must be cheaper than present timber in equilibrium. Timber is therefore discounted. Surely, therefore, the same should be true of life saving. Future life saving is cheaper than present life saving; so life saving should be discounted. But this contradicts my earlier remark that it should not be discounted because it is a constant-wellbeing commodity. So there is a puzzle. Which is right?

The answer is that the earlier remark was right: if life saving is a constant-wellbeing commodity, it should not be discounted. Life saving in the future will make the same contribution to wellbeing as life saving in the present. Sure enough, future life saving is cheaper than present life saving, but this is not a reason for valuing it less. The market prices of commodities have a role in valuations only because they measure the relative values of commodities to people. In equilibrium, they will do so, and up to now I have been assuming the economy is in equilibrium. But if life saving produces constant wellbeing, and yet is cheaper in the future, we evidently do not have an equilibrium. With ordinary commodities like timber, there is a market that will move to equilibrium if it is working smoothly. But with life saving there is no such market. Nor is there one for saving people from deformities. We have no reason to discount these commodities at an interest rate that has been established in the market for marketed commodities.

There is more to the puzzle, though. If we can convert a quantity of life saving now into a greater quantity next year, and if life saving next year is just as valuable as life saving now, the conclusion we have to draw is that life saving should be deferred. We should withdraw resources from life saving today, and apply them to saving more lives next year. We should also defer life saving next year in order to save yet more lives the year after. We should defer life saving the year after in order to save still more the year after that, and so on. We will end up postponing all life saving to the indefinite future, which never comes. So we will end up saving no lives at all. If life saving produces constant wellbeing, and yet its price declines with time, this is the conclusion we must draw. But it is a ridiculous one. We have a paradox.

Here is one possible solution. Life saving may not be a constant-wellbeing commodity after all. Undoubtedly, saving some people's lives adds more wellbeing to the world than saving other people's. Saving a twenty-year-old with a long and happy future ahead of her adds more to wellbeing than saving a ninety-year-old with little left to look forward to. We may expect that, by and large, a society will first direct its resources to saving the people with most wellbeing to gain. As it progresses in its ability to save lives, it will start to save people with less and less to gain. In the future, therefore, where more lives are being saved, life saving will, by and large, produce less wellbeing at the margin. Therefore, the more life saving is deferred to the future, the less wellbeing it will produce on average at the margin. Eventually, as life saving is deferred, there will come a point where the lower price of future life saving is matched by its lower benefit in terms of wellbeing. After that, it would be wrong to defer any more life saving. At that point, future life saving is on average genuinely less valuable than present life saving. Life saving should then be discounted.

It is possible that we are in this position already. If we are, life saving is not a constant-wellbeing commodity, and it should be discounted. But we have no reason to think this is so, because there is no market that can be expected to make it so. We cannot rely on a market interest rate. All we can do is consider directly what wellbeing will result from life saving at different dates. If we conclude that life saving will lead to the same amount of wellbeing at every date, as I assumed earlier, it should not be discounted. The same goes for saving people from deformities.

4.7   Disenfranchised generations

My second objection is that for many projects most of the interested parties are not represented in the market. Many projects will affect future generations for centuries or millennia ahead. Nuclear waste will remain dangerous for many thousands of years, and projects for disposing of it must take account of that. Attempts to control global warming will bring their main benefits more than a century from now. But the only people whose values are registered in market prices are those who are alive now. This is surely a very serious gap in the market price method.

One thing might lead you to think not. I suggested in section 4.4 that the main determinant of interest rates is the economy's technology, specifically its fertility. If this is correct, then interest rates would not be much different even if, in some way, future generations came to be represented in the market. Imagine a trust for future generations was set up, able to borrow money against the potential earnings of future generations, and empowered to buy resources for their use. Once the economy settled down to a new equilibrium, interest rates would not have changed much.

So is the disenfranchisement of future generations a significant fault in the market price method of evaluation, or is it not? If enfranchisement would not make much difference to interest rates, surely not: the market price method uses interest rates that are about correct. But actually this reasoning is erroneous. Interest rates would be about the same in the new *equilibrium*, after the economy has settled down. But just after the new trust was set up, the economy would be very far from equilibrium. From the trust's point of view – representing future generations – future commodities would be much more valuable than they seem to us who are participating in the market now. The trust would use its funds to transfer many more resources to the future. It would buy up future commodities, making them more expensive and reducing their own interest rates. When the new equilibrium was achieved, their prices would drop again to their original level, and interest rates would be restored. But in the meantime many resources would have been transferred away from us for the use of future generations. It is only the disenfranchisement of future generations that gives us the share of the world's resources that we have.

With things as they are, then, in our present equilibrium, if we came to take account of the interests of future generations, we would use lower interest rates. We would discount the future less than we do now in the market. If public authorities took account of the interests of future generations, they would use lower interest rates than market rates in their decision making. This would have the effect of transferring resources forward in time for the use of future people.

Should public authorities act this way? The welfare economist A. C. Pigou thought they should. He wrote:

But there is wide agreement that the State should protect the interests of the future in some degree against the effects of our irrational discounting and of our preference for ourselves over our descendants. The whole movement for 'conservation' in the United States is based on this conviction. It is the clear duty of Government, which is the trustee for unborn generations as well as for its present citizens, to watch over, and, if need be, by legislative enactment, to defend, the exhaustible natural resources of the country from rash and reckless spoliation.[18]

On the other hand, some people think a public authority should adopt the values of its constituents. In a democracy, they think, public authorities are responsible to their electorate, which does not include generations not yet born. No doubt the present generation cares about future generations to some extent, and wishes to leave resources for their use. The value the present generation attaches to the wellbeing of future generations will have been embodied in present interest rates, and it would be wrong to give any further value to future generations. Stephen Marglin takes this view. He says:

I want the government's social welfare function to reflect only the preferences of present individuals. Whatever else democratic theory may or may not imply, I consider it axiomatic that a democratic government reflects only the preferences of the individuals who are presently members of the body politic.[19]

Marglin and Pigou are arguing about what the job of a government is – an argument in political philosophy that I do not wish to join in. I shall say something else instead.[20]

Besides the question of what a government ought to do, there is the separate question of which of its actions would have the best results. It is quite possible that the action a government ought to take is not the one that would have the best results. For instance, a government might have a duty to do what its electorate wants, and its electorate might want it to do something that would not have the best results. In this chapter I am concentrating on the question of what would have the best results. That was the question I posed in section 4.2. The problem I laid out was to compare alternative distributions of wellbeing across present and future people, to decide which is better. The market price method of evaluation came up as a possible short cut towards achieving this aim. It was intended to avoid the very difficult process of comparing people's wellbeing directly, but was still meant to determine which distribution of wellbeing is better, weighing together the wellbeing of different people at different times. Marglin suggests, though, that a government's 'social welfare function' should reflect only the preferences of the individuals who are presently members of the body politic. His reason is that he sees the social welfare function as playing a particular role in a democratic political process: helping to determine what a government ought to do. He does not suggest that the social welfare function measures the actual value of the alternative distributions. So his aim is different from the one I have been pursuing in this chapter. I have been looking for a way of aggregating people's wellbeing to determine the overall value of alternative distributions, and for that purpose the wellbeing of future generations needs to be included.

4.8   Imprudence

Market prices indicate the relative values people set on different commodities. In section 4.3, I discussed what 'values' means in this context. I said that, if a person aims to maximize her wellbeing, the value of a commodity to her is the wellbeing she will derive from it. If people generally aim to maximize their wellbeing, then, market prices will indicate what wellbeing people expect to get from commodities. Prices will be some sort of a measure of wellbeing, and the market price method of evaluation has some chance of approximating the pure method.

But if people do not aim to maximize their wellbeing, this will not be so. Imprudence is an important instance. When I say a person is imprudent, I mean she discounts her own future wellbeing; she does not attach as much value to her future wellbeing as she does to her present wellbeing. Figure 4.3 shows indifference curves for an imprudent person. In the example I used for that figure, future wine is 5 per cent cheaper than present wine. In equilibrium the person must adjust her relative values to prices. She therefore values future wine 5 per cent less than present wine, at the margin. But that does not mean an extra bottle of wine in the future would bring her 5 per cent less wellbeing than an extra bottle in the present. As it happens, in the example I assumed it would bring her exactly the same wellbeing. So although future wine is discounted by 5 per cent on the market, it does not bring 5 per cent less wellbeing. The discount rate does not measure wellbeing.

In general, if people are imprudent, the market prices of commodities will not properly represent the commodities' effects on wellbeing. The market price method of evaluation will therefore not correctly indicate the results that would be reached by the pure method. Market interest rates will discount the future too quickly.

What is to be done about this? In section 4.3, I said that many economists would say 'no matter'. If people are imprudent, that is up to them. It is not the job of a public authority to overrule people's own decision making in these matters. So imprudence gives no reason to use a lower discount rate on commodities than the market's rate. Many economists believe that, if people are imprudent, this is a reason for the government to be imprudent too. On the other hand, Pigou thought otherwise. In the passage I quoted in section 4.7, he says the government should protect the interests of the future, not only against our preference for ourselves over future generations, but also against our own 'irrational discounting'.

Once again, I shall decline to enter an argument about the job of the government; that is a matter for political theory. In this chapter, I have been asking what action would have the best result. The pure method of evaluation was intended to answer this question, and the market price method was intended as a short cut to the pure method. If people are imprudent, the market price method will fail as a short cut, because market prices will not measure people's wellbeing. Market interest rates will not correctly indicate which action will have the best results.

The practical importance of this point depends on whether people are typically imprudent. I know of no convincing evidence about that, one way or the other.[21] But it is theoretically important for the following reason. In section 4.4, I explained that, for reasons of technology, future commodities would generally be cheaper in the market than present ones. This implies that consumers, when they are in equilibrium, must value future commodities less than present ones at the margin. I asked how that could happen, and I mentioned only two possible explanations of importance. The first is that the person might plan to consume more commodities in the future than in the present. This makes future commodities less valuable to her at the margin, because of their diminishing marginal value. Extra commodities will bring her less wellbeing in the future than in the present. So in this case future commodities ought definitely to be discounted in public evaluations; the positive market interest rates constitute a genuine reason for discounting. But this case can occur only if the person is increasing her consumption over time. It can occur in a society generally only if the economy is growing, so that people's consumption is generally increasing. In a static economy, this cannot be the explanation of why people value future commodities less than present ones. In a static economy, only the second possible explanation is available, and that is imprudence. But if imprudence is the explanation, the fact that interest rates are positive in the market does not indicate that present commodities produce more wellbeing than future commodities. If wellbeing ought not to be discounted, market interest rates do not then give us a good reason for discounting commodities in public decisions.

When it comes down to it, if wellbeing ought not to be discounted, the only justification there can be for discounting commodities is that future commodities produce less wellbeing than present ones. And that will only plausibly be the case if people will be better off in the future. Whatever happens, technology will almost always ensure that interest rates are positive, but these positive rates will justify discounting only if the economy is growing. This is a severe limitation on our right to discount future commodities.

4.9   Conclusion

Within the market price method of evaluation, there are some good grounds for discounting future commodities. The method itself has its attractions, and it is much more practical than the pure method. But there are also some sound objections to the market price method. The most serious is that it does not take proper account of the wellbeing of future generations.

We cannot put our faith in the market price method in circumstances where the objections are important. It is certainly unreliable for evaluating long-term projects that have large effects on future generations. For instance, it is useless for projects aimed at mitigating global warming. For these projects I think we have no alternative but to fall back on the pure method; no short cut is available. We shall have to do our best to estimate the effects the projects will have on people's wellbeing. Then we shall have to decide whether future wellbeing should be discounted. I have avoided that question in this chapter. The market price method skirts around it, by fixing attention on the discounting of commodities. But it cannot be avoided in the end.[22]

5   Can a Humean be moderate?

5.1   Moderate and extreme Humeans

A Humean believes that no preference can be irrational. It is not irrational to prefer the destruction of the world to the scratching of your little finger, or your own acknowledged lesser good to your greater.

An extreme Humean leaves it at that. A moderate Humean adds a qualification. Although, she says, no individual preference can be irrational on its own, some patterns of preferences are irrational; there are some sets of preferences that a person cannot rationally have together. Rationality, then, does constrain preferences to some extent.

Moderate Humeans recognize two types of constraint on preferences. One is the connection between preferences about means and preferences about ends. Suppose an action A will bring about one result, and B will bring about another, and you prefer the result of A to the result of B, and you have no intrinsic preference between A and B. Then it is irrational for you to prefer B to A.

The other type of constraint is consistency. Moderate Humeans recognize various consistency constraints. One is transitivity: if you prefer an alternative A to B and you prefer B to C, then it is irrational for you to prefer C to A. There are other consistency constraints too. *Decision theory* is generally taken to encapsulate them. Decision theory consists of a number of axioms defined on a person's preferences. Transitivity is one, and there are several others. Each is intended to specify a consistency constraint on the preferences.[1] A rational person is supposed to have preferences that conform to the axioms.

These two types of constraint on preferences really come down to one: consistency constraints subsume means–ends constraints. Indeed, the main

From *Value, Welfare and Morality*, edited by R. G. Frey and Christopher Morris, Cambridge University Press, 1993, pp. 279–86. This chapter was presented at the Conference on Value, Welfare and Morality, Bowling Green, Ohio, April 1990. My thanks to Donald Hubin and Philip Pettit for their helpful comments, and also to many of the participants at the conference. I should particularly like to mention Simon Blackburn, David Copp, David Gauthier, Gilbert Harman, and Edward McClennen.

point of decision theory is to make clear the nature of means–ends constraints. It specifies precisely what is the connection that rationality requires between a person's preferences about ends and her preferences about means. I described this connection just now, but my description was rough and inadequate. For one thing, I mentioned an 'intrinsic preference' without explaining precisely what that means. And, secondly, things are almost never as straightforward as I implied. You can almost never be sure what the result of an action will be; it might be one thing, or something else. Furthermore, the result, whatever it is, will almost certainly be complex. It will almost certainly not be the achievement of some simple end that you want; it will have some features you want and others you do not want. Forming a rational preference between two actions will therefore be a matter of weighing some goods against some bads, and of weighing the probabilities of some results against the probabilities of others. In this, you will be working back from preferences about ends to preferences about means, but the process will not be a simple one. Decision theory is intended to describe how a rational person conducts the complex weighing up that is involved.

The moderate Humean view, then, comes down to this. You may, rationally, have any preferences, provided only that they are consistent with each other. And what consistency requires is spelt out in decision theory.

The extreme Humean view is unappealing. It implies that reason leaves people unequipped for life. For one thing, it leaves them a defenceless prey to Dutch bookmakers, money pump operators, and suchlike sharks.[2] But that is the tip of the iceberg. The extreme Humean view implies that reason cannot guide people even through the most ordinary business of living. When you want a hot shower rather than a cold one, rationality will not even direct you to prefer to turn on the hot tap rather than the cold one.

A moderate Humean wants to avoid this conclusion. She wants to allow reason a role in guiding people through life; she wants it to help determine and modify their preferences. But she still wants the ultimate basis of preferences to be unconstrained by rationality. Her idea is that some preferences can give rational grounds for others. When a person has some particular preferences, reason will require her to have other particular preferences. So the person may have a reason to have some particular preference – and if she does not have it she will be irrational – but the reason will always derive from her other preferences. A moderate Humean respects the fundamental Humean principle that a reason must always derive from a preference. But she supplements this principle with some requirements of 'instrumental rationality', as they are often called. When a person has preferences that are inconsistent with one another, reason requires her to alter some of them, though it does not determine which. The moderate

Humean thinks of decision theory as (in Richard Jeffrey's words) 'a sort of Logic of Decision which individuals can use as an anvil against which to form and reform parts of their preference rankings'.[3]

But in this chapter, I shall argue that the moderate Humean position cannot really be held apart from the extreme one. I hope this will diminish the appeal of the Humean view as a whole.

5.2   A difficulty facing moderate Humeans

The details of decision theory are not universally agreed. Different versions have different axioms. But they do all agree at least on the axiom of transitivity. Transitivity is a minimal condition of consistency; if consistency does not require transitivity, it requires nothing.[4] So we may take it that all moderate Humeans believe rationality requires a person to have transitive preferences. A Humean who does not insist on transitivity is extreme, not moderate. For this reason, I shall concentrate on the transitivity axiom in my argument.

It is an interesting question how a moderate Humean might defend the requirement of transitivity. But that is not the subject of this chapter. I am not concerned with the grounds of the moderate Humean's view, but with whether her view is significantly different from an extreme Humean's.

Think about this example. Maurice, given a choice between going mountaineering in the Alps and visiting Rome, prefers to visit Rome. Given a choice between staying at home and visiting Rome, he prefers to stay at home. But given a choice between staying at home and going mountaineering, he prefers to go mountaineering. Maurice's preferences seem to be intransitive, and therefore irrational. But Maurice has a defence against the charge of irrationality. In describing his preferences, I distinguished only three alternatives: mountaineering, Rome, and home. Maurice, however, distinguishes four:

H_r: Maurice stays at home, when going to Rome was the only other alternative available.

R: Maurice goes to Rome.

M: Maurice goes mountaineering.

H_m: Maurice stays at home, when mountaineering was the only other alternative available.

He points out that transitivity requires him to prefer H_r to M, given that he prefers H_r to R and R to M. But the choice between staying at home and going mountaineering is a choice between H_m and M, and nothing requires him to prefer H_m to M. Maurice's defence, then, is to refine the individuation of the alternatives.

It does not matter for my purposes what Maurice would choose if offered a choice between all three alternatives at once. But it adds a complication worth mentioning. Suppose he would choose Rome. This suggests he does not prefer home to Rome, though I said earlier that he did. So it suggests that Maurice's preferences vary according to what alternatives are on offer.[5] This, like intransitivity, is contrary to the consistency conditions of decision theory. But Maurice can obviously handle this problem in the way he handles intransitivity. He can individuate the alternatives taking account of the choice on offer. He can treat H_r – staying at home when Rome was the only other alternative – as different from staying at home when both Rome and mountaineering were available. This will allow him to arrange his preferences in one big, unvarying order.[6]

Since the same device of fine individuation works for both problems, I shall continue to concentrate on apparent intransitivity. Maurice's defence is available to anyone who has apparently intransitive preferences. Suppose someone, faced with a choice between A and B, prefers A. Faced with a choice between B and C, she prefers B. And faced with a choice between C and A, she prefers C. These preferences seem intransitive. But let us individuate the alternatives more finely. Let us write 'A when B was the only other alternative available' as A_b, 'B when A was the only other alternative available' as B_a, and so on. Then this person prefers A_b to B_a, B_c to C_b, and C_a to A_c. And there is no intransitivity in that. It seems, then, that the requirement of transitivity is really no constraint on preferences at all. Fine individuation of alternatives will always allow a person to wriggle out of it.

That is an overstatement, however. Transitivity *does* constrain Maurice's preferences, despite his fine individuation. Because Maurice prefers H_r to R, and R to M, transitivity requires him to prefer H_r to M. This is a constraint on his preferences. To be sure, H_r and M are not a pair of alternatives that Maurice could ever have a choice between. If he was to have a *choice* between staying at home and going mountaineering, that would be a choice between H_m and M, not between H_r and M. Let us call one of a person's preferences *practical* if it is a preference between a pair of alternatives that the person could have a choice between. Then Maurice's preference for M over H_m is practical, but his preference for H_r over M is nonpractical.

The truth about fine individuation is this. It means that a person's *practical* preferences are not constrained by transitivity. Transitivity imposes constraints on a person's complete pattern of preferences, including her nonpractical ones. But her practical preferences form only a part of her complete pattern of preferences, and these practical preferences can have any pattern at all without conflicting with transitivity.

For the sake of precision, I need to say more about this conclusion. Take the person who prefers A to B, B to C, and C to A. Under fine individuation, she prefers A_b to B_a, B_c to C_b, and C_a to A_c. Consequently, transitivity requires this of her: either she prefers A_b to A_c, or she prefers B_c to B_a, or she prefers C_a to C_b.[7] So if my claim that transitivity does not constrain practical preferences is to be correct, then a preference between A_b and A_c, and other preferences of that sort, cannot be counted as practical preferences. Yet, at first sight, it may look as if the person might actually have a choice between A_b and A_c. She might be presented with this choice: would you like to have a choice between A and B, or alternatively a choice between A and C? If she decides in advance that, whichever of these alternatives she chooses, she will choose A in her subsequent choice, then this may look like a choice between A_b and A_c – between A when the only other alternative available was B, and A when the only other alternative available was C. But this is not really a plausible interpretation of the choice the person is faced with, since the alternatives available to her really include all of A, B, and C. In any case, I do not mean A_b and A_c to be understood in such a way that the choice I described counts as a choice between A_b and A_c. Nor is there any other way a person could have a choice between A_b and A_c. So a preference between these alternatives is indeed nonpractical. Consider Maurice again. Implicitly I have been assuming he is indifferent between R_h and R_m, and also between M_r and M_h. Transitivity consequently requires him to prefer H_r to H_m. And this is a nonpractical preference; Maurice could not have a choice between H_r and H_m.

Transitivity, then, does not constrain practical preferences. And it turns out that none of the other consistency axioms of decision theory constrains practical preferences either. All of them yield to similar treatment by fine individuation. This point is well recognized when applied to the 'sure-thing principle', the central axiom of Leonard Savage's decision theory.[8] It has often been argued that rational people may have preferences that do not conform to the sure-thing principle;[9] many plausible examples have been produced of preferences that seem rational but do not conform. But it has also been recognized for a long time that these examples can be brought into conformity with the sure-thing principle by means of fine individuation, just as Maurice's preferences can be brought into conformity with transitivity. Fine individuation, then, can be used to defend the sure-thing principle against the examples. However, it has been recognized for just as long that fine individuation leaves the sure-thing principle 'empty' (which seems to make it an unsatisfactory defence).[10] What this means, precisely, is that the sure-thing principle does not constrain practical preferences. I do not need to go into the details here.[11] The conclusion is that, because of the possibility of fine individuation, the consistency conditions on preferences do not actually constrain practical preferences at all.

This is a difficulty for the moderate Humean. She wants rationality to guide a person in her practical affairs. But she supposes that rationality is nothing more than consistency. And it now turns out that in practical matters – between alternatives the person might have a choice between – consistency does not guide her preferences at all.

5.3   A Non-Humean response

What inference should we draw?

Let us consider whether Maurice is really rational. Has he really justified his preferences by insisting on fine individuation? Certainly not by that alone. If we thought him irrational to begin with, because of his apparently intransitive preferences, we shall not revise our view just because he points out the formal possibility of individuating the alternatives more finely. He will have to do better than that. Having distinguished H_r from H_m, Maurice puts them in different places in his preference ordering. And this is what he will have to justify to us. He will have to justify his preference between H_r and H_m.

Perhaps he can. Suppose the explanation of Maurice's preferences is this. He is frightened of heights, and therefore he would rather go to Rome than go mountaineering. Sightseeing bores him, however, and therefore he would rather stay at home than go to Rome. But Maurice sees a choice of staying at home and undertaking a mountaineering trip as a test of his courage. He believes it would be cowardly to stay at home, and that is why he prefers to go mountaineering. (He considers it cultured, not cowardly, to visit Rome.)

Is this enough to show that Maurice is rational? I do not know, but I do know what it depends on. If we are to conclude that Maurice is rational, what shall we have to say? We shall have to say he has produced an adequate reason – that one involves cowardice and the other does not – for placing H_m and H_r in different positions in his preference ordering. If, on the other hand, we are to conclude Maurice is irrational, we shall have to deny this. We shall have to say that he has not shown a difference between these two alternatives that is adequate to justify his having a preference between them. Maurice is rational if and only if he is justified in having a preference between H_r and H_m.

Presumably we shall take the view that Maurice is irrational only if we think he is wrong about cowardice, and that actually there is nothing cowardly about staying at home rather than mountaineering. Even if we think this, it would perhaps be unfair to condemn Maurice for irrationality. His preferences stem from a false belief, and there may be nothing irrational about having a false belief. His preferences will be mistaken in a sense, and we might perhaps say they are objectively irrational, but not subjectively so. Furthermore, even if Maurice is wrong about cowardice, we might concede that his preferences are not irrational *in any sense*. They will not be irrational if, because of his incorrect views about cowardice, staying at home will make Maurice feel bad, or if it will make him lose his self-respect. Preserving his self-respect and avoiding a bad feeling are presumably themselves sufficient reasons to justify Maurice's preference for mountaineering, quite apart from the matter of actual cowardice.

But in any case, Maurice definitely cannot be convicted of irrationality except on the grounds that he is not justified in having a preference between H_r and H_m. So long as it is rational for these two alternatives to occupy different places in his preference ordering, Maurice's preferences are rational. To convict him, we shall have to insist on a rational principle of indifference. We shall have to say that the difference between H_r and H_m is not enough to justify Maurice in having a preference between the two: rationality requires him to be indifferent between these alternatives. This rational principle, together with transitivity, is enough to bring home the charge. The rational principle requires him to be indifferent between H_r and H_m, and transitivity requires him to prefer H_r to M. Together they require him to prefer H_m to M, and actually he does not.

It might be thought that a quite different argument can show Maurice's preferences to be irrational. It seems that a money pump could be operated against Maurice, however he may choose to individuate the alternatives he faces. Suppose he has a ticket to Rome. You offer to exchange it, at a small price, for a certificate to stay at home. Maurice will accept. Next you offer to exchange the certificate, at a small price, for a mountaineering ticket. Again Maurice will accept. Finally, you offer to exchange the mountaineering ticket for a ticket to Rome, at a small price. Once more, Maurice will accept. So he will end up where he started, but poorer. If Maurice can be milked in this way, that is popularly supposed to show his preference are irrational.

A money-pump argument may or may not be effective in general; that is no concern of mine in this chapter. But it certainly cannot succeed in this case. For one thing, it proves too much. If it works at all, it will work even if Maurice is right about cowardice, and fully justified in his preferences. But then his preferences are rational, so there must be something wrong with an argument that concludes they are not. And it is plain what is wrong with it. Suppose Maurice is right. And suppose he is now planning to stay at home, having turned down a trip to Rome. Then, if you come and offer him a mountaineering trip, you are by that very action making him worse off. You are, in effect, moving him from H_r to H_m, which is justifiably lower in his preference ordering. Maurice is willing to buy his way out of this position. It is as though you stole his shirt and then sold it back to him. Rationality cannot protect Maurice from that sort of sharp practice. So the fact that he is susceptible to it is no evidence of irrationality. The money-pump argument fails, then.

To generalize the conclusion I have drawn: there must be such things as rational principles of indifference; rationality must determine that some differences between alternatives are not enough to justify a person in preferring one of the alternatives to the other. There must be these rational principles because, if there were not, then rationality would not constrain practical preferences at all. Consistency conditions on their own (transitivity and the other conditions too) cannot constrain them. Rational principles of indifference are needed to give consistency a grip on practical preferences. These rational principles must be concrete and specific, not formal and general like the consistency conditions. They must determine which specific differences between alternatives are not enough to justify a preference.

I am happy with the conclusion that there must be rational principles of indifference. Here is a plausible one, for instance: the mere difference that in H_r Maurice has not rejected a mountaineering trip whereas in H_m he has is not enough to justify Maurice in having a preference between H_r and H_m. If he is to be justified in his preference, there must be some other difference as well. The other difference Maurice claims is that one involves cowardice and the other does not. If Maurice cannot establish the existence of a justifying difference like this, then his claim to rationality fails. In general, it is not rational to have a preference between two alternatives unless they differ in some good or bad respect.[12]

The view that there are concrete rational principles of indifference is not at all unusual. Some ethical theories imply very restrictive principles. Jeremy Bentham, for instance, seems to have believed that pleasure is the only good, and pain the only bad. Consequently, he would presumably have believed that if each of two alternatives gives everybody the same pleasure, and everybody the same pain, it is not rational to have a preference between the two.

5.4   A Humean response

A Humean, on the other hand, cannot be happy with the conclusion that there must be rational principles of indifference. Such a principle denies that certain specific preferences are rational, which is something a Humean cannot allow. She cannot allow that rationality should ever deny a person the right to prefer anything to anything else, provided this preference is consistent with her other preferences.

A Humean must therefore pay the penalty. She will have to accept that rationality does not constrain practical preferences. At first it looked as though the consistency conditions of rationality constrained them. But actually consistency conditions cannot do so without the support of rational principles of indifference. And those the Humean cannot acknowledge.

How severe is this penalty? Does it completely undermine the position of a moderate Humean? An extreme Humean believes that rationality allows a person to have any pattern of preferences whatsoever. Even a moderate Humean, we now see, has to believe that rationality allows a person to have any pattern of *practical* preferences whatsoever. So can she hold herself apart from an extreme Humean?

She can certainly defend her position. In discussing Maurice, I have been considering the constraints of rationality from the outside. I asked whether we could or could not convict Maurice of irrationality. The answer is that, if we are Humeans, we never could. Nor could we convict anyone else, however strange her practical preferences. But a moderate Humean is not interested in rationality as a criterion for condemning people from the outside. She is interested in it as a guide that helps people conduct their own affairs. So am I, of course.[13] The talk about condemnation was only metaphorical. I had in mind that Maurice could ask himself, 'Am I really being rational in preferring H_r to H_m?' He could ask himself, that is, whether some rational principle of indifference requires him to be indifferent between H_r and H_m. If he concludes that this preference is not rational, then he should adjust his practical preferences. This is how I see rationality guiding him.

But the moderate Humean will point out that, when a person is beating out her preferences on the anvil of decision theory, she has access to all of her preferences, not just the practical ones. The consistency conditions certainly constrain all of her preferences taken together. The person may consistently have any pattern of practical preferences at all, but the pattern of her practical preferences will, by consistency, determine a lot about her nonpractical preferences. Maurice, given the practical preferences I ascribed to him, must prefer H_r to H_m, for instance, or else M_h to M_r or R_m to R_h. Conversely, if he has none of these nonpractical preferences, he ought not to have the practical preferences he does have. If he finds himself in this position, reason requires him to change some of his preferences, and he may change one of his practical ones. In this way, the consistency constraints, applied to the whole pattern of a person's preferences, may have practical effects. If a person has a particular pattern of nonpractical preferences, then the consistency conditions will limit the practical preferences she may have.

According to a moderate Humean, then, reason may guide Maurice in forming his practical preferences as follows. Maurice can ask himself, 'Do

I really prefer H_r to H_m?' If he concludes that he does not, reason will bring him to adjust his practical preferences. From the inside, Maurice does not need to ask whether it is *rational* for him to prefer H_r to H_m; no rational principle of indifference is needed. He only needs to ask whether *actually* he has this preference. If he does not, that gives him a reason to alter his practical preferences.

In general, then, people's preferences are not entirely unconstrained by consistency, and the requirement of consistency may have an influence even over their practical preferences. On the basis of their nonpractical preferences, consistency may help to determine the pattern of their practical preferences. So the moderate Humean has a position that is still distinct from the extreme one. That is her argument.

5.5   The nature and epistemology of preferences

I shall try to show that this argument is unsuccessful. A moderate Humean requires practical preferences to be determined or influenced by reasoning based on nonpractical preferences. One possible response would be to deny that nonpractical preferences even exist: if you cannot have a choice, one might say, you cannot have a preference either. If that were so, the moderate Humean would obviously have no leg to stand on. But I think this response goes too far; I think people do, indeed, have nonpractical preferences. My own response, put roughly, will be that, although nonpractical preferences exist, they do not have enough independent substance to serve the moderate Humean's purposes. We are not able to reason from them to determine practical preferences in the way the moderate Humean requires.

What, exactly, *is* it for someone to have a nonpractical preference? If someone prefers A to B, where A and B are such that she could not have a choice between them, what does this amount to? We shall see that nonpractical preferences raise special difficulties. But let us start by asking the same question about preferences in general. What is it for a person to have a preference?

The notion of preference is a flexible one, and several different concepts may be collected under the same name. But for our purposes we can restrict the concept by at least two conditions that preferences must satisfy. The first is that a person must be able to know what her preferences are. Conceivably, we may have some concept of preference (a Freudian one, perhaps) such that we cannot know what our preferences are. But if so, this is not the concept a moderate Humean has in mind. A moderate Humean requires a person to be able to reason on the basis of her preferences to determine what other preferences she should have. Consequently, since preferences play a part in the person's reasoning, she must be able to know what they are. Our account of preferences must therefore supply a satisfactory explanation of how a person can come to know her preferences. This condition, I think, provides the best approach to the concept of preference. By asking 'How can we know what our preferences are?', we can discover what our concept of preference is.

The second condition we require preferences to meet is this. It must genuinely be a condition of rationality that a person's preferences should conform to the consistency requirements of decision theory – transitivity in particular. We must understand preferences in such a way that this is so. I think this condition provides a serious constraint on the notion of preferences, because if preferences are conceived in some popular ways (as feelings, for instance) it is very hard to see why rationality should require them to be transitive. I suspect that this condition could contribute extra support to the conclusions of this chapter. However, I shall actually make no use of it. The reason is that I could not use it without first settling what are the grounds of the consistency conditions, and I do not want to do that. This chapter, as I said earlier, is not about the grounds of the moderate Humean's position. It is about whether the moderate Humean has a distinct position at all. So I shall rely on the first condition only.

Some sort of functionalist account of preference seems very natural – an account like this: a person prefers A to B if and only if she is in a state that typically has the following functional role . . .[14] Then the typical functional role has to be specified. For practical preferences, this is not difficult. At least a major part of the typical functional role of a practical preference is to dispose the person to choose the preferred alternative, if she has a choice.

This account provides a ready explanation of how we can know our own practical preferences and other people's. There is a canonical test of a person's preferences: to see what she chooses when she has a choice.[15] In principle, a person can apply this test to herself, to discover her own preferences. In practice, however, the canonical test is often not available, because the subject never faces the appropriate choice. And in any case, even when it is available, it is often not the most natural test for a person to apply to herself. But I shall not discuss alternative tests now; it will be most convenient to postpone that discussion to section 5.8.

A functionalist account may be available for nonpractical preferences too. But for a nonpractical preference, a disposition to choose A over B can be no part of its functional role, because the person cannot have a choice between A and B.[16] So what is the functional role of a nonpractical preference? More generally: what is it to have a nonpractical preference? To answer, let us examine the ways we may come to know what our nonpractical preferences are.

5.6   Knowing preferences by perception

How does a person come to know her nonpractical preferences? I can think of three answers that might be given.

First of all, preferences might be directly perceptible in some way. Start with practical preferences. These can be independently identified by their tendency to determine choices. But suppose they can also be perceived directly. Suppose, for instance, that, if I scratch statements expressing two propositions in the dust around my feet, and then stand between them, I generally find myself leaning towards the one I prefer. Or suppose that, when I call to mind two propositions, I generally feel drawn to the one I prefer. Then we might take it as part of the functional role of a preference to bring about these leanings or feelings. We should certainly do so if the leanings or feelings themselves played a causal role in my choices. Suppose that when I am faced with a choice, I contemplate the alternatives, feel drawn to one of them, and, as a result of that, make my choice. Then bringing about the feeling would undoubtedly count as one of the functional roles that identify a preference.

And now suppose I have these leanings or feelings even between alternatives that I could not have a choice between. Then the leanings or feelings might well be enough to determine that I have a preference between the alternatives, and what my preference is. This would be a nonpractical preference. I would have a nonpractical preference between A and B, then, if and only if I am in a state that typically brings it about that I lean towards A when I stand between expressions of A and B scratched in the dust, or I feel drawn towards A when I contemplate A and B. So this could be what it is for me to have a nonpractical preference. And it would explain how I can come to know my nonpractical preferences. I have only to observe my leanings or feelings.

If human nature was like this, the moderate Humean's argument would be sound. Maurice would be able to consult his leanings or feelings to determine whether or not he prefers H_r to H_m, or M_h to M_r, or R_m to R_h. If he finds he does not, rationality would require him to make an adjustment in his preferences.

We could draw the same conclusion if a person had perceptible degrees of desire, rather than perceptible preferences. In this case the argument happens to be more complicated, but the complication makes no significant difference. Suppose I could call an alternative to mind, and by an inward glance determine how much I desire it. Suppose this works in such a way that, of two alternatives, I prefer the one an inward glance reveals I desire more. (So for practical preferences, which can be independently identified functionally, my inward glances reveal my disposition to choose.) Then I could determine my preferences by inward glances. The complication is this. If, for each proposition, there is a degree to which I desire it, then my preferences are *necessarily* transitive. If the degree to which I desire A is greater than the degree to which I desire B, and the degree to which I desire B is greater than the degree to which I desire C, then necessarily the degree to which I desire A is greater than the degree to which I desire C. So, if I prefer A to B, and I prefer B to C, then necessarily I prefer A to C. Consequently, there can be no conflict on grounds of transitivity between my practical preferences and my nonpractical preferences. If Maurice has the practical preferences I described for him, then *it follows* that he prefers H_r to H_m, or M_h to M_r, or R_m to R_h. Transitivity is automatically satisfied; it is not a rational constraint on preferences. Nevertheless, there will still be *other* rational constraints on preferences: namely, the other consistency axioms of decision theory. It will still be possible for practical and non-practical preferences to conflict through these other axioms. The moderate Humean's position will still be intact, therefore; rationality may still constrain practical preferences.

The situation I have been describing is possible. It is possible that non-practical preferences (or degrees of desire) might have been directly perceptible, by means of a feeling or in some other way. Certainly, it is not possible that a preference might have *been* a feeling.[17] But nonpractical preferences might have been *perceptible* by feelings, in the way I have described. If this had been so, the moderate Humean's position would have been distinct from the extreme Humean's. But, although it might have been so, actually it is not. So my case against the moderate Humean is only a contingent one. She would have been right if human nature had been different from how it actually is. But, as it happens, she is wrong.

As it happens, nonpractical preferences are not perceptible by feelings. The only evidence I have for this claim is common experience. No doubt there are some feelings associated with preference. Some desires, at least, are accompanied by feelings, such as the violent passion of resentment mentioned by Hume.[18] Perhaps a person can sometimes perceive her preferences between two simple objects of desire by noticing which she feels drawn to. But we are talking about nonpractical preferences. These are inevitably between complex alternatives, which it requires some intellectual effort to understand. It is implausible that a preference between such things could be detected by a feeling. I shall later be suggesting it could be detected by a process that might be mistaken for this one: by weighing up the considerations in favour of the two alternatives. A person who is weighing up considerations could believe herself to be judging which alternative she feels drawn to. The processes are actually quite different, because one is a rational process and the other is not. But they may be superficially similar, and that may help to conceal the implausibility of the view that non-practical preferences are perceived by feelings.

But in any case, I do not think much evidence is needed for my claim. It is widely accepted.[19] Hume himself accepted that many desires cannot be perceived by feelings. Desires, he thought, are often *calm* passions 'which, tho' they be real passions, produce little emotion in the mind, and are more known by their effects than by the immediate feeling or sensation'.[20]

5.7   Knowing preferences by their effects

That was the first way a person might come to know her nonpractical preferences. In the remark of his I quoted just now, Hume suggests a second way: she might come to know them by their effects. He means their outward effects, as opposed to the feelings they generate.

What are these effects? The primary outward effect of a *practical* preference is to dispose a person to make a particular choice. A nonpractical preference is more remote from choice, but we can identify an outward effect nonetheless. If a person has a particular nonpractical preference, that limits the practical preferences it is rational for her to have. Since people are typically rational, it therefore typically limits the practical preferences a person will have. Consequently, a person's nonpractical preferences can be identified through her practical preferences. From Maurice's practical preferences as I described them, we can tell something about his nonpractical preferences. At least if he is rational, either he prefers H_r to H_m, or R_m to R_h, or M_h to M_r.

This way of identifying a person's nonpractical preferences is available to other people besides the one whose preferences they are. For someone else to identify my nonpractical preferences by this method, she must first identify my practical preferences by somehow discovering my dispositions to choose, and then work back from there. But Hume had in mind that I would come to know my own preferences in this way: from their effects. So I, too, would work back from my *own* dispositions to choose. How would I know what I am disposed to choose? Here it seems I have an advantage over other people. I can simply present myself with the choice in my imagination, and see what I decide.

Applying Hume's idea to nonpractical preferences raises a difficulty, though. The idea is that a person's practical preferences are causally *affected* by her nonpractical preferences, and the effects identify these nonpractical preferences. This gives us a functionalist conception of nonpractical preferences: I have a particular nonpractical preference if and only if I am in a state that typically brings it about that my practical preferences have such-and-such a pattern. But why should we believe that there is such a state? Why should we think that practical preferences are in any way affected by a separate range of preferences, the nonpractical ones? Usually, when we identify a mental state by means of its causal functions, we have separate grounds for thinking there is some causal process, of the appropriate sort, at work. A practical preference, for instance, is that mental state, whatever it is, that causes a person to make the choices she makes. And we have grounds for thinking that *some* mental state causes her choices. Consequently, although a practical preference is *identified* by the person's dispositions to choose, we have grounds for thinking it *is* actually something distinct from the disposition. But if a nonpractical preference is to be identified on the basis of practical preferences, we have no grounds for thinking that the state of having a nonpractical preference will be anything different from the state of having practical preferences of a particular form.

A moderate Humean needs a person to be able to reason from her nonpractical preferences to determine, on grounds of consistency, what her practical preferences should be. For this to be possible, her nonpractical preferences must be distinct from her practical preferences. Yet I have just said that, if she identifies her nonpractical preferences by Hume's method, there is no reason to think they will be distinct. Furthermore, even if they are distinct, they will have been identified from her practical preferences on the assumption that her practical preferences are consistent with her nonpractical ones. So they could not possibly give her a reason, on grounds of consistency, for having practical preferences that are different from the ones she actually has.

This difficulty is only the reflection of a much more fundamental objection: a general objection to Hume's suggestion that a passion might be known by its effects. Hume, given the part he assigned to passions in rationality, ought never to have made this suggestion. He clearly meant that a person might know of one of *her own* passions by its effects. And the effects he had in mind were, evidently, the person's acting in accordance with the passion – doing things that satisfy it. But according to his own theory, these effects are mostly produced by the application of reason to the passion. We cast our view on every side, he thought, and discover by reasoning whatever objects are connected to the original object of our passion by the relation of cause and effect. So 'according as our reasoning varies, our actions receive a subsequent variation'.[21] The effects of a passion on action, then, are mediated by reason. A person, however, cannot apply reason in this way unless she already knows what her passion is. Therefore, she cannot know her passion by its effects.

The moderate Humean is *particularly* concerned to explain how reason can guide action. Consequently, she particularly cannot use this account of how we come to know our preferences.

5.8   Knowing preferences by evaluation

Now the third answer to the question of how a person can come to know her nonpractical preferences. This is the one I favour. Suppose A and B are a pair of alternatives that a person could not have a choice between, so her preference between them is nonpractical. I suggest that she finds out which she prefers by estimating the relative goodness of A and B. I suggest that she prefers A to B if and only if she estimates the goodness of A higher than she estimates the goodness of B.

This is expressed a little awkwardly. It would be easier to say: a person prefers A to B if and only if she believes A to be better than B. But David Lewis has shown that cannot be correct.[22] Lewis believes that his demonstration refutes the opinions of an Anti-Humean. In another paper,[23] however, I have argued that it does less than that. It shows only that an Anti-Humean (and everyone else, too) has to be careful about how she expresses her opinions. Preferences do not go by *beliefs* in degrees of good, but by *expectations* of good, and expectations cannot be identified with beliefs. My proposal about the nature of nonpractical preferences, set out more strictly, is that a person prefers A to B (where this preference is nonpractical) if and only if A has, according to her probabilities, the greater expectation of good. But the details of the formulation make no difference to this chapter. And, although an expectation is not a belief, it is compounded out of beliefs. It is in the same ballpark as a belief.

So the epistemology of nonpractical preferences, on my account, is like the epistemology of beliefs. The process of finding out what one's preferences are is like the process of finding out what one's beliefs are. In particular, it is like other matters of estimation: would you say this plate or that teacup is the older?; would you estimate the standard of living to be higher in Germany or Sweden? To answer such questions, you consider the evidence and arguments available to you, and weigh them up as best you can. Maurice, similarly, must ask himself: 'Is H_r really better than H_m?' This will require him to consider whether or not H_m really involves cowardice, whether cowardice is really bad, or whether perhaps the two alternatives are equally good, and so on. All of this is a matter of rational evaluation.

I described this process of evaluation as a process of finding out what one's preference is. But sometimes it may be a process of acquiring a new preference. I doubt there is a definite line between these things. It depends how long and complicated the process is. If it is quick and obvious, it will count as finding out, otherwise as acquisition. But even if it is acquisition, it is finding out too. At the same time as you acquire your new preference, you will come to know what it is. Either way, evaluation brings one to a knowledge of one's preference.

There is an obvious objection to my proposal. Suppose a person estimates the goodness of A higher than the goodness of B. They she ought to
prefer A to B; reason requires her to prefer A to B. I am proposing, also,
that actually she does prefer A to B. So I am eliding the distinction between
having a preference and its being the case that one ought to have a preference. Obviously, though, there is a genuine distinction here. Suppose a
person estimates the goodness of not smoking higher than the goodness of
smoking. Then she ought to prefer not to smoke. But she may actually
prefer to smoke. That is plainly a possibility.

But I am not denying the distinction in general. I am only denying it for
nonpractical preferences. I have said already that a practical preference,
such as a preference for smoking, can be identified by its typical functional
role, which is to bring about a disposition to choose. Typically, a person
who is disposed to smoke prefers to smoke. And it is plain how she, and the
rest of us, know what her preference is; the epistemology of this type of
preference is clear. Then, separately, it may also happen that she estimates
the goodness of not smoking above the goodness of smoking. That can
clearly happen with a practical preference. But with a nonpractical preference, the difference is that we have no plausible epistemology that can bring
a person to know what her preference is between alternatives, independently of how she estimates the goodness of the alternatives.

That is the argument I offer for my proposal. Estimating goodness is, so
far as I can see, the only way we have of coming to know our nonpractical
preferences. I have considered two alternative theories. Each, if it had been
successful, would have supported a different concept of preference from the
one I am proposing. But neither is successful. Consequently, we have to
conclude that to have a nonpractical preference for A over B is nothing
other than to estimate A as better than B.

There is something more to say about smoking. To be sure, a person who
is disposed to smoke prefers to smoke. But, if she estimates the goodness of
not smoking above the goodness of smoking, it would also be natural to say
she prefers not to smoke. She prefers not to smoke but, because of weakness of will, she smokes. Evidently we have two different senses of 'prefer'
here. We have at least two concepts of preference. According to one – call
it the 'evaluative' concept – a person prefers A to B if and only if she estimates the goodness of A above the goodness of B. According to the other
– functionalist – concept, she prefers A to B if and only if she is in a state
that typically leads her to choose A rather than B. The functionalist
concept applies only to practical preferences. But the evaluative concept
applies to both practical and nonpractical preferences. That is to say,
the concept I propose for nonpractical preferences can be applied to
practical preferences too.

Furthermore, the epistemology of the functionalist concept is problematic even for practical preferences. Its canonical test is to see what a person chooses when she has a choice. This test can be carried out for smoking, but for many of her practical preferences a person will not actually have a choice. What can be done then? There is the possibility I discussed earlier that a preference can be perceived, by a feeling or in some other way. But even for most practical preferences, that is not generally plausible. In practice, the best test for other people to use is generally to ask the person herself what she prefers. And the best test for her is to present herself with a choice in imagination, and see what she chooses. Now, how does that work? Normally, by her running through the deliberation she would run through if faced with the choice, and forming an estimate of the goodness of the alternatives. She can then conclude she prefers the one she estimates higher.

As a way of finding out what the person is disposed to choose, this test is unreliable. If she were actually to have the choice, she might choose the alternative that comes lower in her estimation, because of weakness of will. If she understands her own psychology well, she might be able to allow for her own weakness in making the imaginative test. But that allowance may well seem inappropriate to her if she is trying to find out her own preference. The process I have described, without the allowance, is an unreliable test for the functionalist concept of preference, but it is a perfectly reliable test for the evaluative concept. And when it comes to a preference that is remote from choice, the latter seems the most natural concept to apply. So I think that, because of epistemological difficulties, we very often apply the evaluative concept rather than the functionalist one, even for practical preferences.

Compare the conclusions of this section with Mark Johnston's comments, in 'Dispositional theories of value', on David Lewis's chapter with the same title. Lewis considers how a person can come to know whether a thing is valuable. His proposal is that the person should place herself in a position of full imaginative acquaintance with that thing, and see whether she values it. By this he means: whether she desires to desire it. Lewis's dispositional theory of value implies that, if she does, the thing is indeed valuable. Reason plays a part in the process Lewis describes: it is involved in bringing the person into full imaginative acquaintance with the object. But once she has achieved this position, it is simply a causal matter – nothing to do with reason – whether or not she finds herself valuing the object.[24] Johnston, however, argues that it is unreasonable to exclude reason at this point. I am, in effect, adding an argument to Johnston's. How is the person to know that she values, or desires to desire, the object? I can think of no plausible answer if this state of desiring to desire is one that simply imposes itself on the person causally, as Lewis supposes. Most plausibly, a person will find out whether she desires to desire something by considering whether she has reason to desire to desire it. This is a matter of estimating its goodness, and it is a rational process. If she judges it good, that both makes it the case that she desires to desire it, and gives her the knowledge that she does so. Indeed, it makes it the case that she desires it, in the evaluative sense of 'desire'. So desiring to desire is no different from desiring in this sense.

5.9   Conclusion

In section 5.4, I suggested that reason might guide Maurice like this. He can ask himself whether it is rational for him to prefer H_r to H_m. He might conclude it is not, because some rational principle requires him to be indifferent between these two alternatives. If so, he ought to change his practical preferences, because they are inconsistent with indifference between H_r and H_m. But this story does not suit a moderate Humean. According to a moderate Humean, Maurice has only to ask himself whether he *does* prefer H_r to H_m. He need not ask whether it is rational for him to do so. If he does not have this preference, then he ought to change his preferences in some way, and he may be brought to change his practical ones. Rationality guides him that way.

But I have now argued in section 5.8, on epistemological grounds, that Maurice cannot really distinguish the question of whether he does have the preference from the question of whether it is rational for him to have it. To discover whether he has the preference, he will have to estimate the relative goodness of H_r and H_m, and this is the same process as considering whether it is rational to prefer H_r to H_m. Maurice cannot avoid considering the rationality of this preference. Unless he does, rationality can give him no guidance at all.

This by itself may not worry a moderate Humean. A moderate Humean, unlike an extreme Humean, accepts that preferences can be irrational. So she may be willing to concede that Maurice will have to consider whether it is rational to prefer H_r to H_m. But she must insist that, if a preference is irrational, that can only be because it is inconsistent with other preferences. I said that Maurice, in considering whether it is rational to prefer H_r to H_m, will have to consider the relative goodness of H_r and H_m. The moderate Humean need have no objection to that. But, she will have to say, the goodness of the alternatives, from Maurice's point of view, must itself be determined by Maurice's preferences. When Maurice is deciding whether H_r is better than H_m, I said he would have to consider, amongst other things, whether cowardice is really bad. But the moderate Humean will say he only has to consider whether he prefers not to be cowardly. If he does, then, for him, H_r is better than H_m.

But now the moderate Humean has come round in a circle. Her suggestion is that nonpractical preferences can be derived by principles of consistency from other preferences. These other preferences might themselves be nonpractical in the first instance. But, in the end, nonpractical preferences will have to be derived from practical ones if we are to avoid the epistemological problem I have described. So the moderate Humean's suggestion is that nonpractical preferences are determined by consistency conditions from practical preferences. However, she started off (in section 5.4) with the idea that practical preferences might be constrained, through the consistency conditions, by nonpractical preferences. This requires nonpractical preferences to be determined independently, and she has just concluded they are not. We have known since section 5.2 that practical preferences are not constrained, through consistency, simply by other practical preferences. Consistency permits any pattern of practical preferences whatsoever.

I conclude that the moderate Humean cannot sustain her position. She must either become extreme or cease to be a Humean.

Part II

The structure of good

6 Bolker–Jeffrey expected utility theory and axiomatic utilitarianism

6.1 Introduction

In 1955, John Harsanyi proved a remarkable theorem.[1] Assume everybody has preferences that conform to expected utility theory. Assume there are social preferences that also conform to expected utility theory. Finally, assume the social preferences satisfy the Pareto criterion. Harsanyi proved that, given these three assumptions, social preferences can be represented (in the manner of expected utility theory) by a utility function that is the sum of utility functions representing the preferences of the individuals. I call this the 'Utilitarian Theorem'. Section 6.2 of this paper describes it in more detail.

The significance of the Utilitarian Theorem has been much debated.[2] Harsanyi believes it supports utilitarianism.[3] That is, perhaps, an overstatement, but I do think it throws enough light on the foundations of utilitarianism to justify the name I give it. It certainly makes a remarkable link between attitudes to risk and attitudes to inequality, which was Harsanyi's original purpose.[4] But this paper is not about the theorem's significance; I have expressed my own views on that in my *Weighing Goods*. It is about its truth.

A number of proofs have been published besides Harsanyi's.[5] Each is tied to a particular version of expected utility theory, and several rely implicitly on strong assumptions. Harsanyi's own proof assumes that probabilities are objective and known to everyone. Other existing proofs allow for subjective probabilities, but they all assume versions of expected utility theory that derive ultimately from Leonard Savage's.[6] This paper tries out the theorem in the Bolker–Jeffrey version, which is radically different from Savage's. I shall argue in section 6.3 that there are good reasons to test the theorem in

From *Review of Economic Studies*, 57 (1990), pp. 477–502. Reprinted by permission of the *Review of Economic Studies* Ltd. The appendices, which contain proofs, are omitted in this reprinted version, and the text of the paper has also been slightly shortened. I am grateful for the helpful comments I received from W. M. Gorman, Richard Jeffrey, David Kreps, and Adam Morton.

this version. This paper proves the theorem within it. But it also shows the need for stringent assumptions.

One of my main aims is to introduce the Bolker–Jeffrey theory to economists. It has some important attractions compared with Savage's theory. Section 6.4 of this paper describes the theory. But no presentation of the Bolker–Jeffrey theory these days can ignore the strong objections that have recently been raised against it from the direction of 'causal' decision theories (which include Savage's). Section 6.5 explains these objections, using some economic examples. It also argues that, although they may be cogent objections to the theory conceived as a theory of decision, conceived as a theory of valuation they leave it unscathed. The Bolker–Jeffrey theory remains particularly appropriate for Harsanyi's theorem, which is best understood as a matter of valuation rather than decision.

Section 6.6 outlines the proof of the Utilitarian Theorem within the Bolker–Jeffrey theory. This proof requires strong assumptions. Section 6.7 discusses the assumptions, and draws conclusions.

6.2   The utilitarian theorem

Let there be h people. Let each have preferences defined on a set of alternatives involving some uncertainty (the same set for each person). Person i's preferences I shall designate by the symbols $>_i$, $\geq_i$, and $\approx_i$ in the usual way. Throughout this paper, I shall assume that each person's preferences are *coherent,* by which I mean they satisfy the axioms of expected utility theory. I want to allow for different versions of the theory, with different axioms, so I cannot yet define coherence more exactly.

Expected utility theory shows that each person's preferences may be represented by a utility function defined on the domain of alternatives. These utility functions are *expectational.* By this I mean that, if an alternative has uncertain results, its utility is the expectation of the utility of its possible results. Again, the precise meaning of 'expectational' can be defined only within each version of the theory. A person's utility function is not unique; several expectational utility functions will represent her preferences equally well. But all of them will be positive linear transforms, or in the Bolker–Jeffrey theory – see section 6.4 – fractional linear transforms, of each other.

Let there also be social preferences defined on the same set of alternatives. I shall designate them by $>_g$, $\geq_g$, and $\approx_g$. I call them *Paretian* if and only if, for all alternatives A and B,

if $A \approx_i B$ for all i then $A \approx_g B$, and
if $A \geq_i B$ for all i and $A >_i B$ for some i then $A >_g B$.

If the social preferences are coherent they may be represented by an expectational utility function. Once again, many functions, all positive linear or fractional linear transforms of each other, will serve to represent the preferences. Let $U_1, \ldots, U_h$ be utility functions representing the individuals' preferences, and U_g a utility function representing social preferences. Then, if social preferences are Paretian, U_g will be a function of the U_is:

$$U_g(A) = W(U_i(A), \ldots, U_h(A)) \text{ for all alternatives } A.$$

Also, W will be increasing in each argument.

I call the social preferences *utilitarian* if and only if there is an expectational utility function U_g representing social preferences and for each i an expectational utility function U_i representing i's preferences such that

$$U_g(A) = \Sigma_i U_i(A) \text{ for all alternatives } A.$$

Now I can state the theorem that is the subject of this paper:

> *The Utilitarian Theorem.* Suppose that each person has coherent preferences. Then, if social preferences are coherent and Paretian, they are utilitarian.

Harsanyi's original proof of the Utilitarian Theorem took probabilities to be objective and known to everyone. Some other proofs (including mine in this paper) are more general in that they allow for subjective probabilities that may differ from person to person. However, these proofs invariably arrive at the Utilitarian Theorem via a proof of the following:

> *Probability Agreement Theorem.* Suppose that each person has coherent preferences. Then if social preferences are coherent and Paretian, the individual and social preferences must all agree about the probabilities they assign to every event.

So the initial extra generality cancels itself out: probabilities have to be universally agreed anyway.

Nevertheless, the generality achieves something. It is better than simply assuming agreement about probabilities from the start. The Probability Agreement Theorem is important in its own right. It shows that the coherence and Paretian requirements on social preferences are together very stringent. They impose conditions not just on the social preferences themselves, but on individual preferences too. As a general rule, we have no reason to expect individual preferences to agree about probabilities. Unless they do, though, the theorem says that social preferences cannot be both coherent and Paretian. Yet it is natural to think they should be both. Furthermore, coherence and the Paretian requirement are the conditions of the Utilitarian Theorem. So the Probability Agreement Theorem tell us that as a general rule the conditions of the Utilitarian Theorem are mutually inconsistent. It tells us, then, that some work of interpretation needs to be done in order to reconcile the two conditions. Without this work, neither the notion of social preferences nor the Utilitarian Theorem can be properly understood. I have attempted it in my *Weighing Goods*.

In summary, the theorems say that unless individuals agree about probabilities there can be no coherent Paretian social preferences. And when coherent Paretian social preferences do exist, they must also agree about probabilities, and they must be utilitarian.

6.3   The ex-post approach

Existing proofs of the Utilitarian Theorem – those that allow for subjective probability[7] – model uncertainty in a way that is, broadly speaking, Leonard Savage's.[8] In this model there are a number of 'states of nature', any one of which may come about. People have preferences between alternative prospects ('acts' in Savage's terminology). Each prospect associates a particular outcome ('consequence' in Savage's terminology) with each state of nature: if the prospect is chosen and the state comes about, then this outcome will result. This structure is shown in table 6.1. The cells of the table show outcomes A_1, A_2, B_1, and so on.

Each person has preferences amongst the alternative prospects. Expected utility theory tells us that, provided they are coherent, these preferences may be represented by probabilities and utilities. Probabilities are attached to the states of nature; utilities, initially, to outcomes. Derivatively each prospect has a utility too, calculated as the expectation of the utility of its possible outcomes, assessed according to the probabilities. So the utility of prospect A is

$$U(A) = \mu(S_1)U(A_1) + \mu(S_2)U(A_2) + \ldots$$

where μ stands for probability. Of two prospects, the preferred one will have the higher utility.

The utility of a prospect for a person, then, is derived from the utilities of outcomes, and it depends on the person's assessment of probabilities. On the other hand, in the model the utility of an outcome is basic. This leaves open an escape route from the Utilitarian and Probability Agreement Theorems. Many people find the implications of these theorems unattractive. It seems desirable to have coherent social preferences. But according to the theorems this is rarely possible, and, even when it is, the social preferences must be utilitarian in the sense defined in section 6.2. Such utilitarian preferences seem, at least at first sight, inconsistent with the value of equality. Whatever the truth about this – and in this paper I am not going to enquire into it[9] – an escape from these implications is to adopt the so-called ex-post approach to forming social preferences. This approach has been proposed by Peter Hammond and myself, among others.[10]

Table 6.1

		States of nature				
		S_1	S_2	S_3	.	.
	A	A_1	A_2	A_3	.	.
Prospects	B	B_1	B_2	B_3	.	.
	C	C_1	C_2	C_3	.	.
	.	.	.	.	.	.
	.	.	.	.	.	.

The idea of the ex-post approach is that social preferences about prospects should be based on individuals' preferences about the possible outcomes of those prospects, but not necessarily on their preferences about the prospects themselves. So one should require social preferences to be Paretian about outcomes but not about prospects generally. If everyone's preferences assign one outcome a higher utility than another, then so should social preferences, but the same need not be true for prospects. With this looser Paretian requirement, coherent social preferences are easier to come by, and they need not be utilitarian.

The argument for the ex-post approach is that people's preferences about prospects do not depend only on their wants, but also on their beliefs about probabilities. Democratic principles may insist that social preferences should be based on people's wants, but it is quite a different matter to insist they should be based on their beliefs too.

But this argument is open to a powerful objection. People's preferences about prospects doubtless depend on their beliefs as well as their wants, but so do their preferences about anything. The ex-post approach assumes that outcomes can be distinguished from prospects in such a way that preferences about outcomes do not depend on beliefs about probabilities. But it is never certain what good or harm will result from anything. So a person's preferences about anything must depend on her beliefs about the probabilities of its possible results. Take, for instance, one of Savage's examples of a 'consequence' (outcome): a refreshing swim with friends.[11] If I have a refreshing swim with friends I might or might not get cramp, and my preferences about the swim will depend on my beliefs about the probabilities of these results. If I swim and get cramp, I might or might not drown, and my preferences about swimming and getting cramp will depend on my beliefs about the likelihood of these results. And so on. No doubt in a practical decision-making problem of the sort Savage was concerned with, it is often possible to draw a workable distinction between prospects whose value depends on the probabilities of their results, and outcomes that have value in their own right. But this distinction, the objection goes, cannot be sustained in principle. And the ex-post approach cannot be justified without it.

I think this is a strong objection but not necessarily a conclusive one. It may be that actually an appropriate distinction can be drawn between prospects and outcomes. For instance, complete possible worlds are plausible candidates for outcomes. But the objection certainly needs to be taken seriously. We should therefore not rely on conclusions drawn from a version of expected utility theory that takes for granted the distinction between prospects and outcomes.

The Bolker–Jeffrey theory – the idea and interpretation is Richard Jeffrey's, the axiomatization Ethan Bolker's[12] – assumes no such distinction. Indeed Bolker's axiomatization explicitly rules it out, as I shall explain. A good reason, therefore, for trying out the Utilitarian Theorem within this theory is that, in so far as the theorem is true within it, no escape to an ex-post approach is available.

6.4   Introduction to the Bolker–Jeffrey theory

In the Bolker–Jeffrey expected utility theory, preferences, utilities, and probabilities are all defined on the same set of prospects. Jeffrey expresses these prospects as *propositions*, such as 'I have a refreshing swim with friends', and applies the propositional calculus to them. A prospect or proposition may be thought of as a subset of the set of all possible worlds, the subset consisting of worlds where the proposition is true. The operations of propositional calculus correspond to set-theoretic operations. If A is a proposition, $\neg A$ (i.e. not A) is the complement of A. $A \lor B$ (i.e. A or B) is the union of A and B; $A \land B$ (i.e. A and B) their intersection. If A and B are contraries (propositions that cannot both be true) they are disjoint sets.

Let A be 'I have a refreshing swim with friends', B 'I get cramp', and C 'I drown'. Let A_1 be $A \land B$ and let A_2 be $A \land \neg B$. Then $A = A_1 \lor A_2$ (the disjunction of A_1 and A_2), and A_1 and A_2 are contrary propositions. Rules I shall describe later say that, whenever A is the disjunction of two contraries A_1 and A_2,

$$\mu(A) = \mu(A_1) + \mu(A_2)$$

and

$$U(A) = \frac{\mu(A_1)U(A_1) + \mu(A_2)U(A_2)}{\mu(A_1) + \mu(A_2)} = \frac{\mu(A_1)}{\mu(A)}U(A_1) + \frac{\mu(A_2)}{\mu(A)}U(A_2),$$

where μ is probability and U utility. The formula for probability is obviously appropriate. To understand the formula for utility, remember that

$\mu(A_1)/\mu(A)$ and $\mu(A_2)/\mu(A)$ are the probabilities of A_1 and A_2 conditional on A. So the formula says that the utility of A is the expectation of utility given that A is true. In this way utility is expectational.

A feature of Bolker's axiomatization is that the set of prospects is *atomless*. This means that any prospect in the set can always be broken down into a disjunction in the way that A breaks down into A_1 and A_2. For instance, A_1 breaks down into $A_{11} = A_1 \wedge C$ and $A_{12} = A_1 \wedge \neg C$, so that $A_1 = A_{11} \vee A_{12}$. And

$$U(A_1) = \frac{\mu(A_{11})}{\mu(A_1)} U(A_{11}) + \frac{\mu(A_{12})}{\mu(A_1)} U(A_{12}).$$

The assumption is that any prospect breaks down similarly into a disjunction, and has its utility resolved into the expectation of the utilities of its disjuncts. The utility of any proposition, then, depends on probabilities and utilities, on beliefs as well as wants. There are no propositions that play the role of outcomes or consequences and have a utility that is independent of probability judgements. The ex-post approach is therefore not possible within the Bolker–Jeffrey theory.

A major difference between the Bolker–Jeffrey theory and others is this: in the Bolker–Jeffrey theory, when prospects are combined together by the truth-functional operation of disjunction they retain their own probabilities, made conditional on the disjunction. Other theories combine prospects or outcomes by forming gambles. This involves artificially assigning a probability (or a state of nature, which has its own probability) to each outcome. Setting up a gamble, in fact, involves altering causal relations in the world. In practice the sorts of gamble that are required by the theory may be causally impossible. For instance, fine weather tomorrow may be assigned to the state of nature: this coin falls heads on its next toss. But the toss of a coin cannot actually determine what the weather will be. In order to include them in her preference ordering a person has to imagine herself being offered such impossible gambles. The Bolker–Jeffrey theory, on the other hand, assumes that a person retains her actual beliefs about the causal processes in the world. Jeffrey considers this the theory's main advantage.[13]

Take a set $\mathfrak{R}$ of prospects that is closed under the operations of disjunction and negation (or union and complementation). That is to say,

If A and B are in $\mathfrak{R}$ then $\neg A$ and $A \vee B$ are in $\mathfrak{R}$.

$\mathfrak{R}$ is then a *Boolean algebra*.[14] It will contain a unit T and a zero F. T *is* the necessarily true proposition and F the necessarily false one:

$T = A \vee \neg A$ for all A in $\mathfrak{R}$.
$F = \neg T$.

T is the set of all possible worlds and *F* the empty set.

The Bolker–Jeffrey theory takes the field of preferences to be a Boolean algebra $\mathfrak{R}$ with the zero removed. Write this field $\mathfrak{R}' = \mathfrak{R} - \{F\}$. *F*, then, has no place in the preference ordering.

The algebra $\mathfrak{R}$ need not contain every set of possible worlds. In fact we assume that $\mathfrak{R}$ is *atomless*, which rules this out. An atomless Boolean algebra is one whose every element has a non-zero strict sub-element:

> For each $A \in \mathfrak{R}$ other than F there is a $B \in \mathfrak{R}$ such that $B \to A$ and $B \neq A$ and $B \neq F$.

This implies, for one thing, that the algebra cannot contain a set consisting of a single world. I have already described the significance of this assumption of atomlessness. We also assume that the algebra is *complete*. This means that it contains all disjunctions of arbitrary sets of contrary members of itself.[15]

Like other expected utility theories, the Bolker–Jeffrey theory starts from given preferences and shows that, provided these preferences satisfy certain axioms, they can be represented by an expectational utility function. The axioms are: that the preferences are a complete preorder on $\mathfrak{R}'$, that they are continuous in a particular sense, and that they satisfy these two conditions:

(i) Averaging. If *A* and *B* in $\mathfrak{R}'$ are contraries then $A > B$ implies $A > A \lor B > B$ and $A \approx B$ implies $A \approx A \lor B \approx B$.

(ii) Impartiality. If *A*, *B* and *C* in $\mathfrak{R}'$ are pairwise contraries, and $A \approx B$ but not $A \approx C$, and $A \lor C \approx B \lor C$, then for every *D* in $\mathfrak{R}'$ that is contrary to *A* and *B*, $A \lor D \approx B \lor D$.

The averaging axiom says that a disjunction lies somewhere between the disjuncts in the preference ordering. It slightly resembles the independence axiom found in other versions of expected utility theory. The independence axiom implies that a 'probability mixture' of two prospects lies somewhere between the prospects in the preference ordering. But it implies much more than this too, and furthermore it implies it for any probability mixture with any arbitrary probabilities. As I explained earlier, in the Bolker–Jeffrey theory, on the other hand, prospects always carry their own probabilities with them when they combine in a disjunction. Combination with arbitrary probabilities is not allowed. So the averaging axiom is much weaker than independence. The much-criticized independence axiom is not required by the Bolker–Jeffrey theory.

The impartiality axiom is less transparent. Take two contrary propositions *A* and *B* that are indifferent to each other. Form their disjunctions with a third contrary proposition that is not indifferent to them. These disjunctions $A \lor C$ and $B \lor C$ will be indifferent to each other if and only if A and B are equally probable. So a way of testing whether two indifferent propositions are equally probable is to compare together the disjunctions they respectively form with a third, non-indifferent proposition. The impartiality axiom says this test will deliver the same answer whatever third, non-indifferent proposition is used.

Compare Savage's Postulate 4.[16] Savage, too, needs to test whether two events, say E and F, are equally probable. He does this by taking a pair of outcomes, say A and B, that are known not to be indifferent. He forms a gamble $(A, E; B, F)$ in which A comes about in event E and B in F. And he forms the opposite gamble $(B, E; A, F)$. The events are equally probable if and only if these gambles are indifferent. Savage's Postulate 4 says this test will deliver the same answer whatever pair of non-indifferent outcomes A and B are used.

The impartiality axiom is unsatisfactory in one respect. The explanation I have given for it presupposes expected utility theory to some extent. I said that $A \lor C$ and $B \lor C$ will be indifferent (for indifferent A and B and non-indifferent C) if and only if A and B are equally probable. But the reason for this is that the utility of a disjunction is the average of the utility of the disjuncts, weighted by their probabilities. And this reason comes out of expected utility theory. It is unsatisfactory that an axiom from which expected utility theory is supposed to be derived needs to be explained in this way.

Savage's Postulate 4 is in exactly the same position. The gambles $(A, E; B, F)$ and $(B, E; A, F)$ will be indifferent if and only if E and F are equally probable. The reason for this is that the utility of a gamble is the average utility of its possible outcomes, weighted by the probabilities of the events in which they occur. This reason comes out of expected utility theory. But the postulate is one of the axioms from which expected utility theory is supposed to be derived. The impartiality axiom, then, is neither more nor less unsatisfactory than Savage's Postulate 4.

Now we come to the representation theorem:

> *Bolker's Existence Theorem.* Let $\mathfrak{R}$ be a complete atomless Boolean algebra, and let $\geq$ be coherent preference on $\mathfrak{R}'$. Then there is a probability measure μ on $\mathfrak{R}$ and a signed measure ν on $\mathfrak{R}$ such that for all A and B in $\mathfrak{R}'$
> $A \geq B$ if and only if $\nu(A)/\mu(A) \neq \nu(B)/\mu(B)$.

(I shall use the unqualified term 'measure' to include signed measures, non-negative measures, and non-positive measures. By a 'non-negative measure' I mean a measure μ such that $\mu(A) \geq 0$ for all A in $\mathfrak{R}$. By a 'positive measure', I mean a non-negative measure μ such that $\mu(A) = 0$ implies $A = F$.)

Because μ and ν are measures, whenever A and B are contraries (disjoint) then

$$\nu(A \vee B) = \nu(A) + \nu(B)$$

and

$$\mu(A \vee B) = \mu(A) + \mu(B).$$

In the existence theorem the role of utility is played by the quotient of measures ν/μ. Granted the existence of μ and ν, we define utility U on $\mathfrak{R}'$ by

$$U(A) = \nu(A)/\mu(A) \text{ for all } A \text{ in } \mathfrak{R}'.$$

U will then be a properly expectational utility function as required, because if A and B are contraries,

$$\mu(A \vee B) = \frac{\nu(A \vee B)}{\mu(A \vee B)} = \frac{\nu(A) + \nu(B)}{\mu(A) + \mu(B)} = \frac{\mu(A)U(A) + \mu(B)U(B)}{\mu(A) + \mu(B)} \qquad (1)$$

I explained, using the example above, that this formula makes $U(A \vee B)$ the expectation of utility given that $A \vee B$ is true. The measure ν is best thought of as simply a convenient construction, the product of utility and probability.

Notice that the averaging axiom rules out propositions (other than F) that have probability zero. For if A, $B \in \mathfrak{R}'$, $A > B$, and $\mu(B) = 0$, we shall have from equation (1) that $U(A \vee B) = U(A)$, contrary to the averaging axiom. The measure μ is therefore strictly positive (so U is well-defined on $\mathfrak{R}'$). Bolker defends this implication of the axiom by saying that propositions to which a person assigns probability zero can simply be left out of $\mathfrak{R}$.[17] This may be all right for a single person. But in section 6.6, I shall be assuming that everyone's preferences and also social preferences are defined on the same field $\mathfrak{R}'$. So there is a substantive assumption implied here: that all these different preferences attach zero probability to the same set of propositions.

Notice too that, for a similar reason, the averaging axiom rules out infinite values for $\nu(A)$.

Bolker's Uniqueness Theorem. Let μ, μ' be probability measures and ν, ν' signed measures on a complete atomless Boolean algebra $\mathfrak{R}$. Then μ, ν represent the same preferences as μ', ν' if and only if

	$\nu' = a\nu + b\mu$	(2a)
and	$\mu' = c\nu + d\mu,$	(2b)
where	$ad - bc > 0$	(3a)
and	$c\nu(T) + d = 1$	(3b)
and	$c\nu(A) + d\mu(A) > 0$ for all A in $\mathfrak{R}'$.	(3c)

The transformation of μ, ν to μ', ν' transforms utility U to

$$U' = \frac{\nu'}{\mu'} = \frac{a\nu + b\mu}{c\nu + d\mu} = \frac{aU + b}{cU + d} \tag{4}$$

This is a 'fractional linear transformation'. The Bolker–Jeffrey theory allows a wider range of transformations for utility than other expected utility theories, which allow only linear transformations. It also allows transformations of probabilities, which other theories rule out.

Bolker and Jeffrey have given an explanation of why other theories determine utilities and probabilities more tightly than theirs does.[18] Other theories use a richer body of preferences as data on which to construct utilities. Preferences are defined on all gambles in which outcomes are assigned to arbitrary states of nature or assigned arbitrary probabilities. As I explained, such gambles may be causally impossible. In the Bolker–Jeffrey theory prospects always retain their own probabilities; when prospects are combined in a disjunction the probabilities are simply made conditional. It turns out that utilities and probabilities are then more loosely determined.

There is one case, however, where probabilities cannot be transformed, and utilities are confined to positive linear transformations only. This is where the range of U on $\mathfrak{R}'$ is unbounded above and below. Condition (3c) requires that $cU(A) + d > 0$ for all A in $\mathfrak{R}'$. If U is unbounded above and below this is possible only if $c = 0$. Then by (3b) $d = 1$, and by (4) $U' = aU + b$. So any transform of U is also unbounded above and below. I shall call preferences *unbounded* if they are represented by a utility function that is unbounded above and below.

Other decision theories rule out unbounded utilities as impossible. In effect, this is because of the St Petersburg Paradox. Given a sequence of prospects with unbounded utilities, one can construct out of them a gamble that has infinite utility. This is what the St Petersburg game does. And an infinite utility cannot be accommodated within the theory. But to construct such a gamble one needs to assign each outcome an artificially chosen probability. And this, as I have explained, is not allowed in the Bolker–Jeffrey theory. So unbounded utilities are not ruled out in this theory.[19]

Indeed, in the Bolker–Jeffrey theory utility functions that are unbounded *either* above or below are nothing out of the ordinary. They can always be transformed into bounded functions by a suitable choice of coefficients in (2). And any utility function that does not attain its upper or lower bound can be transformed into one that is unbounded above or below.[20] This makes it clear that unboundedness need not imply extreme desirability or undesirability, whatever that might mean.

Functions that are unbounded above *and* below are in a different class, because they cannot be transformed into bounded functions and they permit no transformation of probability. But one thing that is missing, I think, from Bolker's and Jeffrey's accounts of their theory is a characterization of unbounded preferences. What must be special about preferences to make their utility representation unbounded above and below? One feature they must have is to possess no top and no bottom: no prospect preferred or indifferent to every prospect and no prospect to which every prospect is preferred or indifferent. But it is not only unbounded preferences that have this feature. And it is not clear what extra feature unbounded preferences must have. Jeffrey gives a necessary and sufficient condition for preferences to be unbounded, but it is intuitively opaque.[21]

Throughout this paper I shall adopt the convenient normalization that

$$v(T) = v'(T) = 0.$$

Since μ is a probability measure

$$\mu(T) = \mu'(T) = 1.$$

From (2a)

$$v'(T) = av(T) + b\mu(T)$$

and from (2b)

$$\mu'(T) = cv(T) + d\mu(T).$$

So $b = 0$ and $d = 1$. Then (2a), (2b), (4), (3a), and (3c) respectively reduce to:

$$v' = av, \tag{5a}$$
$$\mu' = cv + \mu, \tag{5b}$$

and $\quad U' = aU/(cU+1),$ (5c)

where $\quad a > 0$ (6a)

and $\quad cv(A) + \mu(A) > 0$ for all A in $\Re'$. (6b)

I shall call a transformation *legal* if it meets these conditions.

6.5   Decision versus valuation

Consider this 'twin prisoners' dilemma'.[22] You and your twin are facing a prisoners' dilemma. Table 6.2 shows the benefits (money, say): first in each bracket is your benefit, then hers.

There is no love lost between the pair of you, and you are going to act entirely self-interestedly. But she and you think very much alike, and you know this. So you know that if you act nice she will probably act nice too, and if you act nasty she will probably act nasty too.

Table 6.2

		Your twin	
		Acts nice	Acts nasty
You	Act nice	(5, 5)	(0, 7)
	Act nasty	(7, 0)	(1, 1)

Let A be the proposition 'You act nasty' and B 'Your twin acts nasty.' You know that the probability of B given A, $\mu(A\wedge B)/\mu(A)$, is high. Correspondingly, $\mu(A\wedge\neg B)/\mu(A)$ is low. In the Bolker–Jeffrey theory,

$$U(A) = U(A\wedge B)\mu(A\wedge B)/\mu(A) + U(A\wedge\neg B)\mu(A\wedge\neg B)/\mu(A).$$

So if $\mu(A\wedge B)/\mu(A)$ is high and $\mu(A\wedge\neg B)/\mu(A)$ low, $U(A)$ is near $U(A\wedge B)$. Similarly, if C is 'You act nice' and D is 'Your twin acts nice', $U(C)$ is near $U(C\wedge D)$. But $U(C\wedge D)$ is well above $U(A\wedge B)$ because $C\wedge D$ gets you 5 and $A\wedge B$ only 1. So $U(C)$ will be above $U(A)$.

This suggests you ought to act nice. But to most people this seems to be an incorrect conclusion.[23] Whatever your twin does, you do better by acting nasty. Acting nasty is a dominant strategy, so that acting nice is irrational. The Bolker–Jeffrey theory seems to come to the wrong conclusion in this case. Its mistake is fairly plain. Acting nice gives you evidence that your twin will probably act nice too, because she is like you. In a sense, then, it makes it probable that she will act nice, and so give you a good result. That is why the theory gives acting nice a high utility. But your acting nice does not have any causal influence on how she acts. And that is what counts in deciding what to do. The theory seems to have muddled evidence with cause.

Examples like this have led to a resurgence of 'causal decision theory' in opposition to the 'evidential' Bolker–Jeffrey theory.[24] Savage's theory is the leading example of a causal decision theory. In Savage's theory there must be states of nature whose probabilities are independent of actions. Faced with the twin prisoners' dilemma, a follower of Savage has two alternatives. She may decline to apply the theory at all, perhaps taking the general view that decision theory does not apply to games. Or she may pick some things to serve as states of nature. She may, for instance, take your twin's acts as states of nature from your point of view. They will then have to be assigned probabilities independent of your own acts. And whatever probabilities they are assigned, acting nasty will come out with a higher expected utility for you. Either way, the Bolker–Jeffrey theory's incorrect conclusion is avoided. So, on the face of it at least, we have here a weakness in the Bolker–Jeffrey theory, which causal decision theory does not share.

It is a serious weakness, too, because situations like the twin prisoners' dilemma are common in practice. Many free-rider problems have the structure of a prisoners' dilemma. And in many of them the participants, though not twins, are similar enough for their behaviour to be quite closely correlated. For instance, suppose I, considering my own interest only, am wondering whether to join a trade union. If a lot of people join, we shall all be better off because we shall win benefits. But, however many people join, I should always be better off not joining, because I should get the benefits anyway, and save the dues. I am much like other people, though. So if I join, many other people will probably do so too. The argument I gave for the twin prisoners' dilemma applies here too. The Bolker–Jeffrey theory therefore seems to say I should join. But actually, most people would think, if I am concerned with my own interest only, I should not.

A government, too, may face dilemmas that raise the same difficulty. Take a government faced with a public that has rational expectations. It is wondering whether or not to expand the money supply. Table 6.3 shows how the effects of its actions will depend on what the people expect.

If the government expands the money supply, the people will probably have predicted that, so the result will be inflation. If it does not expand it, they will probably have predicted that too, so the result will be no change. The Bolker–Jeffrey theory, then, will assign a higher expected utility to not expanding. It suggests this is the right thing to do. Dominance reasoning, however, shows that the right thing is to expand. That, at any rate, is the conclusion of most authors who have considered this 'time-inconsistency problem'.[25] This government's dilemma has exactly the form of the 'Newcomb problem',[26] which first led to the renewed interest in causal decision theory.[27]

There may be ways for the Bolker–Jeffrey theory to overcome the weakness I have been describing.[28] But in any case, it is a weakness only when the theory is taken literally as a theory of decision. If it is taken as a theory of valuation, there is no problem. Although, in the twin prisoners' dilemma, you ought to act nasty, it would nevertheless be better for you, in a natural sense, if you acted nice. If, for instance, you were to learn in some way that you were going to act nice, you would be justifiably pleased.[29] That news would tell you that your twin would probably do the same, so that the outcome would probably be a good one. In the other example, it would be better, in a natural sense, if the government kept the money supply constant. This is what the Bolker–Jeffrey theory says, and it makes good sense. It is, furthermore, a sense that causal decision theory cannot recognize. So here, as a theory of valuation, the Bolker–Jeffrey theory has the advantage.

Valuation must be connected with decision in the end. The point of making valuations is to supply reasons for deciding one way or another

Table 6.3

		Expected action	
		Do not expand	Expand
Government's action	Do not expand	No change	Depression
	Expand	Increased employment	Inflation

when there is a decision to be made. But the connection need not be immediate. For instance, before it comes to a decision in some matter, a government may need to make complicated calculations about how good or bad the alternatives are for the people. In these calculations it may be appropriate for it to take 'good' and 'bad' for the people in a sense that is not directly connected with decisions the people make. So there is nothing wrong in general with separating value from decision. And it is useful in our context.

Let us ask: which sort of expected utility theory is it appropriate to apply to the Utilitarian Theorem – a theory of decision or a theory of valuation? The right one to pick is the one that makes the best sense of the theorem's assumptions: coherence and the Paretian assumption.

The Utilitarian Theorem is about individual and social preferences. The notion of preference is elastic, and we can interpret it as best fits the theorem. In one sense, a rational person in the twin prisoners' dilemma will prefer the prospect of acting nasty, since this is what she ought to do. In another sense, she will prefer the prospect of acting nice, since that would be better for her. Let us call these the 'decisional' and 'valuational' senses of 'prefer'. The same distinction applies to social preferences too. Of two alternatives, the one that is socially preferred in the decisional sense is the one the government should choose if it has the choice. The one that is socially preferred in the valuational sense is the better one.[30]

Suppose we pick the valuational interpretation. The Bolker–Jeffrey theory suits this interpretation, and we can expect individual and social preferences, under this interpretation, to be coherent according to the Bolker–Jeffrey theory. What about the Paretian assumption? Look again at the twin prisoners' dilemma. Under the valuational interpretation, you prefer the prospect of your acting nice to the prospect of your acting nasty. Obviously your twin prefers that too. So the Paretian assumption requires that your acting nice should be socially preferred to your acting nasty. And this seems quite right in the valuational sense: it would indeed be better if you acted nice. All the assumptions of the Utilitarian Theorem, then, work well under the valuational interpretation. This means that the Bolker–Jeffrey theory suits the theorem.

Suppose, alternatively, we pick the decisional interpretation. Savage's theory suits this interpretation, and we can expect individual and social preferences, under this interpretation, to be coherent according to Savage's theory. What about the Paretian assumption? I can find no way of setting up an example like the twin prisoners' dilemma so as to give worthwhile scope to the Paretian assumption. I said that Savage's theory can get a grip in the example by treating your twin's acts as states of nature from your point of view. Given that, your acts can be thought of as prospects, and acting nasty has a greater expected utility than acting nice. But to apply the Paretian assumption, we need both players to have preferences over the same prospects. This means we need to define states of nature that are the same for both. And however this is done, prospects will have to be joint acts: yours and your twin's. Your own acts will not be prospects on their own, so it will no longer be possible to say that your acting nasty has a greater expected utility for you. I conclude, then, that if we want to apply the Utilitarian Theorem to examples like this, the decisional interpretation will get us nowhere.

But the valuational interpretation works. I think this shows, at the very least, that this interpretation is as good as the decisional one for the purposes of the Utilitarian Theorem. But the objections I raised to the Bolker–Jeffrey theory earlier in this section apply only when it is taken as a theory of decision. Taken as a theory of valuation, the Bolker–Jeffrey theory is in good shape. It is therefore appropriate to apply it to the Utilitarian Theorem, and section 6.3 offered a good reason for doing so.

6.6   The utilitarian theorem in the Bolker–Jeffrey theory

Let $\Re$ be a complete atomless Boolean algebra. Let its unit be T and its zero F. Let $\Re' = \Re - \{F\}$. Let there be $h + 1$ preference relations $\geq_1, \geq_2, \ldots, \geq_h$, $\geq_g$ on $\Re'$. Write $I = \{1, \ldots, h\}$ and $I^+ = \{1, \ldots, h\} \cup \{g\}$.

> *Assumption 1.* For all $i \in I$, $\geq_i$ is coherent.
> *Assumption 2.* $\geq_g$ is coherent.

Given these assumptions, Bolker's Existence Theorem tells us that for each $i \in I^+$ there is a probability measure μ_i and a signed measure ν_i such that, for all A and B in $\Re'$

$$\nu_i(A)/\mu_i(A) \geq \nu_i(B)/\mu_i(B) \text{ if and only if } A \geq_i B.$$

I explained in section 6.3 that μ_i is strictly positive and ν_i finite. For each i

$\epsilon\ I^+$, normalize v_i to make $v_i(T) = 0$. Write $U_i(A) = v_i(A)/\mu_i(A)$.
   Some definitions:

> $\geq_g$ is *Paretian* if an only if, for all A and B in $\mathfrak{R}'$,

>   >   if $A \approx_i B$ for all $i \in I$, then $A \approx_g B$, and   (7)

>   >   if $A \geq_i B$ for all $i \in I$ and $A >_i B$ for some $i \in I$, then $A >_g B$.   (8)

> $\geq_g$ is *utilitarian* if and only if, for each $i \in I^+$, there is a legal
>   transform U_i' of U_i such that $U_g'(A) = \Sigma_{i \in I} U_i'(A)$.

> $\geq_i$ is *unbounded* if and only if, for each $n = 1, 2, \ldots$, there are A^n
>   and B^n in $\mathfrak{R}'$ such that $U_i(A^n) > n$ and $U_i(B^n) < -n$.

I shall assume:

>   *Assumption 3.* $\geq_g$ is Paretian.
>   *Assumption 4.* For all $i \in I$, there is an $A_i \in \mathfrak{R}'$ such that $A_i \approx_j T$
>   for all $j \in I - \{i\}$ but not $A_i \approx_i T$.

Assumption 4 requires, firstly, that no one is entirely indifferent between all
propositions. And secondly it requires some minimal independence
between different people's preferences.
   Now my first theorem:

>   *Theorem 1.* Under Assumptions 1–4, for each $i \in I$ there is a
>   number $e_i > 0$ such that for all A in $\mathfrak{R}'$:
> $$v_g(A) = \Sigma_{i \in I} e_i v_i(A). \tag{9}$$

The proof of this theorem and all other theorems appear in the Appendices
to the original edition of this paper.[31]
   Now suppose there is *probability agreement,* or more exactly that all
probabilities can be transformed into agreement. That is, suppose for each
$i \in I^+$ there is a legal transform μ_i' of μ_i such that $\mu_i'(A) = \mu_g'(A)$ for all $i \in I$
and all $A \in \mathfrak{R}'$. Then for each $i \in I$ take the e_i from Theorem 1 and let $v_i' = e_i v_i$. Let $v_g' = v_g$. These are legal transformations. Then

$$U_g'(A) = \frac{v_g'(A)}{\mu_g'(A)} = \frac{v_g(A)}{\mu_g'(A)} = \Sigma_{i \in I} \frac{e_i v_i(A)}{\mu_g'(A)} = \Sigma_{i \in I} \frac{v_i'(A)}{\mu_i'(A)} = \Sigma_{i \in I} U_i'(A)$$

So we have this

>   *Corollary to Theorem 1.* Under Assumptions 1–4, $\geq_g$ is utilitarian
>   if for each $i \in I^+$ there is a legal transform μ_i' of μ_i such that $\mu_i'(A)$
> $= \mu_g'(A)$ for all $i \in I$ and all $A \in \mathfrak{R}'$.

Probability agreement, then, is a sufficient condition for the Utilitarian
Theorem. (It is also necessary, but that is not proved in this paper.)
   To establish the Utilitarian Theorem, then, we would need only to estab-

lish a version of the Probability Agreement Theorem: that individual and social probabilities can be transformed to make them all equal. Assumptions 1–4, however, are not enough to ensure that this is true. The most that can be said is that the individual and social preferences must all agree about the probabilities of propositions that everyone finds indifferent to T. (These probabilities cannot be transformed anyway.) Let $\mathfrak{J}$ be $\{A \in \mathfrak{R}': A \approx_i T$ for all $i \in I\}$.

> *Theorem 2.* Under Assumptions 1–4, $\mu_i(A) = \mu_g(A)$ for all $i \in I$ and all $A \in \mathfrak{J}$.

But outside $\mathfrak{J}$ it may not be possible to transform probabilities into agreement.[32] Consequently the Utilitarian Theorem can fail. Before we can prove the Utilitarian Theorem we shall need two major new assumptions:

> *Assumption 5.* For all $i \in I$ and all $A \in \mathfrak{R}'$, there is a $B \in \mathfrak{R}'$ such that $B \approx_i A$ and $B \approx_j T$ for all $j \in I - \{i\}$.
> *Assumption 6.* For all $i \in I$, $\succeq_i$ is unbounded.

Assumption 5 says that there are propositions over the whole range of i's preferences, from top to bottom, that everyone else considers indifferent to T. It says that the different people's preferences are independent of each other in a sense. I shall discuss this independence assumption and Assumption 6 in section 6.7. Assumption 4 contains a minimal independence assumption of the same sort. Note that Assumptions 5 and 6 together imply Assumption 4.

Granted assumptions 5 and 6, the Probability Agreement Theorem can be proved:

> *Theorem 3.* Under Assumptions 1, 2, 3, 5, and 6, $\mu_i(A) = \mu_g(A)$ for all $i \in I$ and all $A \in \mathfrak{R}'$.

(This says probabilities actually agree, not merely that they can be transformed into agreement, because under Assumption 6 probabilities cannot be transformed.) From Theorem 3 and the Corollary to Theorem 1, the Utilitarian Theorem follows immediately:

> *Theorem 4.* Under Assumptions 1, 2, 3, 5, and 6, $\succeq_g$ is utilitarian.

6.7.   Conclusions

The Utilitarian Theorem, as I described it in section 6.1, says that if individual and social preferences are coherent (Assumptions 1 and 2), and if social preferences are Paretian (Assumption 3), then it follows that social preferences are utilitarian. Theorem 4 tells us that Assumptions 5 and 6 are sufficient conditions for the truth of this theorem. Neither would be sufficient on its own.[33] Neither assumption is necessary, but I believe no weaker significant assumptions would be sufficient to establish the Utilitarian Theorem.[34] So our trust in the theorem has to rest on these assumptions. How plausible are they?

Assumption 5 is very demanding. The values people assign to prospects are likely to be correlated to some extent. A nuclear war, for instance, comes near the bottom of most people's scales of preference. But Assumption 5 requires there to be some prospect that is just as bad as this for one person, but that other people regard with equanimity. This is implausible. I doubt the Utilitarian Theorem could be proved on the basis of a much weaker independence assumption than this. My proof depends crucially on the existence of prospects that are very good or very bad for one person and neutral for everyone else. So I doubt if the objectionable feature of Assumption 5 could be eliminated.

Other versions of the Utilitarian Theorem, within other versions of decision theory, also rely on independence assumptions of the same sort. For example, take Peter Fishburn's proof, which assumes objective probabilities.[35] Fishburn assumes that for each person i there are prospects A_i and B_i such that $A_i >_i B_i$ and $A_i \approx_j B_i$ for all j other than i. This is a very weak independence assumption. Indeed, it is equivalent to my Assumption 4. My Corollary to Theorem 1, which assumes probability agreement, corresponds closely to Fishburn's theorem. It, too, requires Assumption 4. For another example, one of Peter Hammond's proofs assumes implicitly that the range of the vector $(u_{11}, u_{12}, \ldots, u_{21}, \ldots, u_{hn})$, where u_{ir} is person i's utility in state of nature r, is a product set ΠS_{ir}, where S_{ir} is the range of u_{ir}.[36] This means that one person's utility in one state can move over the whole of its range whilst the utilities for every other person–state pair remain constant. This is an extremely strong independence assumption. An earlier proof of Hammond's helps itself to variations in u_{ir} without any constraint.[37]

The need for Assumption 6, the unboundedness assumption, is confined to the Bolker–Jeffrey theory, because it makes no sense in other theories. But one might say that an assumption with the same role is already implicit in other theories. The effect of Assumption 6 is to cancel out a sort of extra generality that the Bolker–Jeffrey theory initially possesses beyond other expected utility theories: the wider range of utility transformations it allows. When preferences are unbounded, only linear transformations are possible, as in other theories. I did not expect this conclusion. I expected that having a wide range of utility functions available for representing preferences would actually make it easier to find a social utility function that is the sum of individual functions. But the opposite is true. This suggests to me that a tight determination of utilities may be playing a part in making the Utilitarian Theorem work in other versions of expected utility theory too. As I explained in section 6.4, this tight determination is the result of supposing that a person has preferences over arbitrarily constructed gambles, including gambles that are causally impossible. It may be, then, that social preferences are forced to be utilitarian only because we insist that they should be coherent and Paretian over gambles that are causally impossible. This is some reason to be cautious about the theorem.

It is not easy to assess the plausibility of Assumption 6 itself: that everyone's preferences are unbounded. I said in section 6.4 that Bolker and Jeffrey have not made it clear just what unbounded preferences are like, so it is hard to know whether to expect them to be common or uncommon. But to assume that everyone's preferences are unbounded does seem, at least, to be asking for a large coincidence.

I conclude, then, that the Utilitarian Theorem, though it can be proved within the Bolker–Jeffrey theory, needs to be treated with caution.

In my *Weighing Goods*, I have reinterpreted the theorem in terms of a person's good, rather than her preferences. I take a person's utility to represent her 'betterness relation'

_ is at least as good for the person as _

instead of her preference relation

_ is preferred or indifferent to _.

The notion of betterness applied to uncertain prospects presupposes probabilities that are the same for everyone.[38] The reinterpreted theorem therefore does not require Assumptions 5 and 6. It is shown to be true by the Corollary to Theorem 1. This requires only Assumption 4, the weakest of independence assumptions. I therefore have faith in the reinterpreted theorem.

7   Fairness

This chapter presents a theory about fairness, as it applies to the distribution of goods between people. I shall concentrate particularly on random lotteries. Sometimes a lottery is the fairest way of distributing a good, and my theory explains, better than any other theory I know, why this is so. That is the main evidence I offer for it. But the theory is not limited to lotteries; it is intended to apply whenever goods are distributed between people. I shall use the fairness of lotteries as a guide to fairness in general.[1]

7.1   Choosing between candidates

It often happens that there are several candidates to receive a good, but the good cannot be divided up to go round them all. The good may be very important; it may even amount to the saving of the candidate's life. For instance, not enough kidneys are available for transplant for everyone who needs one. As a result, some people are denied treatment for their kidney failure, and consequently die.

For each candidate, there will be reasons why she should have the good, or some of it. (I mean prima facie reasons, which may be defeated by other reasons.) Amongst them will be the benefits, to the candidate herself and to other people, that will result from this candidate's receiving the good. When the good is the saving of life, these benefits will depend on how much the candidate enjoys her life, what responsibilities she has to other people, and so on. Then there may also be other reasons. One may be desert: some of the candidates may deserve the good, perhaps because of services they have performed in the past. For the moment, suppose all these reasons can be weighed against each other. (I shall question this later.) Then, for some candidates, the reasons why they should have the good will be stronger, on balance, than for others. Let us call one person a 'better' candidate than another if she has stronger reasons in her favour.

From *Proceedings of the Aristotelian Society*, 91 (1990–1), pp. 87–102. Reprinted by courtesy of the Editor of the Aristotelian Society: © 1991.

How should it be decided which of the candidates should get the good? Several procedures might be used. One is to have some authority judge the merits of the candidates, and select the best. But this procedure has its costs. The job of assembling and assessing the necessary information may be expensive and time-consuming. The responsibility of deciding who is to live and who is to die (if that is in question) may be an intolerable emotional burden. Furthermore, the authority may not actually succeed in picking the best candidates. It may choose the candidates who best meet corrupt or prejudiced criteria, rather than the ones who are actually the best.

One procedure that avoids the costs and dangers of deliberate selection by an authority is to apply some fixed rule. (There is a risk of corruption or prejudice in setting up the rule, but not once it is set up.) And it may be possible to devise a rule that goes some way towards selecting the best candidates. For life saving, the rule of picking the youngest will do this. Age will certainly be one of the factors that helps determine which candidates are the best. Other things being equal, it is better to save a younger person than an older, because it does more good to the person who is saved: it gives her, on average, more years of life. So there is some correlation between a person's youth and how good a candidate she is.

A lottery is another procedure that avoids the costs and dangers of deliberate selection. Unlike a well-chosen fixed rule, though, it is no more likely to pick the best candidates than any others. So what advantage can it possibly have over a fixed rule? Plainly, only that it is sometimes fairer. But how can this be so? How can a lottery be fairer than a rule such as picking the youngest, which has a tendency to select the better candidates? Answering this question is the main test that has to be passed by any account of the fairness of lotteries. To answer it properly demands a particular theory of fairness in general; only this theory, which I shall describe in sections 7.3 and 7.4, is able to explain adequately the fairness of a lottery.

7.2   The facts about fairness

Before coming to the theory, I shall first set out what I think it needs to account for: the facts about the fairness of lotteries that need to be explained.

First: a lottery is by no means always fair. It would not, for instance, be a fair way of choosing whom to award the prize in a violin competition. So in explaining the fairness of lotteries we shall need a criterion for distinguishing when lotteries are fair from when they are not.

Secondly: our account of the fairness of lotteries cannot simply be that lotteries are good tie breakers, appropriate only when the reasons in favour of different candidates are exactly balanced. The two examples below show that it is sometimes right to hold a lottery even when reasons are not exactly balanced. In any case, if a lottery were appropriate only for breaking a tie, its value would be insignificant. It will hardly ever happen in practice that reasons balance exactly. And if ever they do, the slightest change in one of them would mean they were no longer balanced. Then, if it was right to hold a lottery only for breaking a tie, it would no longer be right to hold one. So the value of a lottery would be lexicographically dominated by other values. (Section 7.6, however, qualifies this point.)

Furthermore, to say that lotteries are good tie breakers fails to explain their fairness. When there is a tie, it does not matter which candidate is chosen. What is required is simply a means of getting the decision made. A lottery is a handy means, even when no issue of fairness arises. When I cannot decide between two restaurants for dinner, I may toss a coin. This is not in order to be fair to the restaurants, but simply to avoid the fate of Buridan's Ass. When it comes to a choice not between restaurants, but between candidates for some good, a lottery is sometimes more than just a handy means of getting the decision made when there is a tie. It is sometimes a better means than others because it is fairer. We therefore need a separate explanation of why it is fairer.

Thirdly: the fairness of a lottery does not consist solely in the fact that it overcomes the costs and dangers of deliberate selection by an authority. I have already explained that selection by a fixed rule is likely to be a better way of doing that. And even when it is possible to choose the best candidates deliberately, without cost and without corruption or prejudice, there is still sometimes a case for a lottery. The following two examples make this point, and also the second point mentioned above.

The first example is about games. Most games begin by holding a lottery to settle which player starts in the most favourable position (playing white, say). Fairness requires this. But normally some players will be better candidates for the favourable position than others, as I defined 'better candidate' in section 7.1. For instance, usually more joy will be caused in total by the victory of one player rather than another, so a greater expectation of benefit would result from giving that player a favourable start. Let us suppose there is a referee who, without prejudice or corruption, is easily able to pick out the best candidate. It would still be wrong to leave the decision to the referee rather than a lottery.

The second example is a dangerous mission. Someone has to be sent on a mission that is so dangerous she will probably be killed. The people available are similar in all respects, except that one has special talents that make her more likely than the others to carry out the mission well (but no more likely to survive). This fact is recognized by her and everyone else. Who should be sent? Who, that is, should receive the good of being left behind?

It could plausibly be thought that the right thing is simply to send the talented person. But it is also very plausible that doing so would be unfair to her, and that fairness requires a lottery to be held amongst all the candidates. These two views are not incompatible. It may be that fairness requires a lottery, so that it would be unfair not to hold one, but that in this case fairness is outweighed by expediency, so that on balance it is right to send the talented candidate without a lottery. This depends on the circumstances. If it is vital that there should be no slip in the execution of the mission, the unfairness will be tolerable. But if a less-than-perfect performance is acceptable, more importance can be given to fairness. In some circumstances, fairness will win, and a lottery should be held.

7.3   Claims

Those, then, are the facts. How can they be explained? In this section and the next, I shall present my theory of fairness. I mean it to apply to the distribution of any sort of good, whether indivisible or not. In section 7.5, I shall come back to indivisible goods and lotteries.

When a good is to be distributed, for each candidate there are reasons why she should have some of it. These reasons together determine what ought to be done: how the good should be distributed. But how, exactly, do the reasons combine together to determine what ought to be done? As I shall put it: how do reasons *work*? There are various views about this.

One is *teleology*. Teleology claims that the good ought to be distributed in whatever way maximizes overall benefit.[2] So the only sort of reason it recognizes for a particular candidate to get the good is a benefit that would result. Imagine the good being distributed one unit at a time. Each unit should go to the candidate whose receiving it would produce the most benefit; this will normally ensure that overall benefit is maximized when all the units are eventually distributed. At each stage, the reason for giving a particular unit to one candidate is the benefit that would result; the reason for giving it to the next candidate is the benefit that would result from that; and so on. All these reasons should be weighed against each other, and the unit allocated to the candidate for whom the reason is strongest. So we can say that reasons are combined together by *weighing up*. This is how reasons work in teleology. Weighing up goes along with maximizing.

Other views disagree with teleology. One, for instance, claims that some reasons are side constraints. A *side constraint* determines directly what ought to be done; it is not subject to being weighed against other reasons. *Rights* are often thought to be side constraints. Suppose that, amongst the candidates for a good, one has a right to some part of it. Suppose it is her income, for instance, which she has earned. Then side-constraint theory says simply that she should have it; no question of weighing arises. The theory may acknowledge the existence of teleological reasons too, which work by weighing up. It may allow that weighing up is appropriate amongst other candidates, but not for a candidate who has a right.

I am going to describe a third type of reason, which works in a third way. To introduce it, I shall first draw a distinction of a different sort amongst the reasons why a candidate should get the good: some of these reasons are duties *owed to the candidate herself*, and others are not. I shall call the former *claims* that the candidate has to the good.

The distinction between claims and other reasons is easy to grasp intuitively. Take the dangerous mission, for example. One candidate is more talented than the others. This is a reason for allotting to the others the good of staying behind. But the other candidates' lack of talent gives them no *claim* to this good. It may be right to leave them behind, but it is not owed *them* to do so. Whatever claim they have to this good, the talented candidate has it also.

The distinction can appear even within teleology – indeed within utilitarianism. All utilitarians think that if a person would benefit from having some particular good, that is a reason why she should have it. But some utilitarians think this reason is a duty owed to the person – a claim – and others think it is not. William Godwin, for one, thought it was a claim. 'Every man', he said, 'has a right to that, the exclusive possession of which being awarded to him, a greater sum of benefit or pleasure will result than could have arisen from its being otherwise appropriated.'[3]

The difference is nicely brought out by the attitude of utilitarians to changes in the world's population. Henry Sidgwick[4] believed an action was right if it maximized the total of good enjoyed by people in the world. So he believed one should promote growth in population if the extra people brought into existence will have good lives, and no harm will be done to people already living. But this is clearly not a duty owed to the people who will be brought into existence. One cannot owe anyone a duty to bring her into existence, because failing in such a duty would not be failing anyone. Sidgwick, then, evidently thought that the duty to benefit people is not owed to those people themselves. On the other hand, a utilitarian view promulgated by Jan Narveson[5] is that one should promote the good of existing people or people who will exist, but there is no reason to increase the total of good in the world simply for its own sake. So the fact that the extra people will enjoy good lives is no reason to increase the world's population. Narveson is evidently motivated by the thought that, whatever duty there is to promote a person's good, it must be owed to the person herself. Consequently, there can be no duty to bring a person into existence.

It is clear, then, that there is a distinction between claims and other reasons. It is not so clear which particular reasons are claims and which are not. Even utilitarians, I have been saying, disagree about this. And if we recognize nonutilitarian reasons, there is further scope for disagreement. If we accept *desert* as a reason why a person should have a good, it is perhaps an uncontroversial further step to take it as a claim. But *need* is more controversial. If a person could benefit from a good, that is no doubt a reason why she should have it, but, despite Godwin, we may be reluctant to accept it as a claim. If, however, the person needs the good, perhaps we would accept that. Perhaps, for instance, a person who needs a kidney has a claim on it. But this is controversial.

In this chapter, I am not going to engage in controversy over which reasons are claims and which are not. I shall take it for granted that some are: that some reasons why a person should have a good are duties owed to the person. And I shall concentrate on asking how these reasons, whichever they are, *work*. How do claims combine with each other and with other reasons in determining what should be done?

7.4   What claims require

Some teleologists, as I say, recognize the existence of claims. But they suppose claims work by weighing up, just like other reasons. They think that the right thing to do, and the right way to distribute a good, is determined by the balance of reasons, whether claims or not. They throw claims and other reasons all together on to the same scales, in the same maximizing calculation.

But the fact that conflicting claims are duties owed to different people gives rise to an alternative intuition. Simply weighing claims against each other may not seem enough. Weighing up is the treatment we would naturally give to conflicting duties owed to a single person. Applying it between different people may not seem to be giving proper recognition to the people's separateness.[6]

In particular, weighing up claims does not seem to give proper attention to *fairness*. Take the example of the dangerous mission again. All reasons are evenly balanced, apart from the special reason for sending the talented candidate: she will perform the mission better. So weighing up reasons must conclude in favour of sending this candidate. But that seems unfair to her. It might be the right thing to do under pressure of expediency, but nevertheless it seems unfair. The talented candidate has a claim to the good of being left behind, and her claim is as strong as anyone else's. Yet when it is weighed against other people's claims, and the further reason that she will perform the mission better, her claim is overridden. Weighing up seems to override claims, rather than respect them.

It is fairness that matters here because the particular business of fairness is to mediate between the conflicting claims of different people. But I need to qualify this remark slightly. Certainly, fairness is concerned *only* with claims, and not with other reasons. Suppose there is some reason why a person should have a good, but she has no claim to it. Then if she does not get the good, that may be wrong, but she suffers no unfairness. It cannot be unfair to deny her a good she had no claim to in the first place. On the other hand, it is possible that some claims are outside the domain of fairness, and work in different ways from the one I shall be describing. I shall say more about this possibility later, and for the time being I shall ignore it. I shall assume that all claims are mediated by fairness.

Weighing up claims is not enough, then, because it does not give proper attention to fairness. It would not even be enough to give claims extra heavy weight in the course of weighing up. The example of the dangerous mission shows this, too. However much weight is given to claims, each person's claim to the good of staying behind is still the same. So the claims will all balance, and the talented person will still be sent, because of the extra reason. But this is unfair to her.

What, then, *does* fairness require? It requires, I suggest, that *claims should be satisfied in proportion to their strength*. I do not mean 'proportion' to be taken too precisely. But I do mean that equal claims require equal satisfaction, that stronger claims require more satisfaction than weaker ones, and also – very importantly – that weaker claims require some satisfaction. Weaker claims must not simply be overridden by stronger ones.

This suggestion merely extends and tightens up a principle that is often taken for granted: that people identically situated should be treated identically. Economists call this the principle of 'horizontal equity'.[7] It is, like my generalization of it, inconsistent with teleological maximizing. To see why, imagine two people have equal claims to some good, but that, if the good is divided between them, less benefit will be produced in total than if it is all given to one. Then maximizing implies it should all go to one, but horizontal equity says it should be divided.

The heart of my suggestion is that fairness is concerned only with how well each person's claim is satisfied *compared with* how well other people's are satisfied. It is concerned only with relative satisfaction, not absolute satisfaction. Take a case where all the candidates for a good have claims of equal strength. Then fairness requires equality in satisfaction. So if all the candidates get the same quantity of the good, then fairness has been perfectly achieved, even if they each get very little, or indeed none at all.

To be sure, all is not well if they get none at all. For each claimant there is at least one reason why she should have some of the good: the reason that constitutes her claim. Claims should be satisfied, therefore. But it is not *unfair* if they are not, provided everyone is treated proportionally.

Everyone's claim to a good should, prima facie, be satisfied. Indeed, if there is any reason, whether a claim or not, for a person to have some of a good, she should have some. Call this the 'satisfaction requirement'. Normally, this requirement cannot be fully met for everyone. What does it require then? I suggest it requires maximizing of satisfaction. This implies that, to meet this requirement, claims will have to be weighed against each other and against other reasons; I think weighing up and maximizing are appropriate for the satisfaction requirement. But then *also* fairness requires that claims should be satisfied in proportion to their strength. Claims therefore give rise to two separate requirements: they should be satisfied, and they should be satisfied proportionally.

It will normally be impossible to fulfil both requirements completely. Consequently, the two will themselves have to be combined together in some way, to determine what should be done, all things considered. Here again, I suggest that weighing up is appropriate: the demands of fairness should be weighed against the demands of overall satisfaction. In some circumstances, no doubt, it will be very important to be fair, and in others fairness may be outweighed by expediency.

In summary, claims work like this. Together with other reasons, they go to determine the satisfaction requirement by weighing up. And claims together determine the fairness requirement by the proportionality rule. Then the fairness requirement is itself weighed against the satisfaction requirement.

Evidently, claims in my theory do not work as side constraints; they do not necessarily prevail. This may be a limitation of the theory. I defined claims as duties owed to people, and it may be that within this class there are some claims that are genuinely side constraints. If some claims are side constraints, they are not covered by my theory. My theory is limited to the subclass of claims that work in the way I have described. Call these 'fairness-claims'. It might be a convenient piece of terminology to say that fairness is a subdivision of *justice*, and that justice is concerned with all claims, but fairness only with fairness-claims.

Consequently, I cannot pretend to have defined claims independently of the notion of fairness, and then shown how fairness applies to them. The subclass of claims I am talking about is partly identified by the way they work, and this is itself determined by the theory of fairness. Nevertheless, I believe the subclass of fairness-claims picked out this way is an important one. It may even include all claims. And for brevity I shall continue to use the term 'claim' for fairness-claims only.

The merit of the theory is that it shows a way claims can work, without simply being weighed up in the manner of teleology, and also without being treated as side constraints. Robert Nozick argues for side-constraint theory largely on the grounds that teleology is mistaken. He concedes that these grounds are inadequate if there is a third alternative.[8] My theory of fairness offers one.

It shows how a claim can stop short of a *right*, considered as a side constraint. This fills a significant gap. It seems implausible that anyone has a right to a research grant from, say, the Ford Foundation. But if the Ford Foundation decides to distribute research grants, it should surely deal fairly with the applicants. Someone who was rejected on inadequate grounds would have a just complaint. But how can this be, if she had no right to a grant in the first place? My theory explains how. If her application is good enough, she has a fairness-claim. Consequently, *if* other people are receiving a grant, she should receive one too. In 'Claims of need', David Wiggins considers just what sort of a claim is generated by need. Again, it seems implausible that a person has a right to whatever she needs. So what can her claim be? I suggest it might be a fairness-claim, which implies that, *if* needed resources are being distributed, the person should have a share.

7.5   Claims and lotteries

Now let us concentrate once more on cases where the good to be distributed is indivisible, and there is not enough to go round.

Take a case, first, where all the candidates have equal claims. It would be possible to satisfy their claims equally, as fairness requires, by denying the good to all of them. There may be occasions when it is so important to be fair that this is the right thing to do. But it would totally fail to meet the satisfaction requirement, and normally the demands of fairness will not be enough to outweigh this requirement completely. It will be better to use as much of the good as is available.

In that case, the candidates' claims cannot all be equally satisfied, because some candidates will get the good and others will not. So some unfairness is inevitable. But a sort of partial equality in satisfaction can be achieved. Each person can be given a sort of surrogate satisfaction. By holding a lottery, each can be given an equal *chance* of getting the good. This is not perfect fairness, but it meets the requirement of fairness to some extent.

It does so, of course, only if giving a person a chance of getting the good counts as a surrogate satisfaction of her claim. This seems plausible to me. After all, if you have a chance of getting the good you may actually get it. It is quite different from merely giving the claim its proper weight against other reasons; that does not satisfy it in any way. Suppose, in the example of the dangerous mission, that the talented candidate was sent because of her talents. She could make the following complaint. She has as strong a claim to staying behind as anybody else. Her claim was weighed against other reasons. But this overrode her claim rather than satisfied it. It was never on the cards that she might actually get the good she has a claim to. But if she was sent because a lottery was held and she lost, she could make no such complaint.

Next, take a case where several people have claims to a good that are roughly, but not exactly, equal. Perhaps, for instance, they all need the good, but not exactly equally. And suppose again that there is not enough to go round them all. Fairness requires satisfaction in proportion to their claims. So if the good goes to the people with the strongest claims, the others will not have been fairly treated; their claims will have been over-ridden. And if it goes to other people, the unfairness will be worse. So unfairness is once again inevitable. But once again it can, if the circumstances are right, be mitigated by giving everyone a chance of getting the good. Ideally, each person's chance should be in proportion to the strength of her claim: the lottery should be unequally weighted. (At first, it is particularly puzzling how a weighted lottery could be fair.[9] If it is fair for some people to have a greater chance than others, that means they more ought to have the good. So why not let them have it without a lottery? My theory explains why not.) But even a lottery at equal odds may be fairer than giving the good directly to the candidates with the strongest claims. This depends on a complicated judgement. The result of a lottery will generally be that the good goes to candidates who do not have the strongest claims. This is less fair than the result of giving it directly to those who do. The likelihood of this less fair result will have to be weighed against the contribution to fairness of the lottery itself. But it is clear that, if claims are close to equality, holding a lottery will be fairer than not.

A subsidiary point. We have agreed that fairness requires everyone to have an equal chance when their claims are exactly equal. Then it is implausible it should require some people to have no chance at all when their claims fall only a little below equality.

When claims are equal or roughly equal, then, a lottery is *fair*. Whether it is *right* to hold one is then a matter of weighing the fairness it achieves against the likelihood that it will not meet the satisfaction requirement, which in this case requires the best candidates to be selected. The conclusion will depend on how important fairness is in the circumstances. But there will certainly be some circumstances where it is better to hold a lottery than to choose the best candidates deliberately.

A lottery should be held when, first, it is important to be fair and, secondly, the candidates' claims are equal or roughly equal. These conditions may occur quite often. They do not require an exact balance of all considerations; claims may be equal or roughly equal even when other considerations are not balanced at all. Consider, for instance, a life-saving medical treatment such as a kidney transplant. It seems plausible that, in a matter of life and death, fairness is particularly important. And it seems plausible that everyone has a claim to life, even if on other grounds some are much better candidates than others. Maybe older candidates have weaker claims than younger, since they have already received a greater share of life. But, even so, the candidates' claims may be nearly enough equal to make a lottery appropriate.[10] This explains why a lottery may be better than the rule of picking the youngest. If an older person has a claim to the treatment, even if it is a weaker claim than a younger person's, it demands proportional satisfaction. A lottery provides at least a surrogate satisfaction: a chance. But the rule of picking the youngest gives no sort of satisfaction at all. It simply overrides the claims of older people. So it is less fair.

That is how my theory of fairness explains the value of lotteries. It satisfactorily accounts for the facts set out in section 7.2.

7.6   Other accounts of fairness

I know no alternative theory that explains the value of lotteries as successfully as mine. I cannot review all the alternatives here, but I do need to deal with one that may seem promising at first.[11]

In section 7.1, I spoke of the 'best' candidates for a good, as though the notion was clear-cut. But when the judgement between candidates depends on comparing reasons of different sorts, it often seems impossible to weigh the reasons against each other in a precise way. How, for instance, when comparing candidates for life-saving treatment, should one's *joie de vivre* be weighed against another's family responsibilities? The impossibility might be in the nature of things: some reasons might simply be incommensurable with each other. Or it might be practical: we might have no practical way of making the comparison accurately, even though in principle the reasons might be commensurable.

This indeterminacy suggests the following defence of lotteries. A group of candidates might not be exactly tied – all equally as good as the others – but even so none might be definitely a better candidate than the others. Or it may be that some members of the group are actually better candidates than others, but we cannot in practice know which. Suppose there is only enough of the good for some of this group. Then, just as a lottery has a natural role as a tie breaker when there is an exact tie, it may be appropriate here for the same reason. Here we have a tie within the limits of comparability. And whereas I said in section 7.2 that an exact tie will be very rare, a tie within the limits of comparability may be common. For life-saving medical treatment, for instance, once the medically unsuitable candidates, and perhaps the very old, have been eliminated, it may be that all the remaining candidates are tied within the limits of comparability. We may not be competent to judge between them.

However, I do not think this argument accounts adequately for the value of lotteries. For one thing, it does not explain their *fairness*. As I said in section 7.2, the role of a tie breaker is simply as a device for getting the decision made. No question of fairness need arise. The new argument merely extends this role to a wider domain: a device is needed to get the decision made when the weighing up of reasons has gone as far as it can.

Furthermore, if there is no separate reason why a lottery is fair, it is doubtful that it is even going to be the best way of breaking the tie. A fixed rule may well do better, for the reason I gave in section 7.1: it has some tendency to pick better candidates. Picking the youngest may well do better in the case of life-saving treatment. To be sure, this reason is more questionable in our present context. I said in section 7.1 that, in an arbitrary group of candidates for life saving, the younger ones are more likely to be better candidates than the older. Now, though, we are not dealing with an arbitrary group, but with a group that is tied within the limits of comparability. A candidate's youth is one of the considerations that should already have been taken into account in admitting her to this group. Within the group, therefore, the younger people should generally have fewer other considerations in their favour than the older ones; on balance, they should be no more likely to be good candidates. However, I doubt that in practice, when a lottery is defended on grounds of incomparability, it will often be for a group of people chosen in this finely balanced way. For instance, the group may consist of all the candidates except the medically unsuitable and the very old. For such a group, picking the youngest would be a better tie breaker than a lottery. In any case, this argument from incomparability provides no reason why a fixed rule should be *worse* than a lottery. It fails the test I mentioned at the end of section 7.1.

8   Is incommensurability vagueness?

8.1   Indeterminate comparatives

Which is more impressive: Salisbury Cathedral or Stonehenge? I think there is no determinate answer to this question. The dyadic predicate 'more impressive than' – the comparative of the monadic predicate 'impressive' – seems to allow indeterminate cases. Many comparatives are like that. Amongst them are many evaluative comparatives, such as 'lovelier than', 'cleverer than', and the generic 'better than'.

For many comparatives, the indeterminacy arises because the comparison involves several factors or dimensions, and it is indeterminate exactly how the factors weigh against each other. The impressiveness of a building depends on some combination of its size, its importance in the landscape, the technological achievement it represents, and more, and it is indeterminate how these factors weigh against each other. Many evaluative comparatives are indeterminate for this reason. They depend on a combination of values, and it is indeterminate how the values are to be weighed. The values are *incommensurable*, we say.

Not all indeterminate comparatives arise from incommensurable dimensions, however. 'Redder than' can also be indeterminate, even though it presumably does not involve several factors. Compare some reddish-purple patch of colour with some reddish-orange patch, and ask which is redder. The answer may be indeterminate.

From *Incommensurability, Incomparability and Practical Reason*, edited by Ruth Chang, Harvard University Press, 1998, pp. 67–89. Copyright © 1998 by the President and Fellows of Harvard College. Reprinted by permission of Harvard University Press. This chapter was written while I was a Visiting Fellow at the Australian National University in 1993. I owe a large debt to Adam Morton; his paper 'Hypercomparatives' was the source of many of my arguments. I was also greatly helped by Linda Burns's book *Vagueness*, but unfortunately this chapter is handicapped by having been written before Timothy Williamson's *Vagueness* was published. Had Williamson's book been available, it would have led me to formulate my arguments differently, but they would have led to substantially the same conclusions I have received valuable comments from many people, including Luc Bovens, Ruth Chang, Dorothy Edgington, Sven Danielsson, James Griffin, Frank Jackson, Douglas MacLean, Philip Pettit, Joseph Raz, John Skorupski, Susan Wolf, and Crispin Wright.

To make it clear: when I say a comparative '*F*er than' is indeterminate, I mean that for some pairs of things, of a sort to which the predicate '*F*er' can apply, there is no determinate answer to the question of which is *F*er than which. Neither is *F*er than the other, and nor are the two equally *F*. This chapter is about the logical structure of indeterminate comparatives, and in particular whether they are vague. The analysis is intended to apply to all indeterminate comparatives, but my chief interest is in the structure of evaluative and moral comparatives. I am particularly interested in the structure of 'better than'. I shall argue that the indeterminacy of betterness is commonly misrepresented; it does not take the form that is most commonly assumed for it.

8.2   Standard configurations

I am going to set up a standard framework to use in the investigation. Before doing so I need to make a few preliminary points about the structure of comparatives. First, two formal features of the structure:

> *Asymmetry of* '*F*er than'. For any x and y, if x is *F*er than y, then y is not *F*er than x.
> *Transitivity of* '*F*er than'. For any x, y, and z, if x is *F*er than y and y is *F*er than z, then x is *F*er than z.

I think these are principles of logic. If '*F*er than' is indeterminate, that is no reason to doubt them. They are only conditional statements. Asymmetry requires that *if* x is *F*er than y, then y is not *F*er than x. With an indeterminate comparative, it may turn out for some xs and ys that x is not *F*er than y and nor is y *F*er than x; this is consistent with asymmetry. Transitivity requires that if x is *F*er than y and y is *F*er than z, then x is *F*er than z. If it turns out that neither x is *F*er than y nor y *F*er than x, then in this case transitivity is vacuously satisfied.

My next point is that no comparative I can think of is indeterminate between every pair of things. For some pairs of colour patches, it is indeterminate which is redder than which, but for other pairs, one of the pair is determinately redder than the other. A red patch is determinately redder than an orange patch, for instance. Salisbury Cathedral is determinately more impressive than Bath Abbey. For most comparatives '*F*er than', we can form whole *chains* of things, each of which is *F*er than the next in the chain. A well-chosen chain may run from things that are very *F* to things that are not at all *F*. For instance, we could form a chain of colour patches, each redder than the next, starting from a pure red and running through orange to a yellow with no red in it at all. Churches could be arranged in a chain, each more impressive than the next. The chain might start with St

Peter's, and end with some unimpressive chapel. Stonehenge would not be included in this chain.

Take some chain ordered by '*F*er than'. Then take something that is not included in the chain, and compare it with each of the things that are in the chain, one by one, asking which is *F*er. It may turn out that there is no determinate answer for any member of the chain. Compare Cantor's diagonal proof that the real numbers are uncountable with churches in a chain. Which is more impressive? You might conclude that proofs and churches in general are so different that they can never be determinately compared in terms of their impressiveness. Maybe so and maybe not. Things that are very different from the members of a chain are less likely to be comparable to these members than are similar things. But things that are not too different will normally be comparable to some extent. For instance, take a reddish-purple patch and compare it with the chain of patches I described that runs from red to yellow. The purple patch will be determinately comparable with some members of the chain. Patches at the top of the chain are redder than the purple patch, and the purple patch is redder than patches at the bottom of the chain. But somewhere in the middle there may well be patches where the comparison is indeterminate. To take another example, I think St Peter's is more impressive than Stonehenge, and Stonehenge is more impressive than the gospel chapel in Stoke Pewsey, but for some churches in the chain the comparison with Stonehenge will be indeterminate. So as we move down a chain from top to bottom, comparing its members in *F*ness with some object outside the chain, we may start in a zone where the members of the chain are *F*er, then move into a zone where the comparison is indeterminate, and finally come to a zone where the other object is *F*er.

The aim of this chapter is to investigate what exactly goes on in the zone of indeterminacy. What is true of things in that zone, and what is not true? To focus the discussion, I shall concentrate on a particular type of example, which I shall call a 'standard configuration'. Here is one of the type. Take a chain of colour patches ranging from red through orange to yellow, each patch redder than the next. In fact, let the patches form a continuum: a smooth band of colour graded from red at the top to yellow at the bottom. Compare small patches or points of colour from this band with a single reddish-purple patch, and consider which is redder. At the top are points redder than the single patch and at the bottom points the single patch is redder than.

A *standard configuration* for a comparative '*F*er than' consists of a chain of things, fully ordered by their *F*ness and forming a continuum, and a fixed thing called the *standard* that is not itself in the chain. At the top of the chain are things *F*er than the standard, and at the bottom things the standard is *F*er than. I shall refer to the things that make up the chain as 'points', whatever sort of thing they are.

Two matters of clarification. There may be a zone of indeterminacy between the members of the chain that are *F*er than the standard and those that the standard is *F*er than, and I am particularly interested in cases where there is one, but the definition of a standard configuration does not require there to be one. The second point is that the continuum of points may not exist in fact; we may simply imagine it. For instance, actual churches do not form a continuum, but we can imagine a continuum of churches. Also, I have not defined what I mean by a 'continuum'; I hope I may leave that to intuition.

The colour example is a standard configuration, and here is another. Suppose you have a choice between two careers, and you are wondering which is better. By this I mean: which would be the better one for you to take up. One offers travel and adventure, the other security and a regular income. Let us take the adventurous career as the standard, and form a continuous chain out of the other by varying the amount of income it offers. At the top of the chain are secure careers with a very high income, and let us suppose these are better than the adventurous career. At the bottom are secure careers offering poor incomes, and let suppose the adventurous career is better than those. In the middle there may be a zone of indeterminacy.

A third example. A government is wondering whether to preserve a stretch of rainforest, or open it up for commercial exploitation. Take as the standard the policy of preserving the forest. We can make a chain out of the exploitation option by imagining a range of economic benefits that might arise. Suppose that, if the benefits are enormous, exploitation is better, and, if the benefits are minute, preservation is better. Somewhere in between may be a zone of indeterminacy.

A standard configuration is illustrated in figure 8.1. Graphed against points in the chain, the figure shows truth values for the statements 'This point is *F*er than the standard' and 'The standard is *F*er than this point'. At the top of the chain is a zone of points with the property that they are *F*er than the standard and the standard is not *F*er than them. At the bottom is a zone of points with the property that the standard is *F*er than them and they are not *F*er than the standard. That is a constant feature of any standard configuration. But what happens between the top and the bottom zones? There are a number of possibilities, which I shall describe in turn. In sections 8.9 and 8.10, I shall discuss which of the possibilities are realized in actual English comparatives.

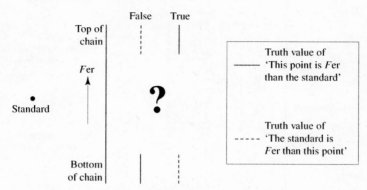

Figure 8.1 A standard configuration.

8.3   No indeterminacy

The first possibility is that there is no more than one point between the top zone and the bottom zone. It may be that, for every point in the chain, either it is *F*er than the standard or the standard is *F*er than it. Alternatively, there may be just one point for which this is not so. In both of these cases there is no indeterminacy. Let us call these type (a) determinacy and type (b) determinacy respectively. Figure 8.2 illustrates either.

In type (b) determinacy, I assume the unique point must be equally as *F* as the standard. That is why I say these cases have no indeterminacy: for every point, either it is *F*er than the standard, or the standard is *F*er than it, or it is equally as *F* as the standard. What justifies this assumption? Not much, I am sorry to say, but here is my reason for adopting it.

Take a standard configuration, and suppose one point in the chain is equally as *F* as the standard. Since higher points are *F*er than this point, and this point is equally as *F* as the standard, it follows that higher points are *F*er than the standard. This is an application of the principle:

> *Extended transitivity of 'Fer than'*. For any *x*, *y*, and *z*, if *x* is *F*er than *y* and *y* is equally as *F* as *z*, or if *x* is equally as *F* as *y* and *y* is *F*er than *z*, then *x* is *F*er than *z*.

This is a small extension of the transitivity principle, and I take it too to be a principle of logic. The same extended transitivity implies that if one point in a chain is equally as *F* as the standard, then the standard is *F*er than all lower points.

So if one point is equally as *F* as the standard, then for every other point in the chain, either it is *F*er than the standard or the standard is *F*er than it. I am inclined to believe the converse. That is: if, for every point in a continu-

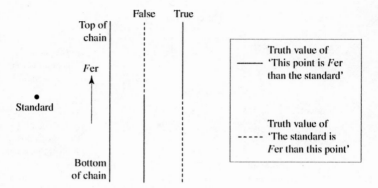

Figure 8.2 No indeterminacy.

ous chain bar one, either it is *F*er than the standard or the standard is *F*er than it, but for one point this is not so, then I am inclined to believe this one point must be equally as *F* as the standard. In fact, I am inclined to believe that 'equally as *F* as' is not an independent notion at all, but can be defined in terms of *F*er than. I would say that '*x* is equally as *F* as *y*' means that *x* is not *F*er than *y*, and *y* is not *F*er than *x*, and anything that is *F*er than *x* is also *F*er than *y*, and *y* is *F*er than anything *x* is *F*er than. This is the basis of my assumption that, in type (b) determinacy, the unique point is equally as *F* as the standard. I have no argument for it, but I can think of no counterexample.

8.4   Hard indeterminacy

The next possibility is that there is more than one point in the chain such that it is not *F*er than the standard and the standard is not *F*er than it. All the points with this property form a central zone.

None of them can be equally as *F* as the standard. If one was, I showed in section 8.3 that all points above it would be *F*er than the standard and the standard would be *F*er than all points below it. Then only this one point would have the property that it is not *F*er than the standard and the standard is not *F*er than it. But our assumption is that there is more than one point with this property.

The whole central zone, then, constitutes a zone of indeterminacy. If there is more than one point in the chain such that it is not *F*er than the standard, and the standard is not *F*er than it, I shall say that '*F*er than' has *hard indeterminacy*.

Hard indeterminacy is not vagueness. It is definite that points within the zone of indeterminacy are not *F*er than the standard and the standard is not *F*er than them. However, it is natural to think there is often something vague about an indeterminate comparative. Take 'redder than', for instance. 'Redder than the standard' is a monadic predicate, and it is natural to think it may be vague, like the predicate 'red'. Start from the top of the chain in the standard configuration I described, which runs from red to yellow. Points at the top of the chain are red, and it seems implausible that as we move down the chain we encounter a sharp boundary that divides these points that are red from those that are not red. Similarly, points at the top are redder than the standard (which is reddish-purple and not in the chain itself), and one might find it implausible that, as we move down the chain, we encounter a sharp boundary that divides these points that are redder than this standard from points that are not redder than it. Instead, it seems there may be a zone of vagueness between the points that are redder than the standard and those that are not. For many comparatives 'Fer than', it seems plausible that there is an zone of vagueness between points that are Fer than the standard and points that are not. There seems also to be an area of vagueness at the bottom of the zone of indeterminacy, between points the standard is not Fer than, and those it is.

Is vagueness like this compatible with hard indeterminacy? At first it seems it should be. Hard indeterminacy simply says there is a zone where points are not Fer than the standard and the standard is not Fer than them. The vagueness I have just described is around the borders of this zone. The suggestion is that the borders are vague rather than sharp. The zone of indeterminacy is bordered by zones of vagueness – at first, there seems nothing wrong with that. However, oddly enough, it turns out that this cannot be so. The boundaries of the zone of indeterminacy must be sharp rather than vague, for the following reason.

Take any point somewhere around the top boundary of the zone of indeterminacy. Clearly, it is false that the standard is Fer than this point, since this is false for all points in the zone of indeterminacy and above. If it is also false that this point is Fer than the standard, then the point is squarely within the zone of indeterminacy. If, on the other hand, it is true that this point is Fer than the standard, then it is squarely within the top zone. So if there is really a zone of vagueness, for points in this zone it must be neither true nor false that they are Fer than the standard. But now we can apply something I call the *collapsing principle*:

> *The collapsing principle, special version.* For any x and y, if it is false that y is Fer than x and not false that x is Fer than y, then it is true that x is Fer than y.

This principle is crucial to the argument of this chapter. I shall defend it in the next section, and here I shall simply apply it. I have just said that, for a point in the zone of vagueness, if there is such a zone, it is false that the standard is Fer than it, but not false that it is Fer than the standard. Then

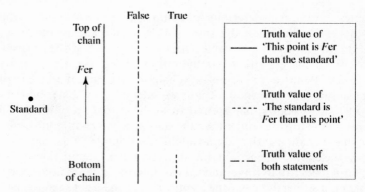

Figure 8.3 Hard indeterminacy.

according to the collapsing principle, it is true that it is *F*er than the standard. This implies it is not in a zone of vagueness after all. So there is no such zone.

Figure 8.3 shows hard indeterminacy. As we move down the chain from the top, starting with points that are *F*er than the standard, we suddenly come to ones that are not *F*er than the standard. Later, having found only points that the standard is not *F*er than, we suddenly encounter ones that the standard is *F*er than.

A comparative that has hard indeterminacy is a strict partial ordering without vagueness.

8.5   The collapsing principle

The proof in the previous section depended crucially on the collapsing principle. Now I need to justify it. My only real argument is this. If it is false that *y* is *F*er than *x*, and not false that *x* is *F*er than *y*, then *x* has a clear advantage over *y* in respect of its *F*ness. So it must be *F*er than *y*. It only takes the slightest asymmetry to make it the case that one thing is *F*er than another. One object is heavier than another if the scales tip ever so slightly towards it. Here there is a clear asymmetry between *x* and *y* in respect of their *F*ness. That is enough to determine that *x* is *F*er than *y*.

I find this obvious, and here is a thought-experiment to reinforce its obviousness. Suppose you had to award a prize to either *x* or *y* for its *F*ness. Suburbs in Canberra are named after great Australians, and each new suburb has to go to the greatest Australian who does not yet have a suburb. Suppose there are two candidates for the next suburb, and you have to decide between them. Suppose that, on investigating their cases, you conclude it is false that Wye is a greater Australian than Exe, but that it is not false that Exe is a greater Australian than Wye. This is not at all like the case where you conclude that Wye and Exe are equally great Australians, because then it is not clear who should get the suburb; you should probably toss a coin. Nor is it like the case where you conclude that neither Wye nor Exe is greater than the other and they are not equally great either. This is a case squarely in the zone of indeterminacy. In this case, it is once again not clear who should get the suburb, just because neither candidate is better than the other. Perhaps you should toss a coin in this case too, or perhaps some other procedure would be right. But when it is false that Wye is greater than Exe, but not false that Exe is greater than Wye, you need not hesitate. It would be quite wrong to give the suburb to Wye. Since the prize was for being the greater Australian, it could not be so obvious who should win unless that person was the greater Australian.

When it is false that y is Fer than x but not false that x is Fer than y, then if you had to award a prize for Fness, it is plain you should give the prize to x. But it would not be plain unless x was Fer than y. Therefore x is Fer than y. This must be so whether actually you have to give a prize or not, since whether or not you have to give a prize cannot affect whether or not x is Fer than y.

8.6   Soft indeterminacy

What other options are there for the structure of a comparative 'Fer than'? No other option can allow the existence of points in the chain such that they are not Fer than the standard and the standard is not Fer than them (that is: such that it is false that they are Fer than the standard and false that the standard is Fer than them). That would be hard indeterminacy. But it might be possible for there to be points such that it is neither true nor false that they are Fer than the standard, and neither true nor false that the standard is Fer than them. There could be a zone of indeterminacy composed of points like this. I call this case *soft indeterminacy*.

None of the points in the zone of indeterminacy can be equally as F as the standard, since if a point was equally as F as the standard it would be false that it was better than the standard, whereas it is not false. Therefore, the zone of indeterminacy must have more than one point in it. If there were only one point, I argued in section 8.3 that it would have to be equally as F as the standard. But I have just said this is impossible.

Unlike hard indeterminacy, which has no vagueness, soft indeterminacy is entirely vagueness. The zone of indeterminacy is also a zone of vagueness. For any point in the zone, it is vague whether or not it is Fer than the standard, and vague whether or not the standard is Fer than it.

The possible structures of a softly indeterminate comparative are severely limited. Once again, it is chiefly the collapsing principle that limits them. One limit is that, for any point, it is neither true nor false that it is Fer than the standard if and only if it is neither true nor false that the standard is *F*er than it. So the entire zone of indeterminacy necessarily has vagueness of both sorts; the comparison is vague taken either way. Here is the proof. First, suppose some point is *F*er than the standard and it is neither true nor false that the standard is *F*er than it. Since this point is *F*er than the standard, the asymmetry of '*F*er than' implies the standard is not *F*er than it. This contradicts that it is neither true nor false that the standard is *F*er than it. Secondly, suppose a point is not *F*er than the standard and it is neither true nor false that the standard is *F*er than it. From this supposition, the special version of the collapsing principle, stated in section 8.4, implies that the standard is *F*er than the point. That contradicts that it is neither true nor false that the standard is *F*er than it. The rest of the proof is a matter of ringing the changes.

Another limit on the structure of softly indeterminate comparatives is imposed by a more general version of the collapsing principle. My statement of this version needs a preface. I intend it to be neutral between competing theories of vagueness. It uses the expression 'more true than', but this is not to be read as implying the existence of degrees of truth as they are usually understood. Its meaning is wider. For instance, if P is true and Q is false, then I would say P is more true than Q. If P is neither true nor false, and Q is false, again I would say P is more true than Q. In this case, P is certainly less false than Q, and I intend 'more true' to include 'less false'. If P is definitely true and Q is not definitely true, I would again say that P is more true than Q. In general, I will say P is more true than Q whenever P in any way rates more highly than Q in respect of its truth. Now, the principle is:

> *The collapsing principle, general version.* For any x and y, if it is more true that x is *F*er than y than that y is *F*er than x, then x is *F*er than y.[1]

The argument for it is the same as the one I gave in section 8.5 for the special version. Remember that this principle is specifically about reciprocal comparative statements. I do not endorse the general claim that if any statement P is more true than another statement Q then P is true, nor the different specific claim that if P is more true than its negation $\neg P$ then P is true. If someone is more dead than alive, I do not believe she is necessarily dead.

The general version of the collapsing principle implies that for no point in the zone of indeterminacy can it be more true that the point is *F*er than the standard than that the standard is *F*er than it. Nor can it be less true. This leaves open several possibilities, corresponding to different theories of vagueness. One theory is that when statements are vague they have no truth value. Figure 8.4 illustrates how soft indeterminacy will appear from this point of view; I have called it type (a) soft indeterminacy. Evidently, it is

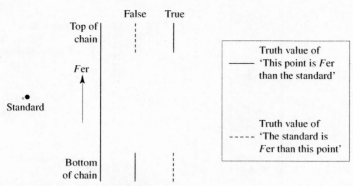

Figure 8.4 Type (a) soft indeterminacy.

consistent with the collapsing principle. According to other theories, vague statements may have some other truth value besides true or false. It would be consistent with the collapsing principle for 'This point is *F*er than the standard' and 'The standard is *F*er than this point' to have the same truth value throughout the zone of indeterminate. It might be 'indefinite', say, or some particular degree of truth. Figure 8.5 illustrates this possibility. I have called it type (b) soft indeterminacy.

8.7 Incomparable truth values

Both types (a) and (b) of soft indeterminacy fail to capture one natural intuition. For any point in the zone of indeterminacy, it is neither true nor false that it is *F*er than the standard. But intuition suggests that in some sense or other the statement 'This point is *F*er than the standard' is more true for points near the top of the zone than for points near the bottom. For points near the top, indeed, it seems it must be almost true they are *F*er than the standard, and for points near the bottom it seems this must be almost false.

This intuition clearly implies that statements can be true to a greater or lesser degree. So in order to discuss it, I shall have to give up my attempt to be neutral amongst competing theories of vagueness. For this discussion, I shall take it for granted that there are degrees of truth. Anyway, the study of comparatives suggests there are. Suppose *x* is redder than y. This implies that *x* has redness to a greater degree than *y* has it, so there are degrees of redness.[2] But it seems also to imply that *x* is red more than *y* is red, which in turn surely implies that '*x* is red' is truer than '*y* is red', so there are degrees of truth. I shall say more about this in section 8.8. Other sorts of comparisons perhaps point more clearly to degrees of truth, because they

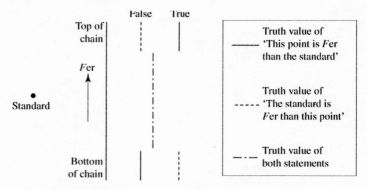

Figure 8.5 Type (b) soft indeterminacy.

more clearly compare statements. 'It's raining more than it's snowing' seems clearly to imply that 'It's raining' is truer than 'It's snowing.'

One intuition, then, is that as we move from point to point up through the zone of indeterminacy, 'This point is *F*er than the standard' becomes progressively more true and 'The standard is *F*er than this point' progressively less true. At first, this intuition seems to be inconsistent with the collapsing principle. It seems to imply that, as we move up through the zone, we must eventually encounter points for which 'This point is *F*er than the standard' is more true than 'The standard is *F*er than this point.' But then the collapsing principle will kick in and say these points must actually be determinately *F*er than the standard: they are not in the zone of indeterminacy after all.

However, a point made by Adam Morton can be used to show this need not happen.[3] It may be that the truth values of 'This point is *F*er than the standard' and 'The standard is *F*er than this point' are incomparable throughout the zone of indeterminacy, but nevertheless one of these statements may increase in truth value as we move up through the zone and the other decrease. The reason this seems impossible at first is that we traditionally think of degrees of truth as numbers between zero and one. At least, we assume they are linearly ordered. If degrees are linearly ordered, every degree is comparable with every other. But degrees are not linearly ordered, and there really are incomparable degrees.

The evidence that there are incomparable degrees is this. I have already assumed that, if *x* is redder than *y*, '*x* is red' is truer than '*y* is red'. We know already that in many cases it is indeterminate which of *x* and *y* is redder. In those cases it must be indeterminate which of '*x* is red' and '*y* is red' is truer. So, because comparatives can be indeterminate, degrees of truth can be incomparable. Given that, there is no reason why it should not be indeterminate which of 'This point is *F*er than the standard' and 'The standard

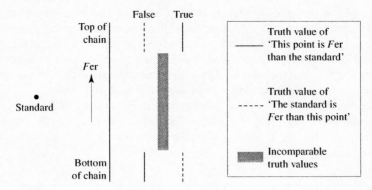

Figure 8.6 Type (c) soft indeterminacy.

is *F*er than this point' is truer. This gives us a type (c) of soft indeterminacy. I have illustrated it as well as I can in figure 8.6, but the illustration is inadequate because I can find no way of showing the truth values of the two statements varying through the zone of indeterminacy.

Type (c) indeterminacy raises a more complex question. If it is indeterminate which of two statements – specifically, 'This point is *F*er than the standard' and 'The standard is *F*er than this point' – is truer, just what sort of indeterminacy is this? This is a question about the structure of the comparative 'truer than': does it have hard or soft indeterminacy in this application? I suggest it has soft indeterminacy, on grounds of uniformity. The statement '*x* is *F*er than *y*' implies '*x* is *F*' is truer than '*y* is *F*'. So if '*F*er than' is softly indeterminate, 'truer than' must be softly indeterminate between statements of the form '*x* is *F*'. My suggestion is that it is also softly indeterminate between statements of the form '*x* is *F*er than *y*' (such as, 'This point is *F*er than the standard') or equivalently between statements of the form '"*x* is *F*' is truer than '*y* is *F*''. I also suggest it is softly indeterminate between statements at the next level of complexity: statements of the form '"'*x* is *F*' is truer than '*y* is *F*'' is truer than ''*y* is *F*' is truer than '*x* is *F*.'"' In fact, I suggest we find only soft indeterminacy as we iterate to infinity.[4] My reason is that I would expect 'truer than' to have a uniform structure wherever it is used.

Type (c) soft indeterminacy satisfies our intuitions to some extent, but not completely. One intuition is that, as we move up through the zone of indeterminacy, it becomes progressively more true that the points we encounter are *F*er than the standard, and progressively less true that the standard is *F*er than them. Type (c) indeterminacy reconciles this idea with the collapsing principle. But another intuition is that, as we get near the top of the zone, it becomes nearly true that the points we encounter are *F*er than the standard, and nearly false that the standard is *F*er than them. I think this really is inconsistent with the collapsing principle. If one statement is nearly true and another nearly false, it is surely undeniable that the first is truer than the second. Other degrees of truth might be incomparable, but the degrees 'nearly true' and 'nearly false' are plainly comparable. So the intuition suggests that, for points near the top of the zone, it is truer that they are Fer than the standard than that the standard is Fer than them. This drags in the collapsing principle in the usual way, and leads to a contradiction. So, even in type (c) indeterminacy, at the boundary of the zone of indeterminacy, 'This point is Fer than the standard' changes its truth value sharply. At the top boundary its value drops from true to some degree that is not nearly true.

8.8   Supervaluation

The most widely held theory of vagueness is supervaluation theory.[5] If we take this theory on board, what can we add to the analysis?

When a term is vague, there are various ways it could acceptably be made sharp. Suppose 'Fer than' is vague – softly indeterminate that is – and in particular suppose it is vague whether x is Fer than y. Then if 'Fer than' was sharpened in one direction, x would be Fer than y, and, if it was sharpened in another direction, y would be Fer than x. I shall confine the word 'sharpening' to sharpenings that are complete: they are not themselves vague, that is to say. According to supervaluation theory:

> *Supervaluation.* A statement containing a vague term is true if and only if it is true under all acceptable sharpenings of the term.

The sharpenings of a vague comparative 'Fer than' will be comparatives. Since they are not themselves vague, they must either be fully determinate, or have hard indeterminacy. Which will it be? I cannot rule out either possibility on logical grounds. A vague comparative may have as its sharpenings both determinate comparatives and comparatives with hard indeterminacy. Alternatively, a vague comparative may have only determinate comparatives as its sharpenings. However, I can show that no vague comparative can have only comparatives with hard indeterminacy as its sharpenings; at least some of its sharpenings must be determinate.

Here is the demonstration. Suppose every sharpening of 'Fer than' has hard indeterminacy. Then each sharpening has two 'switch points' as I shall call them. The lower switch point is where 'The standard is Fer than this point' switches from true to false as we move up the chain; the upper switch point is where 'This point is Fer than the standard' switches from false to true. For every sharpening there is a gap between these switch points. Now think about the top end of the zone of indeterminacy. Every sharpening must have its upper switch point within the zone. So every sharpening must have its lower switch point a definite distance below the top of the zone. Consequently, there will be some points within the zone that are above the lower switch point of every sharpening. (I shall ignore the mathematical possibility that there might be a sequence of sharpenings such that the distance between their switch points tends to zero; this is uninteresting.) For these points, every sharpening makes it false that the standard is Fer than them. That is, every sharpening makes it true that the standard is not Fer than them. Consequently, it is definitely true that the standard is Fer than them. But in the zone of indeterminacy this is not so. So there is a contradiction.

Why does it matter what sort of indeterminacy the sharpenings have? If all the sharpenings of a softly indeterminate comparative were determinate, we could draw a striking conclusion. In every sharpening of 'Fer than', it would be true of every point that either it is Fer than the standard, or the standard is Fer than it, or that it and the standard are equally F. Since this would be true of every point in every sharpening, according to supervaluation theory it would simply be true of every point. Even when 'Fer than' is softly indeterminate, it would nevertheless be the case for every point that either it is Fer than the standard, or the standard is Fer than it, or it and the standard are equally F. This may seem puzzling, since for any point in the zone of indeterminacy, we know already it is not true that the point is Fer than the standard, and it is not true that the standard is Fer than the point, and it is not true that the point and the standard are equally F. Since none of these three things is true, how can their disjunction be true? The answer is: in the same way as the law of the excluded middle is true according to supervaluation theory. If F is vague, then for some x it may not be true that x is F nor true that x is not F. Nevertheless, according to supervaluation theory, the disjunction is true: x is either F or not F, since this disjunction is true in every sharpening.[6]

So, if every sharpening of a softly indeterminate comparative were determinate, the contrast between hard determinacy and soft determinacy would be particularly stark. In hard indeterminacy, no point in the zone of indeterminacy is Fer than the standard, and nor is the standard Fer than it, and nor are it and the standard equally F. In soft indeterminacy, for every point, either it is Fer than the standard, or the standard is Fer than it, or it and the standard are equally F.

Now, what version of soft indeterminacy does supervaluation theory support? Many supervaluationists refuse to recognize degrees of truth,[7] and that suggests they would adopt type (a) as their version. But we may make a small and readily acceptable addition to the theory:

Greatervaluation. One statement *P*, containing a vague term, is truer than another *Q* if *P* is true in every sharpening that makes *Q* true, and also true in some sharpening that does not make *Q* true.

When people dislike the idea of degrees of truth, I think that is generally because they assume degrees must be linearly ordered. Greatervaluation does not imply that.

I only offer greatervaluation as a sufficient condition for *P* to be truer than *Q*. It is not a necessary condition, as this example shows. Compare a reddish-orange patch with a pure orange patch. The former is redder than the latter. Consequently, it is more true that the former is red than that the latter is red. However, there is no sharpening of the language in which it is true that the former is red.

Now, take a pair of points, one higher in the zone of indeterminacy than the other. Any sharpening that makes the lower point *F*er than the standard will also make the higher point *F*er than the standard, but there will be some sharpenings that make the higher point *F*er than the standard and the lower point not *F*er than the standard. So according to greatervaluation, it is more true that the higher point is *F*er than the standard than that the lower point is. Similarly, it is more true that the standard is *F*er than the lower point than that it is *F*er than the higher point. As we move up through the zone, then, it becomes progressively more true that the points we encounter are *F*er than the standard, and progressively less true that the standard is *F*er than them. This implies type (c) indeterminacy, so greatervaluation supports this type.

8.9   Ordinary comparatives are softly indeterminate

I have now laid out the possible structures a comparative might have. What structures do we find amongst our ordinary comparatives? I particularly want to ask what is the structure of 'better than'.

Without doubt, there are comparatives that have no indeterminacy. 'Heavier than' is one.

Are there comparatives with hard indeterminacy? A comparative with hard indeterminacy is a strict partial ordering without vagueness. There are plenty of such orderings around; the question is whether any of them are the comparatives of monadic predicates.

It may be possible to construe some of them artificially as comparatives, by deriving monadic predicates from them. For instance, let us say that one object is mucheavier than another if and only if it is more than one kilo heavier than the other. Then the relation 'mucheavier than' is a strict partial ordering without vagueness. Let us say it is the comparative of a monadic predicate 'mucheavy'. Then 'mucheavy' is a predicate whose comparative has hard indeterminacy. However, I am not convinced that the predicate 'mucheavy' really exists. The only property of objects that is involved in the relation 'mucheavier than' is their heaviness. The objects have no separate property that a predicate 'mucheavy' could refer to, and that suggests there is no such predicate. I do not think 'mucheavier than' is the comparative of any predicate; instead it is a fragment of the genuine comparative 'heavier than', the comparative of 'heavy'.

Or take another example of a strict partial ordering without vagueness. Let us say that one option is 'Pareto-better' than another if and only if it is better for someone and not worse for anyone. Pareto-betterness defined this way is a strict partial ordering, and for the sake of argument let us assume it is not vague. Could we define a monadic predicate 'Pareto-good' to have 'Pareto-better than' as its comparative? Once again, I am doubtful. The only property of options that seems to be in play is their goodness. Pareto-betterness is best understood as a partial, sufficient criterion for 'better than', the comparative of goodness, rather than as itself the complete comparative of anything. There are people who think that Pareto-betterness is actually a *complete* criterion for betterness, so that one option is better than another if and only if it is better for someone and not worse for anyone. These people do not try to construct an artificial predicate out of the relation 'Pareto-better than'. Instead they think that 'better than', the comparative of the natural predicate 'good', happens to be extensionally equivalent to 'Pareto-better than'. If they were right, 'better than' would have hard indeterminacy, but I shall say in section 8.10 why I think are wrong.

These examples suggest to me that constructing artificial comparatives with hard indeterminacy may not be as easy as it seems. But I do not insist they cannot be constructed. Perhaps they can. I am interested in our ordinary, natural comparatives. Do any of them have hard indeterminacy?

I find it implausible that any do. My reasons are these. First, the difficulty of finding artificial comparatives with hard indeterminacy suggests to me there is something fishy about hard indeterminacy in general. A comparative with hard indeterminacy is incomplete, and that suggests it may be a fragment of a complete comparative rather than a comparative in its own right. Secondly and more importantly, I showed in section 8.4 that if a comparative has hard indeterminacy it cannot be vague. I find it implausible that indeterminate comparatives are not vague at all.

If a comparative has hard indeterminacy, then, as we move down from the top of a chain in a standard configuration, there comes a point where 'This point is Fer than the standard' suddenly changes from true to false. So the monadic predicate 'Fer than the standard' is sharp and not vague. I find this implausible for indeterminate comparatives. Why? I do not think it is as obvious as the vagueness of many predicates. Take 'red', for instance. If we move down a continuous chain of colour-patches from pure red to yellow, it seems obvious that there is no point in the chain where the patches suddenly cease to be red. Therefore, 'red' is vague. But a predicate of the form '*F*er than the standard' cannot be quite so obviously vague, because it will not be vague everywhere. Taker 'redder than the standard', for instance. Take the chain of colours from red to yellow, and for a moment let the standard be a patch that exactly matches some point in the chain. Then higher points are redder than the standard and lower points are not redder than the standard, and the transition is sharp. Since there is a sharp transition for certain standards, it is not perfectly obvious that there is no sharp transition for other standards.

Notice first about this example that it has no indeterminacy. The point in the chain that exactly matches the standard is equally as red as the standard. Higher points are redder than the standard, and the standard is redder than lower points. So this is not an example of hard indeterminacy. Moreover, I am sure there is no sharp transition when the standard is, say, reddish-purple, and does not match a point in the chain. The reason is that, if there is a sharp transition, I cannot tell where it is. I know no way of detecting where it is, and I know of no one who can detect where it is. If there is a point of transition, it is undetectable, and I do not believe redness can have an undetectable boundary of this sort. The same goes for every other natural indeterminate comparative I can think of, including evaluative ones.

I think ordinary indeterminate comparatives are softly indeterminate. Admittedly, even soft indeterminacy has a sharp boundary of a sort. There is a sharp boundary between points where 'This point is *F*er than the standard' is true and points where it is not true. I find it hard to believe in a sharp transition of this sort. It is the collapsing principle that demands it, and this implication of the principle is paradoxical. The principle implies there are sharp boundaries where there seem to be none. I am recommending soft rather than hard indeterminacy as the lesser of two evils. It certainly is the lesser evil. In soft indeterminacy the sharp transition is between points where 'This point is *F*er than the standard' is true and points where it is not true. In hard indeterminacy it is between points where this statement is true and points where it is false. So the transition in soft indeterminacy is not so abrupt. Furthermore, in type (c) soft indeterminacy, 'This point is *F*er than the standard' becomes less and less true as we move down through the zone of indeterminacy. This makes the transition even softer. In this respect type (c) is the least paradoxical type of soft indeterminacy.

8.10 Other views

Many authors have described indeterminacy in a way that implies or suggests it is hard. Remember that in section 8.4 I defined a comparative '*F*er than' to have hard indeterminacy if and only if there is more than one point in a chain such that it is not *F*er than the standard and the standard is not *F*er than it. I explained in section 8.4 that none of these points can be equally as *F* as the standard, and I explained in section 8.3 that if there is only one point in a chain such that it is not *F*er than the standard and the standard is not *F*er than it, then it will be equally as *F* as the standard. So '*F*er than' has hard indeterminacy if and only if there is a point in the chain such that it is not *F*er than the standard, and the standard is not *F*er than it, and it is not equally as *F* as the standard. But most authors take it for granted that indeterminate comparatives will satisfy a condition like this. For instance, Christopher Peacocke argues that 'redder than' is indeterminate, and says of two colour-patches that 'neither is red to a greater degree than the other, nor are they equally red'.[8] Joseph Raz says that when *A* and *B* are incommensurable it is generally 'false that of *A* and *B* either one is better than the other or they are of equal value'.[9] When goods are incommensurable, I myself have said 'neither alternative will be better for the person and they will not be equally good for her either'.[10] I could find many more examples. All these authors seem to imply that indeterminacy is hard.

But I doubt if many of them are seriously attached to this view. For one thing, there is a way of reading most of their statements that makes them consistent with soft indeterminacy. When Peacocke says that neither object is red to a greater degree than the other, and nor are they equally red, I read him as meaning it is false that either object is red to a greater degree than the other and false that they are equally red. But he could also be read as saying it is not true that either object is red to a greater degree than the other, and not true that they are equally red. This allows the possibility that these statements are neither true nor false, which is consistent with soft indeterminacy. (Raz, though, deliberately rules out this alternative reading.) More important, these authors have not realized that hard indeterminacy in a comparative is incompatible with vagueness. I am sure that, once they realize it, they will have no inclination to believe in hard indeterminacy any more. I do not expect much controversy about my claim that indeterminacy is normally soft.

There is a tradition in economics – inspired by Amartya Sen – of representing certain comparatives by means of strict partial orderings without vagueness.[11] For instance, Sen himself uses a strict partial ordering to represent 'more unequal than' (applied to distributions of income),[12] and in another place to represent 'socially preferred to', which I take to mean simply 'better than'.[13] This seems to imply hard indeterminacy. But actually I do not think Sen necessarily has hard indeterminacy in mind. Let us look at one of his arguments.[14]

Suppose we have to compare various alternative arrangements for society, where some are better for some people and others better for others. To judge which are better than which, we have to weigh some people's good against others'. Suppose we cannot do this weighing precisely, but we can do it roughly. There is a range of weights we might give to each person; we should use weights from this range, but it is not precisely determined which. If, for each person, we picked one weight from her range, so we had a set of weights, one for each person, that set would determine a complete ordering of the options. If we picked a different set of weights, that would determine a different complete ordering. Suppose we go through all the combinations of possible weights; each will determine a complete ordering. Now let us say one option is 'clearly above' another if and only if it is above the other in all these orderings. 'Clearly above' is then a strict partial ordering without vagueness, and Sen takes it to represent betterness. Does this mean he thinks 'better than' is not vague?

I can see no evidence for that. Sen says one option is better than another if it is clearly above the other, but I doubt he would insist that one option is not better than another if it is not clearly above the other. If neither of two options is clearly above the other, he does not tell us his views about their relative goodness.

If he had to tell us, it would be most natural for him to adopt soft indeterminacy. His explanation of how betterness comes to be a partial ordering is close to supervaluation theory. When applied to alternative arrangements for society, we can say that 'better than' is vague because it is indeterminate how we should weigh together the good of different people. Within the appropriate range, each set of weights constitutes a sharpening of 'better than'. Supervaluation says it is true that one option is better than another if and only if it is true in all sharpenings. Apparently Sen agrees. Supervaluation also says it is true that one option is not better than another if and only if *that* is true in all sharpenings. Sen does not state a necessary condition for one option not to be better than another, but it would be natural for him to agree to this too. If he did, he would have adopted soft indeterminacy. When Sen says betterness is a partial ordering, I do not think that is meant to be a complete account of betterness. If the account were consistently completed, it would amount to soft indeterminacy.

But what of the hard-liner who believes one person's good can never be weighed against another's to determine what is better overall? Suppose this person thinks one option is better than another if and only if it is better for someone and no worse for anyone. Between any pair of options that are not related in this way, suppose she thinks it false that either is better than the other or that they are equally good. She thinks the relation I called earlier 'Pareto-better than' is actually the whole of 'better than', the comparative of 'good'. It is a strict partial ordering, and let us suppose once again it is not vague. This person unequivocally thinks that 'better than' has hard indeterminacy.

My answer to this person is that her position is too implausible to be correct. I could understand someone who thinks there is no such thing as goodness, viewed from a neutral perspective, so that no option could ever be better than another. I mean: plain better, rather than, say, better for a particular person. But our hard-liner recognizes the existence of goodness; she simply thinks it can never be determined by weighing one person's good against another's. Now imagine some piece of good fortune could befall either of two people. Suppose neither of them has any particular entitlement to it. One would scarcely benefit from it at all because she has already received her fill of good fortune. The other would benefit tremendously; the good fortune would lift her from grinding poverty to a comfortable and enjoyable life. Would it be better for the first to receive the good fortune or the second? If you do not believe in goodness, you will think this question meaningless. But if you recognize goodness, you cannot plausibly deny the question has an answer: the second person. So, if goodness exists, then sometimes it can be determined by weighing together the good of different people. Once you acknowledge that, you will have to recognize borderline cases where it is indeterminate precisely how different people's good should be weighed. You will have to acknowledge vagueness in 'better than', and that makes it softly indeterminate.

8.10   Conclusion

So indeterminate comparatives are softly indeterminate, and that includes 'better than'. What conclusions can we draw? I shall talk about betterness only.

One is that the commonest formulations of indeterminateness are incorrect or at least misleading. When it is indeterminate which of two things is better, people commonly say that, of two options, neither is better than the other and they are not equally good either. This suggests it is false that either is better than the other, and false that they are equally good. But in a standard configuration, when a point in the zone of indeterminacy is compared with the standard, it is not false that it is better than the standard, and it is not false that the standard is better than it. Indeed, there are grounds for saying that either one is better than the other, or they are equally good. These grounds come from supervaluation theory.

In section 8.8, where I introduced supervaluation, I showed that some of the sharpenings of a particular comparative must be fully determinate. But I could not rule out on logical grounds the possibility that some of them might have hard indeterminacy. But by now I think I can plausibly rule it out on other grounds. I have not found any indubitable cases of hard indeterminacy even amongst artificial comparatives, and I very much doubt that any exist amongst natural comparatives. So it seems reasonable to doubt that they exist amongst the sharpenings of vague comparatives. If so, all sharpenings of 'better than' must be fully determinate. In that case, I explained in section 8.8 that, for every point in a chain, either it is better than the standard, or the standard is better than it, or it is equally as good as the standard.

When it is indeterminate which of two things is better, their goodness is in a sense incomparable. But the conclusion I have just drawn makes it clear that in other senses it is not incomparable. Even if you reject this conclusion of supervaluation theory, just recognizing that soft indeterminacy is a sort of vagueness should make you recognize a sort of comparability. When it is indeterminate which of two things is better, it is not true that one is better than the other, but it is also not false. Furthermore, if the indeterminacy is type (c), then it is true to some degree that one is better than the other. And if one of the things improves a little, it will then be more true that it is better than the other. All these are facts about the things' comparative goodness.

9 Incommensurable values

9.1 The idea of incommensurability

You might join the army or you might become a priest. Which would be better? Intuitively it seems this question may have no determinate answer; the values realized by these two careers seem to be so very different that they cannot be weighed against each other in a precise way. In some circumstances there will be a determinate answer to the question – for instance if you do not believe in God and like guns. But, in more balanced circumstances, it will not be determinate which is the better option. This phenomenon of indeterminacy is often called the 'incommensurability' of values. It is often thought to be a central feature of ethical life.

James Griffin has taken up the subject of incommensurability several times during his career.[1] He is not enthusiastic about its importance, and even casts some doubt on its existence.[2] He points out, first, that what many philosophers have called 'incommensurability' is not really that at all, or ought not to be called that. 'Incommensurability' ought to be reserved for cases where alternatives are 'incomparable' as Griffin puts it, by which he means that they cannot be put in an order. When a philosopher says the value of free speech is incommensurable with the pleasure of eating pizza, she means that free speech is immeasurably more valuable than this pleasure. That is to say, free speech and this pleasure *can* be ordered, emphatically. A small amount of free speech is better than any large amount of pizza-pleasure. This is not really incommensurability but extreme commensurability. Griffin mentions other misuses of the term too. If we set the misuses aside, and concentrate on true incommensurability, he thinks it may be hard to find any.

From *Well-Being and Morality: Essays of Honour of James Griffin*, edited by Roger Crisp and Brad Hooker, Oxford University Press, 1999. Reprinted by permission of Oxford University Press. I received penetrating comments on this chapter from Brad Hooker, Ruth Chang, Roger Crisp, David Donaldson, Ingmar Persson, Franz Prettenthaler, Jonathan Riley, and John Skorupski and the editors of this volume. The comments were so penetrating, and the subject so difficult, that I was able to take account of only a few of them in this chapter. They set me a programme for future work.

So values are commensurable in Griffin's sense if alternatives can be ordered. It is not the values themselves that can be ordered. Griffin is not interested in ordering enjoyment and understanding – to take two of his examples of values. These values cannot be ordered – neither is better than the other – because they come in various amounts. Wren's enjoyment in designing St Paul's is better than understanding Article iv of section 3.8 of Regulation 294 issued by DG65 of the European Union, whereas understanding evolution is better than enjoying a pizza. So we cannot order the values of enjoyment and understanding themselves. But we might be able to order events that realize these values, such as designing St Paul's or eating a pizza. Each event realizes one or more values to some degree. If the values are commensurable, that means they can be measured on the same scale. So a degree of one can be compared, as greater or less, with a degree of the other. Consequently the events can be ordered. We often need to compare other things besides events, so for generality I shall say that 'options' can be ordered, without specifying what sort of options. To claim that values are commensurable is to claim that options can be ordered.

Ordered with respect to what? Their goodness. Values are goods of different sorts, which contribute to the goodness of the options that realize them. To say that values are commensurable is to say that options are ordered by their goodness.

Griffin himself sometimes seems not to have recognized clearly enough that it is options rather than values themselves that need to be ordered. As part of his argument against incommensurable values, he mentions that we can and do compare values. 'We can and do compare pain and accomplishment. If the pain is great enough and the accomplishment slight enough, we should not consider this accomplishment worth the pain.'[3] But this is beside the point. Undoubtedly, *some* amount of pain-avoidance can be compared with *some* amount of accomplishment; indeed there may be no two values such that some amount of one cannot be compared with some amount of the other. Perhaps all values are commensurable in this sense. But we are not interested in comparing values themselves; we need to compare options that realize values. Options realize values to various degrees. A great accomplishment achieved with a little pain is better than painlessly accomplishing nothing. And painlessly accomplishing nothing is better than very painfully accomplishing very little. But if pain and accomplishment are to be thoroughly commensurable, *any* amount of pain-avoidance must be comparable with *any* amount of accomplishment, so that all options that realize pain-avoidance or accomplishment to any degree can be ordered by their goodness.

Still, despite this slip, Griffin does correctly identify the question of commensurability as a question of ordering options. Actually, the ordering of options is a more fundamental and more general matter than commensurability. To ask whether values are commensurable is implicitly to make a presumption about the way individual values combine together to determine the overall goodness of an option. It is to presume that the goodness of an option is determined by the various values it realizes, acting independently of each other. If that is so, and if these independent values are commensurable – so they can be measured on the same scale – then they can be added up to determine the overall value of the option. But actually the value of an option may be determined in a complex fashion by the interaction of values with each other and with other features of the option that are not themselves values. If values and other features interact like this, the notion of commensurability is obscure. But the question of ordering remains clear. However complex the determination of goodness, we can ask whether options are ordered by their goodness. This question of ordering is the subject of this chapter, though I shall use the terms 'commensurability' and 'incommensurability' loosely to refer to it.

Actually, I shall be asking two questions. First, are options always ordered by their goodness? Secondly, if they are not, how important is that fact in ethics? Section 9.4 aims to answer the first question, and section 9.10 returns to it; sections 9.5 to 9.10 aim to answer the second. But before coming to the two substantive questions, I need to deal with some formal matters in sections 9.2 and 9.3. I have suggested that options might or might not be ordered by their goodness. What, exactly, is the difference?

9.2   The standard configuration

I find a particular formal device useful for answering this question; I call it a 'standard configuration'.[4] Take the career example again. You have a choice between joining the church and joining the army. In practice there is bound to be a great deal of uncertainty about how each of these careers will progress if you choose it. But for simplicity let us ignore that; imagine each can be accurately predicted. So you have a choice between a particular career as a soldier, which is mapped out in detail, and a particular career as a priest, also mapped out. Now, imagine variations in the church career that make it better or worse. For instance, imagine the community becomes more religious, which makes for a better career, or less religious, which makes for a worse one. Think of a whole sequence of imaginary church careers, each a little bit better than the previous one in the sequence. I shall call this sequence a 'chain'. Next, fill in the spaces in the chain till we have fully continuous variations in goodness as we move along it. For instance, imagine continuous variations in the community's religiousness. Then our chain can be represented as a continuous line like this:

$\leftarrow$ worse   better $\rightarrow$
Possible careers as a priest

Each point on the line stands for a particular possible career. Each career on the line is better than every career that lies to its left. A standard configuration consists of a continuous chain like this, together with a single alternative that I call the 'standard'. In our example, the standard is the career available to you in the army. We hold that constant, while comparing it with all the various careers in the chain. In a standard configuration, the chain must be sufficiently long that the worst options in the chain are worse than the standard and the best options are better than the standard.

The choice of careers is only an example. Standard configurations can be drawn up in other contexts too. Suppose you are choosing between dinner and a film. You can hold the film constant as standard, and form an imaginary chain of dinners that varies continuously from grim to superb. In general, then, a chain is like this:

$\leftarrow$ worse   better $\rightarrow$
Possible options

As we move from left to right along a chain, two things are essential for my purposes. First, there is improvement all the way: every option is better than every option to its left. Secondly, the improvement is continuous. Joseph Raz thinks this may not always be possible.[5] He suggests some values may not be continuously variable; they can change only in discrete steps. Myself, I can think of no values that are discrete like this. But even if there are some, we can still always change the goodness of an option in a continuous fashion, because options need not realize only one value. We can simply add or subtract amounts of some value that is not discrete. For instance, the service at dinner might be quicker or slower; that is a quality that can certainly vary continuously. I am sure there are at least some continuous values. So I see no difficulty in assuming the chain is continuous.

9.3   Definitions

Now we have the standard configuration, let us start to compare the options in the chain with the standard – in the example, the church careers with the army career. At the left of the line there are options that are worse than the standard; they form the 'worse zone', as I shall call it. At the right are options that are better than the standard; they form the 'better zone'. What happens in between? There are three possible cases. There may be more than one option between these zones – between options that are better than the standard and those that are worse. There may be just one. Or there may be none. This third case is genuinely possible, but it is not important for this chapter and I shall say no more about it.[6] So we have two cases to consider.

In the first, where more than one option lies between the worse zone and the better zone, there must be many that do. If there are two options between those zones, any option in the chain that lies in between these two options must also lie between the zones. So there will be an intermediate *zone* of options between the worse and better zones. The cases we need to consider, then, are, first, where there is an intermediate zone and, secondly, where there is just a single intermediate option.

Take some intermediate option. Suppose it happens to be equally as good as the standard. Then any option better than it (to its right on the line) would be better than the standard, and any option worse than it (to its left) would be worse than the standard. It would therefore be the only intermediate option between those that are better than the standard and those that are worse. So if there is more than one intermediate option – an intermediate zone – no option within this zone can be equally as good as the standard.

In this argument, I assumed that if one option is better or worse than another, and the other is equally as good as a third, then the first is, respectively, better or worse than the third. This is part of the meaning of 'equally as good as'. (It is a extension of transitivity.) It prevents any option in an intermediate zone from being equally as good as the standard.

But if there is only a single intermediate option, nothing of this sort prevents it from being equally as good as the standard. In this case, indeed, I think it must be equally as good as the standard. The slightest improvement or deterioration in this option would make it better or worse than the standard. If a choice is so finely balanced that the slightest change in one of the alternatives can make the difference between its being worse and its being better than the other, surely the alternatives are equally good.

Indeed, I think we may *define* a single intermediate option to be as good as the standard. I propose this as a definition of 'equally as good as': one option A is equally as good as another B if and only if any possible option that is better or worse than A is also, respectively, better or worse than B, and any possible option that is better or worse than B is also, respectively, better or worse than A. (This definition does not state explicitly that A is neither better nor worse than B, because that is implied by the rest.) This is an acceptable definition because it meets the formal condition that 'equally as good as' must satisfy as a semantic matter: it must be an *equivalence relation* – it must be transitive, reflexive, and symmetric.

The definition has the effect that, when there is just a single intermediate option, it must be equally as good as the standard (except in some peculiar cases). The picture is, then:

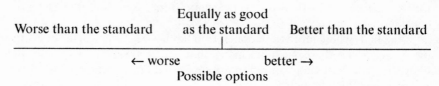

Let us call this 'the equality case'.

Next, let us define one option A to be 'incommensurate' with another B if and only if it is not the case that A is better than B, and not the case that B is better than A, and not the case that A and B are equally good. We have found that, if there is an intermediate zone, all the options in it are incommensurate with the standard. Let us call this the 'incommensurate case'. Its picture is:

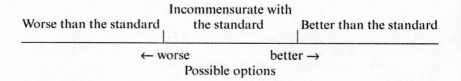

To sum up: we have only one primitive relation to deal with – 'better than'. 'Equally as good as' and 'incommensurate with' are defined in terms of that. The difference between them is fixed by the structure of the 'better than' relation. This relation picks out the zone of options that are better than the standard and the zone of options that are worse than the standard. If it leaves only one option in a chain intermediate between these zones, this option is equally as good as the standard. If it leaves an intermediate zone, the options in this zone are incommensurate with the standard. The difference between equality and incommensurateness is simply whether there is one intermediate option or many. There is no further, intuitive distinction between the two.[7]

My definition of 'equally as good as' may seem unsatisfactory, because it may seem to deny a significant possibility. When there is only a single intermediate option between the worse and better zones, there may seem to be two possibilities for it: it might be equally as good as the standard or it might not be. When I defined it to be equally as good as the standard, I was denying the second possibility.

However, I do not think this is unsatisfactory; I think it is correct. I see no genuine second possibility. What real difference could there be between a case where this intermediate option is equally as good as the standard and a case where it is not? Presumably, the difference would have to show up in some practical way: it would have to make some difference to your decision making, if you ever had to make a choice between this option and the standard. Now, it certainly makes a practical difference whether there is a single intermediate option or a whole intermediate zone; I shall explain why in section 9.8. But when we are anyway dealing with just a single intermediate option, I see no real difference. Various things would be true if you had to make the choice between the intermediate option and the standard: it is not the case that you ought to choose the intermediate option, nor that you ought to choose the standard; choosing either would not be wrong; it is not determinate which you ought to choose; and so on. But all of these things are true simply because neither alternative is better than the other; none of them indicates a difference between their being equally good and their not being equally good. I shall say more about this in section 9.7.

9.4   Is there incommensurability?

Having set up the definitions, we can turn to substantive questions. The first question I mentioned at the end of section 9.1 is: are options necessarily ordered by their goodness? As I have now formalized it, this question has become: does the incommensurate case really exist, or is it only a technical possibility? Let 'commensurabilism' be the view that it does not exist. We can now see that commensurabilism is implausible. It is very stringent because it requires a sharp division between options that are worse than the standard and those that are better. There is at most one intermediate option. But this is implausible in, for instance, the careers example. It is implausible that a tiny change in the conditions of a church career could make all the difference between this career's being worse than soldiering and its being better. This example seems to have an intermediate zone; it seems to fit the incommensurate case.

At first, one might think commensurabilism could be supported by the epistemicist theory of vagueness. Take a vague predicate such as 'red'. Most people believe there are borderline cases between things that are red and things that are not red. Of these borderline cases, we cannot say definitely that they are red, nor that they are not red. But *epistemicists* about vagueness believe there is a sharp boundary between red and not red, despite appearances. All coloured things are either red or not, and for apparently borderline cases we are simply ignorant which they are. Although epistemicism is intuitively unattractive, there are arguments in its favour; epistemicists believe their theory is the only way to avoid certain logical problems that afflict other theories of vagueness.[8] So if epistemicism implied commensurabilism, it would give commensurabilism support.

But epistemicism does not imply commensurabilism. Consider the predicates 'better than soldiering' and 'worse than soldiering'. Epistemicism implies that these predicates have sharp borderlines. A tiny improvement in the career of a priest takes us across the borderline from a career that is worse than soldiering to one that is not worse than soldiering, and from one that is not better than soldiering to one that is better than soldiering. In the incommensurate case, epistemicism implies that the borderline between the worse zone and the incommensurate zone is sharp, and so is the borderline between the incommensurate zone and the better zone. But it does not rule out the existence of an incommensurate zone. Only if these borderlines had to coincide would this be ruled out. Epistemicism does not imply that they coincide, so it gives no support to commensurabilism.

Given that, I think we may safely reject commensurabilism because of its sheer implausibility. I shall go on to the second of the two questions mentioned at the end of section 9.1: given that commensurabilism is false, and options are not necessarily ordered by their goodness, what importance does that have for ethics? I can now express this question more precisely: how ethically significant is the difference between the equality case and the incommensurate case? Sections 9.5 and 6 consider two arguments about this that have to do with the form of the betterness relation. Sections 9.7 to 9.10 consider the importance of the difference for practical decision making.

9.5   Rough equality

Griffin does not support commensurabilism as I have defined it. For example, he would accept that there may be a range of careers as a priest that are intermediate between those that are better than soldiering and those that are worse. So he accepts there are incommensurate cases. However, he seems to think they are all, or at least mostly, cases of 'rough equality'. We might call Griffin a 'rough commensurabilist'. Evidently he thinks the difference between equality and incommensurateness is not very important.

What does 'rough equality' mean, exactly? Griffin presents an analysis,[9] but we do not need to analyse the concept very far in order to see that rough commensurabilism is implausible. So long as 'roughly equal' has something like its ordinary meaning, this must be true: two options that are each roughly equal in goodness to a third cannot differ very much from each other in their goodness. They do not have to be roughly equal in goodness to each other; that would follow if rough equality was a transitive relation, but (as Griffin points out) it is not. Nevertheless, they plainly cannot differ very much in their goodness. Griffin is evidently assuming that no incommensurate zone can be very wide. But there seems to be no reason why it should not be. We would generally expect the zone to be narrow when we are comparing similar types of thing, and wide when we are comparing very different things. Between joining the Northumberland Rifles and the Fifth Lancers, the zone may be narrow, but between the church and the army it may be very wide. A mediocre career in the church may not be definitely worse than a career in the army, and a successful career in the church may not be definitely better than a career in the army. But a successful career in the church is much better than a mediocre one. It follows that not all careers in the incommensurate zone are roughly equally as good as a career in the army.

To make this argument, I have presumed we have some scale of goodness. It need only be a rough scale, just enough to give sense to such expressions as 'much better', 'do not differ much in their goodness', and so on. The idea of rough equality itself presumes a rough scale, so I have taken one for granted in arguing against it.

Commensurabilism is very implausible because it presumes there is no intermediate zone at all, but at most one intermediate option. Rough commensurabilism is less implausible, but implausible nonetheless because it presumes the intermediate zone is narrow. If we are to believe it, at least we need from Griffin an argument why this zone should be narrow.

9.6   Vagueness

Griffin does make one point that I think is intended as such an argument. He claims that incommensurability is vagueness.[10] When two options are incommensurate, we cannot say either is better than the other. This leaves open several possibilities. Griffin's view is that, although we cannot assert 'This one is better', we also cannot deny it, and although we cannot assert 'That one is better', we cannot deny that either.

Take the career example again. Griffin believes the predicates 'better than soldiering' and 'worse than soldiering' are vague. Unlike the epistemicists, he believes this means there is no sharp borderline between priest-careers that are better than soldiering and those that are not, nor between priest-careers that are worse than soldiering and those that are not. More than that, he thinks these borderlines overlap and extend across the whole incommensurate zone. The consequence is that, although we cannot assert of a career within this zone that it is better than soldiering, we cannot deny it either. Also, although we cannot assert it is worse than soldiering, we cannot deny that either. The incommensurate zone is a zone of vagueness.

Joseph Raz disagrees. He thinks that, of a career in the indeterminate zone, we can deny it is better than soldiering and deny it is worse than soldiering too.[11] The issue between these views is a fiddly question of logic. As it happens, I think Griffin is right and Raz wrong, but since the arguments are fiddly I shall not present them here.[12]

The real difference of opinion between Griffin and Raz is not the fiddly one about logic, but that Raz thinks incommensurability is important, and Griffin thinks it is not. They both seem to take it for granted that, if incommensurability was vagueness, it would not be important. That is why they disagree about whether it is indeed vagueness.

But if incommensurability is vagueness, why should that make it unimportant? Raz says it would merely be an instance of the general indeterminacy of our language.[13] That is true; at least, vagueness is a common feature of our concepts. But why should it make it unimportant? If 'better than' is vague, I see no reason why that should not be a significant feature of ethics. Vagueness in general is not unimportant in ethics. The vagueness of 'person' is a very important feature of several ethical problems.

I think Griffin believes that if the incommensurate zone is a zone of vagueness, then it cannot be very wide, and that would make it unimportant. It would support his contention that options within the zone are roughly equal to the standard in goodness. But vagueness can be very extensive. The Southern Ocean is a vague expanse of water whose boundaries with other oceans are indeterminate to the extent of a thousand miles or so. So the claim that incommensurability is vagueness does not support the claim that it is rough equality.

I think the question of vagueness is a red herring when we are interested in the importance of incommensurability. It does not provide an argument why the incommensurate zone must be narrow, and it does not suggest independently that incommensurability must be unimportant.

The real question about importance is whether incommensurability makes an important difference to practical decision making. In the next section I shall turn away from the formal questions of vagueness and rough equality to consider decision making directly. In doing this, I shall assume that incommensurate zones exist, and that they need not be small. We have found no reason for doubting either of these assumptions.

9.7   Practical decision making

What implications does incommensurability have for how we ought to act? What ought we to do when faced with a choice between two options that are incommensurate in their goodness? To smooth the way for answering this question, let us make the assumption that the goodness of the options is the only consideration relevant to the choice. This is to assume *teleology*; teleology is the view that how one ought to act is determined by the goodness of the available options. Nonteleological theories deny this. For instance, some nonteleological theories hold there are rules of right action – deontic rules – that are not determined entirely by the goodness of the options. To get a clear view of the importance of incommensurability, let us set nonteleological theories aside.

Granted teleology, when you are faced with a choice between two options, if one is better than the other, you ought to choose the better one. It would be wrong to choose the other. But if the two options are either incommensurate or equally good, what then? We cannot say that you ought to choose one, nor that you ought to choose the other. Choosing either would not be wrong. It is not determinate which you ought to choose. Reason, as it were, leaves you on your own. You must simply decide without the guidance of reason.

This is mysterious in one way. Rational creatures have to be able to decide without the guidance of reason, and it is mysterious how we can do that. Buridan's Ass could not manage it; how can we? It is not simply a matter of choosing which we like, since we may not like either of the options any more than the other. So how do we choose? One might be tempted to use this mystery as an argument against incommensurability. One might argue that reason simply cannot leave us in the lurch like this; there must always be something we ought to do.[14] But if this were a valid argument, it would work just as effectively against equality of goodness as against incommensurability. Since equality of goodness is surely possible, the argument must fail. It leaves us with the mystery of how we choose. But I have no need to solve this mystery, because it applies equally to the incommensurate case and the equality case; it does not distinguish them.

If you are faced with a choice between two options, and they are equally good, it does not matter which you choose. If they are incommensurate, it does matter. People often identify this as the practical importance of the distinction: one type of choice matters and the other does not. But actually this remark is a mere tautology. To say a choice between two options does not matter – literally, and not simply that it does not matter much – is simply to say the options are equally good, and to say it does matter is simply to say they are not equally good.

I conclude that, when we think about an isolated choice between two options, there is nothing in practical decision making that is different between the incommensurate case and the equality case. To find a difference we need to look further. In section 9.3, I distinguished the cases by means of a structural feature of betterness that does not show up in an isolated choice like this. Using the device of the standard configuration, I made the distinction depend on whether there is an intermediate zone or a single intermediate option, between options that are better than the standard and those that are worse, or just one. So this structural feature is where we should look for a practical difference between the cases. The difference must depend on there being an intermediate zone rather than a single intermediate option.

9.8   A puzzle

Here indeed there is a significant difference. Decision making in the incommensurate case, but not the equality case, can lead to a puzzle. Suppose two careers are open to you: a career in the army and a good career as a priest. Suppose they are incommensurate in their goodness. Then choosing either would not be wrong. You have to choose without the guidance of reason, and suppose you choose the army: you commit yourself to the army career, and give up the chance of a good career in the church. In doing so you are doing nothing wrong. But then suppose another opportunity comes up to join the church, this time in much worse conditions. You now face a choice between the army or a much less good career as a priest. Suppose these two, also, are incommensurate. Choosing either would not be wrong. You have to choose without the guidance of reason. Suppose this time you choose the church. Once again you do nothing wrong. But though you have not acted wrongly in either of your choices, the effect of the two together is that you end up with a much worse career in the church than you could have had. Surely rationality should be able to protect you from this sort of bad result; surely there is something irrational in what you have done. Yet apparently neither of your decisions was irrational. This is puzzling.[15]

No such bad result could have emerged had you only been choosing amongst options that are equally good. Suppose you have a choice between A and B, and the two are equally good. Suppose you choose B. Next suppose you have a choice between B and C, which are also equally good, and you choose C. Neither of your choices is contrary to reason. But in this case you are no worse off with C than you would have been with A. A and C must be equally good because the relation 'equally as good as' is transitive. On the other hand, the relation 'incommensurate with' is not. So we have identified a practical difficulty that arises in the incommensurate case but not in the equality case. This certainly makes the difference significant.

The puzzle is that rational decision making leaves you worse off than you could have been. But what is puzzling about that? The same thing can happen in ways that are not puzzling at all. For example, you might rationally make a decision that could be expected to lead to a good result, but by sheer bad luck it might lead to a bad result. The example I described can also be interpreted in a way that is not puzzling. You might just change your mind between one decision and the next. Having chosen the army, you might decide that was a mistake, and make the best of a bad job by taking up the only church career that is still available. Then you would not have acted irrationally. Nor is it puzzling that you end up worse off than you could have been.

The puzzle arises only if, when you make the second choice of a poor church career rather than the army, you do not at the same time repudiate your first choice of the army rather than a good church career. If at one single time you are willing to endorse both decisions, then you are certainly in a puzzling condition.

9.9   Bayesianism

Compare a similar puzzle that arises in a different context. Suppose you are at a horse race, knowing absolutely nothing about the horses. You have no information whatsoever about which is likely to win; indeed you do not even know the number of entries in the race. You find the bookies offering even odds on Gorgeous to win. Having no reason not to, you place a £10 bet on Gorgeous. In that, you are doing nothing wrong. Next you find even odds are also offered on Screaming Angel to win, and, having no reason not to do this either, you place a £10 bet on it. Again, you are doing nothing wrong. Finally, you find even odds offered on Intravenous to win, and you place a £10 bet on Intravenous too, once more doing nothing wrong. By these three bets, you have guaranteed yourself a loss of at least £10. You have accepted what is known as a 'Dutch book' against yourself. This is puzzling, since you have done nothing wrong. (Let us abstract from the fun of the game and assume your only object is to make money.)

Once again, there are ways this can happen that are not at all puzzling. For instance, you might change your mind about the horses' chances as the afternoon progresses. Having bet on one horse, you might decide another is more likely to win and bet on that one, resigning yourself to losing on the first, and hoping to recoup some of your losses. But you are in a puzzling condition if you are willing to endorse your bets on the three horses at the same time.

Here is a Bayesian solution to the puzzle. Your bets are in fact irrational. True, none is individually irrational, because you have no reason not to bet on each of the horses individually. But each bet you place on a horse implies you have a particular degree of belief in that horse's winning. When you bet on Gorgeous at even odds, that implies you believe to some degree at least as much as a half that it will win. You have no reason either to have this belief or not to have it, so it is rational for you to make the bet or not to make it. But you should only make it if in fact you do have this degree of belief in the horse's winning. Similarly, you should bet on Screaming Angel only if you believe to a degree at least as much as a half that Screaming Angel will win, and you should bet on Intravenous only if you believe to a degree at least as much as a half that Intravenous will win. Now, it is irrational to believe to a degree at least as much as a half that Gorgeous will win, and to a degree at least as much as a half that Screaming Angel will win, and to a degree at least as much as a half that Intravenous will win. So your three bets together are irrational.

Let me put this Bayesian argument in better order. Bayesians think, first, that reason imposes particular constraints on the combinations of bets you should make. These are constraints of consistency, and they are laid down in the 'axioms' of Bayesian theory. The grounds for the axioms are that, if you do not stick to them, you will be vulnerable to traps such as Dutch books.

Bayesians next claim that bets imply particular degrees of belief. For instance, betting on a horse at particular odds implies a particular degree of belief in its winning. They then demonstrate mathematically that, if your betting is consistent according to the axioms, it implies a consistent pattern of beliefs. Otherwise it implies an inconsistent pattern. 'Consistent' here means conforming to laws of probability. For instance, your degrees of belief in various horses winning a race must not add up to more than one. This consistency of belief gives further support to the consistency requirements of the axioms: bets that are consistent according to the axioms can be interpreted in terms of consistent beliefs.

The upshot is that, if you are to be rational, you must act according to some probability beliefs or other. This is so whether or not there are rational grounds for some beliefs rather than others. If there are none – for instance if you know nothing about the horses – you should still have beliefs. As it is often put, you should have subjective probabilities and act on them. This is so even if there are no objective probabilities, so reason does not determine which subjective probabilities you should have. Reason still determines that you should have some.

9.10   Reasons and intentions

We might take a similar Bayesian line about the career example. Neither of your decisions – to join the army rather than to take up a good career as a priest, and to take up the less good career as a priest rather than join the army – is irrational on its own, but they are irrational in combination. Your decisions should be consistent with each other in particular ways, because otherwise you may find yourself in traps such as the one that actually caught you. Just as Bayesians interpret betting decisions as implying beliefs, we can interpret your decisions as implying values. Your first choice in the example implies that you value a career in the army at least as highly as a good career in the church. On the other hand, your second choice implies that you value a less good career in the church at least as highly as a career in the army. So these two decisions imply inconsistent values. Consistent decisions will imply a consistent value system. In this case, the objective facts of goodness do not determine what values you ought to adopt. They do not determine whether you should value an army career higher than a good church career, or a less good church career higher than an army career. So reason does not determine what your subjective values should be. But it does determine that you should have some and act according to them.

This Bayesian line is commensurabilist in a sense. Values may be objectively incommensurable, but subjectively they should not be. Objective values may leave room for subjective choices, but to act consistently you need to settle on subjective values for yourself, and these must have no incommensurability. Moreover, this is a sort of commensurabilism that many people might find credible even if they agree with my claim in section 9.4 that commensurabilism is implausible. They might think objective commensurabilism is implausible, but the need for consistency in decisions gives grounds for subjective commensurabilism. Whatever the objective facts, we need to create fully commensurable value-systems for ourselves. This conclusion would have made a pleasant ending for a chapter in honour of James Griffin.

However, I am sorry to say I shall have to end with doubts about it. There is a good objection to the Bayesian line. When you make your decisions in the career example, there is no reason to think you are reflecting your values. You have to decide between one career and another. If there are no grounds for your decision, you have to make it all the same, without grounds. Consequently, the fact that you make it does not show you have grounds.[16] In particular, your decision need not imply a subjective system of values that gives it grounds. The same objection may be raised against the Bayesian line on probability. You have to choose whether or not to bet on Gorgeous. Since you have no information relevant to its chances of winning, you have no grounds on which to base this decision. You have to decide, so you decide without grounds. The fact that you decide to bet does not show you have grounds for doing so. In particular, it does not show you believe to a degree greater than a half that Gorgeous will win.

Bayesians might not be troubled by this objection. To avoid a Dutch book, you must certainly act *as if* you have a consistent pattern of beliefs. Whether you actually have one or not might not particularly concern a Bayesian. If the Bayesian favours a behaviourist or functionalist notion of belief, she will think you do indeed have consistent beliefs, because acting consistently is a criterion for having consistent beliefs. But Bayesians are more concerned with the rationality of your behaviour than with the state of your mind, and they may be perfectly content so long as you act as if you have consistent beliefs.

But I am not satisfied by this casual response. Having bet on Gorgeous and Screaming Angel, Bayesians think you ought not to bet on Intravenous, unless you have repudiated your previous bets. So they think you have some reason not to bet on Intravenous. But what could that reason be? It can only be that you believe, to a degree at least as much as a half, that Intravenous will not win. Your belief must be substantive enough to generate a reason for you. We may have a notion of belief that entitles us to attribute to you particular beliefs on the basis of your previous bets. But could these beliefs be reason-giving for you? Could your previous bets give you a reason not to bet on Intravenous? I doubt it. You have no information about the horses that could justify you in having particular beliefs and acting on them. Your placing a bet gives you no information either. So how could placing a bet make it the case that you now have a belief, and that this belief gives you reason to act in a particular way? I doubt it could.

Similarly, I doubt that your decision to join the army, in preference to a good church career, necessarily makes it the case that you value the army career more highly than the church career. I recognize that decision making can sometimes stimulate you to form values, and it may even be a way of forming your values, but I doubt it is necessarily so. You have to act, whether or not you form values that determine how you should act. Consequently, I do not see how your first decision gives you a reason not to make your second one (not to choose a poor church career rather than the army). True, it is common nowadays to think that decisions are themselves reason-giving.[17] For example, if you have decided on some end, that gives you a reason to take an appropriate means to this end. In a similar way, your decision to join the army rather than take a good church career could give you a reason not to take a worse church career rather than join the army. But I think this common opinion is incorrect. If you have no reason to pursue some end, even if you have decided to do so, you have no reason to take some means to this end. I do not believe decisions create reasons.

So I doubt the Bayesian idea. But since it was a solution to a puzzle, I need an alternative. The one I have to offer is only a suggestion, which will have to be worked out properly another time. Take the means–end connection again. Deciding on an end gives you no reason to take a means to it, but in a different way it does commit you to taking a means. Deciding on an end is itself deciding to take some means to it. Deciding to go to the cinema is itself deciding to take some means of getting there. To put it another way: intending an end is intending some means to it. So the movement from end to means is not mediated through reasons but through intention. The difference is important. You can intend a means to an end without its being the case that you ought to take a means to this end, and even without your believing you ought to. Moreover, there is absolutely nothing wrong with changing your mind and deciding not to (unless you have already invested some effort). On the other hand, if you had a reason to take the means, there would be something wrong with changing your mind.

Similarly, if you decide to join the army rather than take a good job as a priest, that in itself is plausibly a decision not to take a worse job as a priest rather than join the army. You can change your mind, but not without repudiating your earlier decision. So I suggest the connection between the two decisions is mediated by intention rather than reason. One intention implies another. The structure of intentions – what intention is implied by what – and the nature of this implication still need to be worked out.

The Bayesian solution implies that subjective values must be commensurable, because it assumes only commensurable values can resolve the puzzle I mentioned. My alternative does not require even subjective values to be commensurable. The puzzle can be resolved by the structure of intentions, rather than by the structure of values. I suggest incommensurability of values is indeed an important phenomenon in ethics, which cannot be dissolved away by the Bayesian method.

10 Goodness is reducible to betterness: the evil of death is the value of life

10.1   Utility theory and betterness

The methods of economics can contribute in many ways to the study of ethics. One way is that utility theory can help to analyse the *structure of goodness*.

At least, utility theory can help to analyse the structure of *betterness*, the comparative of goodness. Betterness is a mundane matter. We very commonly discuss which things are better or worse than others. We say that sun is generally better than rain; we wonder whether it would be better to move to a new job or stay in the old one; we debate about which is the best way of coping with the sufferings of refugees. Betterness and worseness are common topics of our ordinary conversation. To put it more formally, between objects from some range we may be considering, there is a betterness relation denoted by:

    _ is better than _,

where each blank is to be filled in with the name of an object. Utility theory can help to analyse the structure of this relation.

What do I mean by the *structure* of a betterness relation? One structural feature is that a betterness relation is necessarily transitive. If A is better than B, and B is better than C, then A is necessarily better than C. I think this is a fact of logic, because for any property F, its comparative relation denoted by '_ is *F*er than _' is necessarily transitive. Betterness is therefore an ordering. But this is only one of its structural features. There are others, which utility theory can help to reveal.

Utility theory was originally designed as a theory of rational preferences. It consists of a number of axioms that are intended to apply to *preference relations*. A person P's preference relation is denoted by:

    P prefers _ to _.

From *The Good and the Economical: Ethical Choices in Economics and Management*, edited by Peter Koslowski and Yuichi Shionoya, Springer-Verlag, 1993, pp. 70–84. Reprinted by permission of the editors. I should like to thank Jeff McMahan, Derek Parfit, and Hans-Peter Weikard for their helpful comments.

The blanks are, again, to be filled in with the names of objects. Utility theorists claim that, provided a person's preferences are rational, they will
conform to the axioms of the theory. Different versions of the theory have
different axioms, but every version includes transitivity as an axiom. The
point of utility theory is that, granted the axioms, useful theorems can be
proved about the structure of a person's preferences.

Utility theory is only a formal structure. Although it was intended for
preference relations, it can be applied to any relation that satisfies the
axioms. I believe betterness relations satisfy these axioms, or many of them
at least; I have already said they necessarily satisfy transitivity, for instance.
That is why I think utility theory can be useful in analysing the structure of
good.

That utility theory applies to betterness is a matter of the *form* of the
betterness relation: it conforms to the axioms. I am not suggesting there is
necessarily any *substantive* connection between betterness and preferences.
For instance, I am not suggesting it is necessarily good for a person to have
her preferences satisfied. Whether or not that is so is a separate question.

This chapter is not about the details of applying utility theory to betterness. It is about a possible limitation of the whole idea. Preferences constitute a two-place relation rather than a one-place property. Since utility
theory was originally designed for preferences, it is only available as a tool
for analysing a relation and not a property. Consequently, it may be suitable for analysing the betterness relation, denoted by '_ is better than _', but
inadequate for analysing the goodness property, denoted by '_ is good'. So
there may be structural features of goodness that cannot be captured in
utility theory. In order to bring utility theory to bear on the problem, I
started by announcing I was going to concentrate on the structure of betterness rather than good. In doing that, I may have missed out something
important.

Because economists are used to working with preferences, they naturally
think in comparative terms. I have suggested taking over utility theory to
analyse betterness in a formal fashion, but economists have been doing the
same thing informally for a long time. They use, for instance, the concept
of 'social preference'. When an economist says that A is socially preferred
to B, she often means simply that A is better than B. Rightly or wrongly,
she evidently thinks of betterness as a sort of preference. This has the
advantage of opening it up automatically to exactly the analysis by means
of utility theory that I have been recommending. I think that is very useful.
On the other hand, it constrains the economist to think of goodness only
in terms of its comparative, betterness. This might be a limitation of the
approach.

But actually, I do not think it is a limitation at all. I think that goodness is actually fully reducible to betterness; there is nothing more to goodness than betterness. I think economists are right to think in comparative terms, and they miss nothing by doing so. I think some philosophers have occasionally found themselves chasing red herrings because they have not had the economist's instinct to work with comparatives. There are some examples in section 10.5 below. Thinking in comparatives is one of the lessons economics can teach to philosophy.

Section 10.2 of this chapter explains more exactly what I mean when I say goodness is reducible to betterness. It explains the alternative possibility, that there might be absolute degrees of goodness and an absolute zero of goodness. Section 10.3 considers some senses in which goodness has an absolute zero, but shows that goodness is reducible to betterness nonetheless. Section 10.4 describes a sense of goodness that is genuinely irreducible, but argues it is not the right sense to use in ethics. Section 10.5 describes some of the difficulties philosophers have been led into when pursuing the idea of irreducible goodness. From section 10.3 onwards, the context of my discussion will be the value of life and the evil of death. Questions of life and death raise the idea of absolute goodness most urgently, and they are the main subject of this chapter.

10.2   The idea of absolute goodness

Let us say a property F is 'reducible to its comparative' if any statement that refers to the property has the same meaning as another statement that refers to the property's comparative, Fer than, instead. I think goodness is reducible to its comparative. Anything that can be said using 'good' can be said using 'better than'. To put it another way, if you knew everything about betterness – of every pair of alternatives, you knew whether one was better than the other, and which – then you would know everything there is to know about goodness. There is nothing more to goodness than betterness. So there is in principle nothing about the structure of goodness that cannot be captured within utility theory.

When I say there is nothing more to goodness than betterness, you might think I mean to say that goodness is an ordinal property rather than a cardinal one. But I do not mean that. I am not concerned with ordinality and cardinality in this chapter. I consider both to be features of betterness. Betterness is a cardinal concept if we can make sense of amounts of betterness: if we can sensibly ask how much better one thing is than another. More precisely, if it makes sense to say A is better than B to a greater extent than C is better than D, then betterness is cardinal. If not, betterness is ordinal. All this is a matter of the structure of the betterness relation. Whether there is more to goodness than betterness is a different matter.[1]

It is a matter of whether there are absolute degrees of goodness. Some properties have absolute degrees, and consequently cannot be reduced to their comparatives. One example is the property of *width*. Many statements that mention width can be reduced to others that mention only comparative width, but not all can. 'The Mississippi is wide' can be reduced; it means the same as 'The Mississippi is wider than a typical river.' But the statement 'An electron has no width' cannot be reduced in this way. You might at first think it means simply that nothing is less wide than an electron. But actually it means more than that; the fact that an electron's width is specifically zero has a significance over and above the fact that nothing is less wide. Width is not reducible to its comparative because there is an absolute zero of width.

Width has an absolute zero. Other properties have absolute degrees of other sorts beside zero. *Correctness*, for instance, has an absolutely maximal degree. An arithmetical calculation can be absolutely perfectly correct, and this fact about it cannot be expressed in terms of comparative correctness. But for goodness, I take it that, if it has absolute degrees of any sort, it will surely have an absolute zero. If it does, there will also be absolutely positive and negative degrees: things that are better than the absolute zero will be absolutely good; things that are worse, absolutely bad.

To test whether goodness can be reduced to its comparative, I shall therefore look for an absolute zero of goodness. However, if goodness does have an absolute zero, it will certainly not have one in quite the way width has. If it does have a zero, goodness is likely to have a structure more like the structure of *attractiveness*. Things are ordered by the comparative denoted by '_ is more attractive than _'. Towards one end of the ordering are positively attractive things; towards the other negatively attractive or positively repellent things. In between are things with zero attractiveness. So the zero of attractiveness is in the middle of the ordering, whereas width has its zero at the end. Still, the zero ensures that attractiveness, like width, is an irreducible property. 'Pandas are attractive' cannot be replaced with a comparative statement. No doubt, the zero of goodness, if it has one, will also be somewhere in the middle of the betterness ordering. And goodness may resemble attractiveness in another way too. The zero of attractiveness is doubtless vague; it will occupy some vague position in the middle of the ordering. If goodness has an absolute zero, that may well be vague too.

In looking for an absolute zero of goodness, we must not be too hasty. Goodness may have absolute degrees of a sort, whilst still being reducible to its comparatives. In section 10.3, I shall describe various ways in which this can happen.

10.3   Reducible senses of goodness

Are there absolute degrees of goodness? Suppose we have the betterness relation fully worked out over some range of objects; we have all the objects arranged on a scale from the worst to the best. Once that is done, can we sensibly ask the question: where on the scale is the zero point? If there is a zero, objects above it will be good, and objects below it bad. Can we can divide the objects into the good one and the bad ones?

The answer is that we can indeed make this division in various sensible ways. Here is one. When we are assessing the goodness of something, there is often an obvious standard of comparison. Given that, we may say the thing is good, and simply mean it is better than the obvious standard. The obvious standard depends on the sort of objects we are assessing. If they are actions or events, the obvious standard is generally what would other- wise have happened. 'It is a good thing you remembered the corkscrew' means it would have been worse if you had forgotten the corkscrew. Alternatively, if the objects are propositions, the obvious standard for a particular proposition is its negation. When we say a proposition is good, we mean it is better than its negation. In *The Logic Of Decision*, Richard Jeffrey works out this idea formally, and shows how it determines a zero for goodness that always lies between the goodness of a proposition and the goodness of its negation.[2]

The existence of obvious standards of comparison gives us absolute degrees of goodness of a sort. But these degrees are themselves determined by the betterness relation, so they do not prevent goodness from being reducible. 'X is good' reduces to 'X is better than the standard.' Once you know which things are better than which, you know all there is to know about the goodness of things.

When the objects we are considering are not events or propositions, but people's lives, there is another way to make sense of the question which are good and which bad. Questions of life and death very easily raise thoughts about absolute good and bad. The rest of this chapter concentrates on these questions.

People lead lives of different lengths and different qualities. Some lives are better than others. There is a betterness relation between lives, that is to say. This relation arranges lives on a scale from the worst to the best. Having done that, we may still have reason to ask what point on this scale divides good lives from bad ones. This is because we may want to know whether it is a good or a bad thing that a life of a particular quality is lived at all. As the question is commonly put, is a particular life *worth living*? For instance, is it a good or a bad thing that people are born to live in desperate poverty, or to suffer some genetic disease? Between lives that are worth living and those that are not is a quality of life that we might naturally count as zero on the scale of goodness. So here is an idea of absolute zero for goodness.

But whether a life is good, or worth living, is once again a matter of comparing one thing with another. Precisely which comparison is in question depends on the context. Sometimes we may ask, of a particular person now alive, whether her life is good. In that context, to say her life is good generally means it is better for the person that she should continue to live rather than die now. Or it may mean it is better, not necessarily for the person but from some impersonal point of view, that she should continue to live. In either case, to say the life is good reduces to a comparative statement of betterness. The relevant comparison is between one possible life and another: on the one hand a shorter life, coming to an end now, and on the other a longer life that continues into the future. This comparison determines the zero of goodness in this particular context. Goodness reduces to betterness.

In another context, to say a person's life is good or worth living means it is better that the person should live her life than that she should never have lived at all. Here the comparison that gives sense to goodness is not a comparison between lives. I started by supposing we have lives ranked from the worst to the best. To fix a zero in the ranking, in the sense I am now considering, we have to go outside the ranking itself. We need to compare not lives, but worlds: we must compare a world in which a life is lived with one in which it is not lived. But still, this is a comparative judgement of betterness. It is true that, if you knew only which lives are better than which, you would not know which lives are good in this sense. You would need a wider knowledge of betterness than that. Still, if you knew all about which things are better than which, you would know which lives are good and which are not. Goodness reduces to betterness once again.

All these are ways of making sense of a zero of goodness. None of them is any reason to doubt that goodness reduces to betterness. But there is another possible way, and this one would make betterness irreducible. I shall come at it indirectly, through a discussion of Derek Parfit's notion of a life worth living.

10.4   Naturalism

In Part IV of *Reasons and Persons*, Derek Parfit considers the value of adding people to the world's population. He uses the idea of a good life or a life worth living throughout his discussion. What exactly does he mean by it? I suggested some possible meanings in section 10.3. One suggestion was that a life worth living is a life such that it is better that this life is lived than that it is not. But this is evidently not Parfit's meaning. At one point, he considers the view that 'though . . . a life is worth living . . . it would have been in itself better if this life had never been lived'.[3] Parfit treats this as an intelligible opinion, but if 'worth living' had the meaning I suggested, it would be self-contradictory.

Parfit also speaks of a life worth living as one that 'has value to the person whose life it is'.[4] This could point to another of the meanings I suggested for 'worth living': that a life is worth living if it is better for the person that her life continue than that she should die. But this is not Parfit's meaning either. Whether a life is worth living in this sense may change from one time in a person's life to another. If a person lives happily when young, but experiences acute suffering for some months before she dies, her life may be worth living in this sense when she is young, but not during those last months. But in his discussion of population, Parfit only considers the value of lives as a whole. He has no place for values that change over time. So this cannot be his meaning.

The expression 'has value to the person whose life it is' might also suggest a third possible meaning: a life is worth living if it is better for the person that she lives than that she should never have lived at all. I have not mentioned this as a possible meaning before, because I think it makes no sense. At least, it cannot ever be *true* that it is better for a person that she lives than that she should never have lived at all. If it were better for a person that she lives than that she should never have lived at all, then if she had never lived at all, that would have been worse for her than if she had lived. But if she had never lived at all, there would have been no her for it to be worse for, so it could not have been worse for her. Parfit seems to agree.[5] So this is not his meaning either.

At this point, Parfit says:

Causing someone to exist is a special case because the alternative would not have been worse for this person. We may admit that, for this reason, causing someone to exist cannot be *better* for this person. But it may be *good* for this person.[6]

Parfit here seems to be explicitly denying that goodness can be reduced to betterness. But we have still not discovered what he means by this irreducible 'good'. Explicitly, he identifies a good life with a life worth living,[7] but what does he mean by that?

There may be a clue in the examples he uses throughout his discussion of population. Parfit does not accept hedonism, but he often assumes hedonism for the sake of argument in his examples. Hedonism says that the only good thing in life is pleasure, and the only bad thing pain. Given hedonism, we can define an *empty* life as one that contains neither pleasure nor pain. And we can still use the same idea of emptiness even if we drop hedonism. Suppose we have a list of the good and bad things in life; no doubt the list will include pleasure and pain, but it may include other things as well. Then we can define a life as empty if it contains none of these good or bad things.

The idea of good and bad things in life can be defined in terms of betterness; it does not depend on any absolute notion of good. Something – pleasure, for instance – is a good thing if and only if a life that has more of it is better than one that has less, other things being equal. However, once we have identified the good and bad things in life, they present us with a plausible absolute zero for goodness. It is plausible to take an empty life to have zero goodness, so that a positively good life is one that is better than an empty life. This idea exploits the natural zeros of good and bad things – the natural zero of pain, for instance – to give us a zero for goodness. This zero is certainly not reducible to betterness; it is defined in terms of the zeros of the good and bad things.

Parfit seems to think of a life of zero goodness, or a life that is just not worth living, in this way. For instance, when describing lives that are not much above the zero, he says:

A life could be like this either because it has enough ecstasies to make its agonies seem just worth enduring, or because it is uniformly of poor quality. Let us imagine the lives . . . to be of this second drabber kind. In each of these lives there is very little happiness.[8]

If this is indeed what Parfit means by 'a good life' or 'a life worth living' – a life that is better than an empty life – it would explain why he thinks goodness cannot be reduced to betterness.

G. E. Moore would have called this account of the absolute zero of goodness 'naturalistic'.[9] The account depends on some particular theory of good: before we can define an empty life, we must first identify the good and bad things in life. This theory of good is not necessarily naturalistic in Moore's sense. A naturalistic theory is one that claims 'good' *means* some natural thing: 'good' means pleasure, say, or something else. But when we say that particular things in life are good – pleasure amongst them – we are simply saying that a life containing more of these things is better than a life containing fewer of them. We need not claim this is true in virtue of meaning. The meaning of 'better' may be determined independently, in some quite different way. However, our theory of good has supplied us with a naturalistic notion of zero goodness. According to this idea, 'a life of zero goodness' *means* a life that is neither better nor worse than an empty life. As yet, in following Parfit, we have not found any other meaning for zero goodness; this is the only meaning we have found. The natural zeros of the good and bad things in life have given us a naturalistic zero for goodness.

Naturalism is subject to Moore's open-question argument.[10] Here is a version of the argument, adapted to our context. Suppose some person lives an empty life; suppose, indeed, she is unconscious throughout her life and has no pleasures and pains for that reason. We might ask: would it have been better if this person had never lived? We might plausibly reach the answer: yes.[11] If we did, we would surely say this empty life was a bad one. Since it would have been better if the life had not been lived, it is a bad thing that it is lived, so we should surely say it is a bad life. According to the account of meaning I have given, however, it is not a bad life; it has zero goodness because empty lives necessarily have zero goodness. Even if we concluded it is not bad that this empty life is lived, it is certainly an intelligible question whether or not it is bad. Therefore, it cannot be the case that an empty life is neither good nor bad simply in virtue of meaning. Yet that is implied by the naturalistic account of zero goodness. So this account must be wrong.

I am convinced by the open-question argument in this application. I do not think it shows that the naturalist account is strictly wrong; it is no doubt acceptable to speak of zero goodness in the naturalistic way. But the argument displays a rival sense of zero goodness for lives. In the rival sense, a life has zero goodness if it is neither better nor worse that it is lived than that it is not lived. This is one of the senses I mentioned in section 10.3. When it comes to ethics, it is goodness in this sense that we are concerned with: is it a good or a bad thing that a particular life is lived? Therefore, in ethics, this second sense must have priority over the first. And whatever we understand by zero goodness, the argument certainly shows we cannot have a naturalistic meaning for the term 'worth living'. We must not call a life worth living if it is an open question whether or not it is a good thing that it is lived.

I suggest a different terminology. Let us distinguish a person's wellbeing from her good. Let us treat her wellbeing as a natural property; it is made up of the good and bad things in her life. Wellbeing in this sense has a natural zero given by the natural zeros of the good and bad things. An empty life, with no good or bad things, has zero wellbeing. But it is an open question whether it has zero goodness. Wellbeing has a natural absolute zero; goodness does not. Goodness is still reducible to betterness.

10.5   The evil of death and the value of life

I have now said what I can to defend my claim that goodness can be reduced to betterness. I have described some senses of goodness that are reducible, and objected to a sense that is not. I now want to give an example of the harm that can be done by neglecting the principle that goodness can be reduced to betterness. Philosophers have always debated the question of whether death is an evil. It seems to me that a good part of this debate has been diverted on to an unsatisfactory course by the search for a holy grail of absolute goodness. My main example will be Thomas Nagel's paper 'Death'. In writing this paper, Nagel was twice misled by the idea of absolute goodness.

He says:

> The fact that it is worse to die at 24 than at 82 does not imply that it is not a terrible thing to die at 82, or even at 806. The question is whether we can regard as a misfortune any limitation, like mortality, that is normal to the species.[12]

Is it terrible to die at eighty-two? Nagel assumes it is better to die at eighty-two than at eighty-one or younger, and worse than at eighty-three or older. Nagel takes this for granted from the start. But this remark about betterness is almost all there is to be said on the subject. Beyond that, 'Is it terrible to die at eighty-two?' is an almost empty question.

It is not quite empty. When we ask whether an event is bad, we are normally asking whether it is worse than the obvious standard of comparison, which is what would otherwise have happened. But when we ask if it is bad to die at eighty-two, that leaves it unclear what would otherwise have happened. This lack of clarity makes it tempting to pursue the question of what we should take as the standard of comparison. Nagel asks whether we should take as our standard what is normal to the species. Other authors have pursued the question at greater length. Jeff McMahan is one. In 'Death and the value of life', he recommends as a standard what would have happened if the person had not died, and he discusses how to interpret this counterfactual condition.

There may be some point in trying to answer this question about the standard of comparison, but it cannot tell us anything significant about the value of living and the evil of dying. It is only a question about what we might mean when we ask 'Is it terrible to die at eighty-two?' What comparison do we have in mind? All the significant facts have been fully stated once we have said what dying at eighty-two is better than and what it is worse than. There is no further significant question whether or not dying at eighty-two is an absolutely bad thing. Nagel concludes his article by saying: 'If there is no limit to the amount of life that it would be good to have, then it may be that a bad end is in store for us all.'[13] What is in store for us is an end that is worse than living longer would have been, and better than dying sooner would have been. That is all. Nagel tries to say more when there is nothing more to be said. That is one way in which he was led astray by the search for absolute goodness.

The second appears in his central argument against the Epicureans. The Epicureans argued that death is not bad for us, and Nagel's main purpose in 'Death' is to answer their arguments. Epicurus says:

Become accustomed to the belief that death is nothing to us. For all good and evil consists in sensation, but death is deprivation of sensation . . . So death, the most terrifying of ills, is nothing to us, since so long as we exist death is not with us; but when death comes, then we do not exist. It does not then concern either the living or the dead, since for the former it is not, and the latter are no more.[14]

There are two arguments contained in this passage. Nagel concentrates on the first. If death is bad for a person, the argument goes, its badness must consist in depriving the person of the good of living. But, as Nagel puts it,

Doubt may be raised whether *anything* can be bad for a man without being positively unpleasant to him: specifically, it may be doubted that there are any evils which consist merely in the deprivation or absence of possible goods, and which do not depend on someone's *minding* that deprivation.[15]

Nagel aims to remove this doubt.[16]

His argument is to reject Epicurus' claim that all good and evil consists in sensation. He argues that there are many sorts of evil that are not experienced. He gives examples. It is bad for a person, he says, to have her wishes ignored by the executor of her will, even though she can suffer no bad experience as a result. It is bad for a person to be ridiculed behind her back, even if she never finds out and suffers no bad experiences as a result. And so on. Amongst unexperienced evils like this Nagel places the evil of deprivation. Death deprives a person of the good she would otherwise have enjoyed, and this is an unexperienced evil.

This is a dangerous argument for Nagel to make. His examples of unexperienced evils are controversial. He makes such contentious remarks as:

A man's life includes much that does not take place within the boundaries of his body and his mind, and what happens to him can include much that does not take place within the boundaries of his life. These boundaries are commonly crossed by the misfortunes of being deceived, or despised, or betrayed.[17]

To answer Nagel, a hedonist like Epicurus would simply deny all this. She would deny it is bad for you to be ridiculed behind your back, and so on. It is unwise of Nagel to rest his case on such contentious grounds. He certainly does not need to. He does not even need to reject Epicurus' hedonism in order to refute his argument. This particular argument of Epicurus' is trivially mistaken.

Suppose hedonism is true, and a person's good is determined entirely by the pleasures and pains she enjoys in her life. Now suppose something happens that causes you to have fewer good experiences – enjoy less pleasure – than you otherwise would have done. That is bad for you. An event is bad for you if it makes your life less good than it otherwise would have been, and that is what this event has done. That is so whether or not you find out what has happened, and whether or not you have any bad feelings as a result. Suppose you win a lottery, but because of a glitch in a computer you never find out you have won, and never receive the prize. If the prize would have given you pleasure, the glitch is bad for you.

A event can be bad for a person even if it does not result in any bad experiences in her life. This is so even if a person's good is entirely determined by the quality of her experiences. One way an event can be bad for someone is to give her a bad experience she would not otherwise have had. Another way is to deprive her of some good experiences she otherwise would have had. Either makes her less well off than she otherwise would have been. We may call a bad event of the latter sort 'a deprivation'. A deprivation cannot fail to be bad, because by definition it makes a person less well off than she would have been. Since death is a deprivation, it is bad for you.

Both Epicurus and Nagel missed this simple point. Why? They must have been mesmerized by the idea of absolute good and bad. They must have assumed that the badness of death must show up as some sort of absolute bad, like a bad experience or something else. But actually the badness of death simply consists in its being worse than staying alive.

Nagel says:

If we turn from what is good about life to what is bad about death, the case is completely different. Essentially . . . what we find desirable in life are certain states, conditions or types of activity. It is *being* alive, *doing* certain things, having certain experiences, that we consider good. But if death is an evil, it is the *loss of life*, rather than the state of being dead, or nonexistent, or unconscious, that is objectionable. This asymmetry is important.[18]

But there is no such asymmetry. If life is good, that means simply that it is better than death, and, if death is bad, that means simply that it is worse than life. What is good about life must be exactly the same as – or perhaps I should say exactly the opposite of – what is bad about death. As Nagel says, what is good about life is that, in life, we enjoy certain states, conditions, or types of activity. What is bad about death is also that, in life, we enjoy certain states, conditions, or types of activity. To be fair to Nagel, I must admit that, in effect, this is what he says. But he presents it as a puzzle needing explanation, whereas it is actually trivially true. Once we recognize that goodness is reducible to betterness, it is obvious.

The passage I quoted from Epicurus contains two arguments intended to show that death is not an evil. The first is that 'all good and evil consists in sensation, but death is deprivation of sensation'. This argument, I have said, is trivially mistaken. The second argument is that 'so long as we exist death is not with us; but when death comes, then we do not exist'. I find this much more significant and persuasive. The real puzzle about the evil of death is not to do with the idea of deprivation, but with time: death deprives us of good, but when? Because he concentrated on the first argument, Nagel failed to do justice to the second

Part III

The value of life

11   Trying to value a life

Many of the enterprises governments engage in cause people's deaths in one way or another. Therefore, those governments that like to give some of their actions the appearance of economic rationality have to fix on a monetary value for a human life. A blossoming literature explains to them the correct way to make this valuation. But, though it blossoms still, I think the roots of the literature are insecure.

Before the discussion can get under way, the whole notion of the 'value' of benefits and costs – values that can be added and subtracted to establish the rightness or wrongness of a government's project – needs to be supplied with both an exact definition and a justification. In this chapter, I shall consider only the familiar interpretation of cost–benefit analysis as a 'compensation test'. Under this interpretation the values of costs and benefits are defined by means of monetary compensation, in a manner I shall specify in a moment. This definition is justified by arguing that, if the benefits of a project exceed its costs when valued this way, the project is a good thing. I must explain.

I think that by now most people recognize the invalidity of the compensation test except when compensation is actually paid, so let us assume it is. Then the test boils down to something rather harmless, the 'Pareto criterion', and it works as follows. Each person who would lose from the project is asked what is the minimum payment of money he would consider full compensation for his loss. This amount is defined as the value of his loss. If the project is carried out it will be paid him, so he is deemed not to have suffered in the end. Each person who would benefit is asked how much money he would be prepared to pay to get the benefit. This amount is defined as its value. Then, if the value of the benefits adds up to more than the value of the losses, the project can be carried out, the gainers can compensate the losers, and no one will end up worse off than when he started.[1] Thus, provided some surplus is left over for somebody, the project is a good thing by the Pareto criterion.

A longer version of this chapter appeared in *Journal of Public Economics*, 9 (1978), pp. 91–100. Reprinted by permission of Elsevier Press. © 1978.

So, from this standpoint, the value of a loss is the amount of money that would compensate the loser. Coming back to the subject of death, let us for simplicity confine our attention to cases where the death in question is to be immediate, and where no bequests are permitted. Then the monetary value of a person's life, to be destroyed by a putative project, must be infinite. For no finite amount of money could compensate a person for the loss of his life, simply because money is no good to him when he is dead. There is nothing esoteric about this; it is an application, if an unexpected one, of the very orthodox notion of value that I have outlined.

But if a death counts as an infinite cost, measured in money, then it seems that a cost–benefit analysis will automatically reject any project that causes anybody's death (except possibly one that also saves lives). That, however, cannot be right. One can imagine a project that is very beneficial to millions of people, saving great suffering, but that is bound to kill somebody during the course of its implementation. Such a project would not automatically be wrong. It cannot be right for a single death to outweigh every other consideration.

So there is a paradox: the theoretically prescribed way to value life appears to lead to an obviously wrong confusion. I believe the first person to acknowledge the difficulty in print was E. J. Mishan,[2] and in trying to resolve it he employed a particular device, which has been taken for granted in the flourishing literature ever since. I shall concentrate my discussion on his arguments. It is because he interprets cost–benefit analysis by means of the compensation test that I have done the same. Mishan's intention is to circumvent the paradox by reducing the value of death to some finite amount. The device he and his successors employ is as follows. Notice, first of all, that on the whole government projects do not kill definite people who are identifiable at the time of launching the project. Instead they increase the risk of dying for a number of people. The monetary value of the increased risk is finite, in the sense that people will accept a finite amount of money as full compensation for it. The compensation that would satisfy the people exposed to extra risk is added up, and this is what is counted as the cost of the project. So, as it were, for purposes of evaluation, death is commuted to risk of death.

The main aim of my chapter is simply to show that this device is illegitimate.

To begin with, it is obvious at once that it cannot be a complete solution to the difficulty. For one can imagine an extremely beneficial project that would involve the certain death of a known person. Even according to Mishan the monetary cost of this would be infinite, but it would nevertheless be wrong to reject such a project automatically. So the paradox is still there in that case, unresolved. I shall show that Mishan's idea is mistaken also in cases when the victim is not definitely known.

If a definite number of people are going to die, can it really make such a vast difference whether or not it is known who they are? Here are some intermediate cases.

(a)   It is not known today who will die as a result of the project, but it is known that the information will be available tomorrow. The project is up for consideration today. It is known today that tomorrow it would be deemed unacceptable by an infinite margin, since the people who would die would accept no finite compensation. Yet today everyone has only a probability of dying. They may be compensated for this by a finite amount that turns out to be less than the benefits. So the project is accepted.

(b)   The names of those who will die have been deposited by a computer in a sealed box. Had the box been opened, the project would have been rejected at once. But it has not, so the project is approved.

(c)   The names are known to the government, but the people have not been told, so they can still be compensated cheaply for the extra risk.

(To put flesh on these first three examples, suppose the proposal is to close down the only treatment centre for a rare disease. The disease is fatal if not treated. Diagnosis is only possible by tests in a government laboratory, and some results are awaited.)

(d)   For another example, imagine two alternative projects that have to be compared. One will cause the death of a single person, and we know who it will be. The other will cause the death of a thousand people, but it is not known which thousand. According to the proposed method, the second project is better. Yet this kills a thousand people instead of one.

(e)   There may be a very small degree of probability that people do not distinguish from no chance at all, so they will accept that chance of being killed without requiring any compensation. Suppose the probability is one in ten million. Then a country with a population of fifty million could kill five people at random, assessing their deaths at no cost at all.

These examples help us to see how Mishan has gone wrong. In (d), for instance, the fact is that a thousand particular people are going to die. It is mere ignorance that they do not know who they are. In (b) the ignorance is plainly removable; it is being unfairly used by the government. The unfairness is especially clear in (c). Generally with future events we think that some, if not all, of our ignorance about them could be removed by looking more closely at the present. If it was wrong to use ignorance as it was used in (b), it is also wrong to use ignorance that could be removed in other ways, for instance by further research. But going further, it can hardly be relevant whether the ignorance is at present removable or not. In (a) we need only wait a day. In every case, it is undeniable that particular people who are alive now will die, and there is no adequate compensation for that. The government, if it follows Mishan's suggestion, really seems to be playing a trick on people's ignorance. Provided it can get in and make the decisions soon enough, before there is much information about who will die, it can get away with causing many more deaths than if it waited. Each project that causes deaths and that is nevertheless accepted is accepted in the knowledge that, were it re-evaluated later, it would be rejected as infinitely wrong. In view of these examples, it does not seem correct to distinguish in value between the deaths of a known and of an unknown person.

To put the argument more directly: if the justification for accepting a project by cost–benefit analysis is that compensation can be arranged so that nobody is harmed, then the justification cannot possibly apply when, after the project has been carried out and the utmost has been done by way of compensation, somebody palpably has been harmed, namely the person who has died.[3]

Mishan says:

A word on the deficiencies of information available to each person concerning the degree of risk involved. These deficiencies necessarily contribute to the discrepancies experienced by people between anticipations and realized satisfactions. For all that, in determining whether a potential Pareto improvement has been met, economists are generally agreed – as a canon of faith, as a political tenet, or as an act of expediency – to accept the dictum that each person knows his own interest best. If, therefore, the economist is told that person A is indifferent between not assuming a particular risk and assuming it along with a sum of money, V, then on the Pareto principle the sum V has to be accepted as the relevant cost of his being exposed to that risk. It may well be the case that, owing either to deficient information, or congenital optimism, person A consistently overestimates his chance of survival. But once the dictum is accepted, as indeed it is in economists' appraisals of allocative efficiency, cost–benefit analysis has to accept V as the only relevant magnitude – this being the sum chosen by A in awareness of his relative ignorance.[4]

This passage is remarkable in many ways. I want only to note, though, that the issue is not whether people know accurately the probability of dying, but whether they know if they are going to die. To know a probability is only a certain sort of ignorance. If people know only the probability of their dying, then the compensation they demand is chosen out of ignorance. We are asked by Mishan to accept the dictum that each person knows his own interest best. We may know our own interest better than other people, but since we do not know the future, we necessarily do not know our own interest accurately. There are some people who will die as a result of the project. Their interest is to refuse every offer of compensation, but they do not know this.

It is often said in defence of proffered techniques for evaluating projects that, although deficient, no better method is available. Something like that seems to be argued in this passage by Mishan: people's decisions are not perfect because of ignorance, but nothing better can be done. No doubt the argument has its applications, but here it is factually in error. It is not true that nothing better can be done. The government can estimate the monetary value of the deaths much more accurately and much more easily than it can be estimated by asking people what compensation they require for the extra risk. Consider any project in which an unknown person will die. Because whoever it is does not know it will be him – because of his ignorance – he is prepared to accept a ridiculously low compensation for letting the project go forward. The government does not know who will be killed either, but it knows it will be someone, and it knows that, whoever it is, no finite amount of compensation would be adequate for him. Therefore, if the cost of the project is to be evaluated as the compensation required by the losers, it must be infinite. It is only the ignorance of the person destined to die that prevents his demanding an infinite compensation. It may be true that sometimes we are forced to make decisions based on imperfect knowledge, if nothing better can be done. But this is one case where something better can be done. The problem caused by imperfect knowledge can easily be eliminated. If there is to be a death, we know at once that the cost, defined as the compensation required for the loss, is infinite. Any other conclusion is a deliberate and unfair use of people's ignorance.

That concludes my main argument. However, I started with the paradox that if life has an infinite monetary value then the false conclusion seems to be entailed that any project that causes death has to be rejected. I have now blocked the most familiar path around the paradox, so it seems appropriate to say something about how it may be resolved in other ways. As a matter of fact there is really no serious difficulty to resolve. What I have to say will seem commonplace and obvious to most people, though some may like to be reminded of it.

If, for some project, the value of the benefits exceeds the value of the costs, then compensation can be fixed up so that nobody loses. So, provided the compensation is paid, the project is a good thing. If, on the other hand, the value of the costs exceeds the value of the benefits, then there is no way of arranging compensation so that nobody is harmed. This, unsurprisingly, is the case for all projects that kill somebody, be he known or unknown. But there is not the least reason to suppose that such projects are necessarily wrong. A project that damages some people's interests while promoting others' could well be, on balance, an improvement. The Pareto criterion simply does not make a judgement in such a case. Some people seem to have believed that, if a project is good, then necessarily it would be possible to arrange compensation so as to make nobody a loser. But there is, so far as I can tell, no warrant for this belief.

There is, then, really no paradox at all. For a project that causes a death, the costs will exceed the benefits, if the calculations are done in money. But that is no reason to reject it. A compensation test can establish that a project should be done (provided the compensation is paid), but not that it should not be done. This means that such a test can never be used to evaluate any project that causes death.

For an analogy, imagine trying to perform a compensation test with roses as the medium instead of money. People cannot be compensated with roses for any major loss. Therefore, according to this method, rather a lot of projects would have an infinite cost. Nevertheless many of them could still be improvements (as we might be able to find out by recalculating their values in terms of money). The point is that roses are an inadequate measure for big costs and benefits. Money is a more powerful measuring instrument, but even the measuring rod of money is not long enough to encompass life and death. I hope this analogy will serve as a reminder that I have made no fancy claim that the value of life is infinite, but simply pointed out a difficulty in measuring it in monetary terms. Let us suppose that no finite number of roses could compensate a person for enduring a day of rain; no one would deduce that a day's fine weather is infinitely valuable.

12 Structured and unstructured valuation

12.1 Introduction and an example

Economists can value things for cost–benefit analysis in two different ways: they can adopt either a *structured* or an *unstructured* approach. In this chapter I shall first explain the difference. Then I shall examine the relative merits of each. One conclusion I shall draw is that we need to distinguish two different aims that cost–benefit analysis could pursue: it could aim to discover what ought to be done, or alternatively it could aim to discover what would be the best thing to do. These are not necessarily the same. I shall argue in favour of the latter. I shall support the structured approach to valuation, because it turns out to be appropriate for this latter aim.

As an example, I shall concentrate on valuing human life. To value life, some economists adopt a structured approach and others an unstructured approach, so this application illustrates the distinction nicely. A classic cost–benefit problem involving life and death is the question of how much it is worth spending on roads to make them safer. If more money is spent on safety, the benefit will be that some people who would have died on the roads will be saved. But if this money is not spent on safety, it will be available for other uses, which will benefit people in other ways. The problem of road safety is a matter of balancing one sort of benefit against the other.

A very schematic version of the problem is illustrated in figure 12.1. The figure is divided into two halves. The left half (A) represents the option of spending on safety; the right half (B) the option of not spending on safety. I assume the society at present contains only two people. If money is spent on safety, I assume both of them will survive to old age. But if the money is not spent, one of the people will soon be killed on the roads. One person will certainly die, but it is not known which of the two it will be. The uncertainty is represented in figure 12.1 by two 'states of nature'. Nature may be such that, if money is not spent on safety, the first person will die, or it may be such that, if the money is not spent, the second person will die. On the other hand, if the money is spent, the state of nature makes no difference.

From *Analyse & Kritik*, 16 (1994), pp. 121–32.

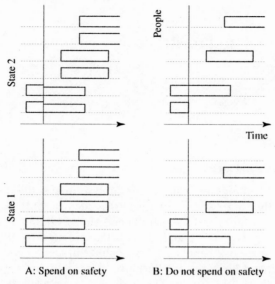

A: Spend on safety   B: Do not spend on safety

Figure 12.1

The figure shows the results of both options in both states, and it shows that the results of spending on safety are the same in both states.

The results are represented by graphs. Each graph has time on its horizontal axis, and a vertical bar marks the present. Each dotted line represents a person, and standing on each is a little graphlet that shows the person's level of wellbeing at all times in her life. A person's graphlet starts when she is born and continues till she dies. Each graph, then, shows a distribution of wellbeing across people and across time. To keep the figure simple, I have assumed that people's wellbeing generally stays constant, so the graphs are generally horizontal straight lines. The presently living people are the bottom two in each graph; they were born before the present. The graphs show that, if money is spent on safety, both the existing people will continue to live, but they will suffer a reduction in their wellbeing. This is because the money will not be available for other beneficial purposes. If the money is not spent on safety, one person's life is shown ending immediately, but the survivor will have a better life than she would have had if the money had been spent on safety.

Besides the two people alive now, the figure shows their children and grandchildren. I intend it to represent something that is typical of young people: if a young person's life is saved, typically she will later have children and indeed a whole line of descendants, who would never have existed had she died. If money is spent on safety, the figure shows two new people in each succeeding generation. But if the money is not spent, one of the presently living people dies before having children, so the figure shows only one new person in each generation. (Evidently, these people reproduce by parthenogenesis.)

That is a schematic illustration of the problem facing a cost–benefit analyst. Practical problems are much more complicated, of course, and often there will be more than just two options available. The analysis proceeds by setting a value on each of the options, and it favours the one that turns out to be the most valuable. As I say, we can distinguish structured and unstructured approaches to making the valuation. I shall start by explaining the unstructured one.

12.2   The unstructured approach

The unstructured approach sets out from the preferences of the various people who are alive at the time of decision making. Each of these people will have preferences about the options that are available, and these are the basic data for the unstructured approach. They are the people's preferences about the options taken as a whole: for instance, their preferences between spending on safety or not spending on safety. I call this the unstructured approach because the economist making the evaluation does not herself take any account of the internal structure of the options. For instance, she takes no account of the way each option distributes wellbeing across time or across states of nature.

At least, she takes no direct account of these things. She does take account of people's preferences between the options, and in forming their preferences the people will presumably take account of the options' internal structure. In this way the structure enters the economist's evaluation indirectly. If an option has uncertain results, then each person's preferences will presumably take account of the uncertainty. In life-and-death cases, each option presents each person with a life of some quality and length, so in these cases the people's preferences will presumably reflect the values they attach to different sorts of lives. Because of uncertainty, in practice each option will present each person with not just one life but a portfolio of possible lives: a different one in each state of nature. The people's preferences should reflect their assessments of these portfolios. For example, in figure 12.1 each person faces two alternatives: on the one hand living a moderately good life for sure, and on the other a chance of dying immediately and a chance of living a very good life. Each person's preferences between the two options should reflect her assessment of the quality of the lives she might lead, and of the uncertainty that faces her.

Because the unstructured approach ignores the structure of the options, it assumes no particular theory about the form of people's preferences. It does not assume they will conform to expected utility theory, for instance. Expected utility theory requires a person's preference to conform to some particular formal conditions when the person is faced with uncertainty, but the unstructured approach does not assume those conditions. Nor does it impose any theory about how a person values her future life: it assumes nothing about how she takes account of its prospective length and quality.

People's preferences amongst the options are the basic data of the unstructured approach, but this approach needs more than the basic data to arrive at an overall valuation for the purposes of cost–benefit analysis. For one thing, it needs a way of aggregating people's preferences together, or weighing them against each other. It needs to do some 'interpersonal weighing', I shall say. The subject of this chapter is the basic data, not the interpersonal weighing, but I need to say something about the interpersonal weighing all the same. Particular views about it are often implicit in the way the basic data are collected in practice. This can obscure the distinction between unstructured and structured approaches, so I need to explain it.

The basic data are the people's preferences. Each person's preferences can be represented by a utility function. A utility function is a function that assigns a number called a 'utility' to each of the options in such a way that one option gets a higher number than another if and only if it is preferred. It represents the order of preferences by means of utilities. The way cost–benefit analysts aggregate different people's preferences together is to add up utilities across people. (This is not generally how they themselves describe what they do, but it is so.) Each person's utility function assigns a utility to each option. Adding these utilities across people gives a total utility to each option, and cost–benefit analysis favours the option that has the highest total.

Because a utility function has to represent only the order of a person's preferences, many different utility functions will represent the same preferences. This means that, before they aggregate preferences by adding utilities, cost–benefit analysts have a choice of which utility function to pick for each person. Naturally, they pick the one they think best serves the purpose of aggregation or interpersonal weighing. I shall give two examples.

One example is the use of 'healthy-year equivalents', which has recently been gaining ground in health economics.[1] For each of the options we are interested in, we can define its healthy-years equivalent (or 'hye') as the number of years of healthy life that the person finds indifferent to the option. The option, remember, may involve some uncertainty: it is a portfolio of various possible patterns of life. We can assume that the person prefers a longer healthy life to a shorter one. So one option will have a greater hye than another if and only if it is preferred. It follows that hyes are utilities. More exactly, the function that assigns to each option its hye is a utility function; it is one of the many utility functions that represent the preferences. Hyes are used by health economists to compare alternative treatments; a treatment that produces more hyes in total is supposed to be better than one that produces fewer. So hyes are added across people. Evidently, these economists believe hyes are appropriate utilities for the purpose of interpersonal weighing. The effect is to count a healthy year to one person as equally as valuable as a healthy year to another. I am not proposing to assess the merits of this idea; I am only offering it as an example of the unstructured approach. It is unstructured because hyes represent each person's preferences about the options as a whole, incorporating uncertainty and all their other features.

A second example is the use of willingness to pay. Pick one of the options and call it 'the status quo'. Then for each option we can define a person's 'willingness to pay' for the option relative to the status quo as the amount of money the person would be willing to pay to have the option instead of the status quo. Let me put this more precisely. If the option came about, then in each state of nature the person would have some particular amount of money. Imagine this option came about, but as well as that imagine the person had a fixed sum of money taken away from her in every state of nature, deducted from what she would otherwise have had. The amount of deducted money that would make her indifferent to the status quo is her willingness to pay for the option. Her willingness to pay for the status quo is zero, and her willingness to pay for some options may be negative.

Normally a person would be willing to pay more to have one option than another if and only if she prefers the former to the latter. So the function that assigns to each option her willingness to pay for it is a utility function for her. It gives a scale of utility in terms of money. It is only one such scale; there is a whole range of 'money-metric utilities', as they are called. First, there is a whole range of willingness-to-pay scales of utility, because each choice of a particular option to serve as the status quo will yield a different scale. And there are other money-metric utilities besides those. One, known as the 'equivalent variation' of the option, is minus the amount of money the person would be willing to pay to have the status quo rather than the option.

Many cost–benefit analysts evaluate an option by adding together different people's willingnesses to pay for the option. They must think that willingness to pay is an appropriate basis for interpersonal weighing. In effect, they must think a pound to one person is as valuable as a pound to anyone else. Willingness to pay is a second example of an unstructured approach to valuation.

12.3   The structured approach

That is the unstructured approach, then. By the structured approach, I mean an approach where the economist takes account of the structure of the options facing the people, and imposes some theory about how the value of an option depends on its structure. This is a vague description so far, and a matter of degree: there are highly structured approaches and less structured approaches.

In practice, every cost–benefit analysis is structured to some degree. Imagine a completely unstructured cost–benefit analysis of, say, a new road. Let it use, say, willingness to pay as the basis for interpersonal weighing, and let us take the option of not building the road as the status quo. To do an unstructured analysis, we would find out from each person what she is willing to pay to have the road, leaving it to her to put together all the different costs and benefits to her of having it. She would have to make her own assessment of the damage the road will do to the environment, of how often she is likely to use the road, of how much time it will save her when she does use it, of how likely she is to get killed while using it, and so on. All of these things will determine her preferences, and how much she is willing to pay to have the road. Few people will make a good job of that sort of assessment, and no cost–benefit analyst in practice uses such raw preferences about the options. Instead she first produces a breakdown of the various benefits and harms that will result from the road. She calculates the saving in time, the change in people's risk of accident, the effects on the environment, and so on. Then she elicits values for the various different components. In all of this, the cost–benefit analyst makes theoretical assumptions. For instance, she makes assumptions about what is valuable about a new road; she assumes its value is to save time and improve safety, say, rather than to let people enjoy the sound their tyres make on the road surface. These are no doubt innocuous assumptions, but still they impose some sort of structure.

But the structured approaches I am thinking of impose more structure than that. What sort of structure do I mean, and what sort of theory should it be based on? There are many different possibilities, depending on precisely what we take to be the objective of our valuation, and I shall come to that later. Clearly, too, whatever theory we impose will need justification. But here are some examples of structures we might impose. First, we could impose some theory of rationality on people's preferences. Doing so would imply that we wished to base our valuation on what people's preferences would be if they were rational, rather than on people's actual preferences. For instance, we could impose expected utility theory, which many people take to be an account of rationality for preferences. Here is how this would work. We would evaluate an uncertain option, from the point of view of each person, by first evaluating the various outcomes that would result from it in the various states of nature, and then calculating their expectation, perhaps adjusted for the degree of riskiness. This structured evaluation would start from the value of outcomes. By contrast, an unstructured evaluation would be based on the people's preferences about the options themselves taken as a whole, incorporating whatever uncertainty is implied.

Another example is that we could impose some sort of structure across time. For instance, we could evaluate each person's life as an aggregate of how good her life is at each time. Perhaps we might assume it is the simple total of the good contained in her life, or perhaps a total discounted for time, or perhaps some other sort of aggregate. Another example: we might impose expected utility theory at the level of our own evaluations. We might insist that the value we attach to an uncertain prospect should be the expectation of the value we assign to the outcomes that will result from it.

Like the unstructured approach, the structured approach will usually be based ultimately on people's preferences. But they will be preferences about different things. Instead of preferences about options treated as a whole, they will be preferences about parts or aspects of options. For instance, a structured cost–benefit analysis of a road will rely on people's preferences about such things as saving time and the loss of a natural landmark, instead of their preferences about the existence of the road together with everything that goes with it. Another example: if we adopt expected utility theory, we might rely on people's preferences about what happens in each of the possible outcomes of an uncertain prospect, rather than their preferences about the prospect as a whole.

A good example of a structured approach in practice in economics is the use of quality-adjusted life years (qalys) to evaluate treatments in medicine. The value of a life is calculated as its length in years, adjusted for the quality of those years: a year in a wheelchair, say, or blind, is counted for less than a year in good health. Qalys impose a structure across time.

Qalys are commonly used by health economists, whereas transport economists generally adopt a less structured approach. To bring out the difference, let us compare how a typical transport economist and a typical health economist would approach the example of road safety illustrated in figure 12.1. Both would ignore the people in future generations who are not yet alive; I shall mention them later, but for the time being I shall ignore them too. The transport economist would start by finding out which of the two options the people prefer as individuals, without worrying about why they prefer them. We cannot tell their preferences from the figure, so we do not know what conclusion the transport economist will come to in this case. The health economist would look at the qalys that will result from either option for the two people, proceeding as follows. She will look at each state of nature separately. Since the states are symmetrical, her results will be the same for both. In each state, she will look to see which option delivers more qalys in total to the two people. As I happen to have drawn the figure, the safety option wins easily in both states. Next the health economist will aggregate across states of nature. In this case that is easy, because safety is better in both states. So the health economist will be in favour of spending money on safety.

People's preferences are implicitly embedded in the health economist's calculations, but they are overlaid by a fair amount of theory. Preferences enter through the scale of wellbeing or quality of life that the health economist will use. I have been taking this scale for granted, but now is the moment to say that is generally derived from people's preferences about different qualities of life. Evidently, the transport economist's method relies on preferences in a more raw form.

This example illustrates a conspicuous division between the way human life is typically valued in two areas of economics: transport and health. For some reason, the traditions are different in the two areas. The main difference is that health economists generally use a structured approach and transport economists an unstructured one. (But remember I have mentioned already a move towards an unstructured approach within health economics, using healthy-years equivalents.) There are other differences too, of course, but I think they are relatively minor. One difference often mentioned is that qalys are not intended for cost–benefit analysis of treatments, only for 'cost-effectiveness analysis'. Qalys are intended to serve as a measure of the benefit that results from a treatment, but not as a measure that is comparable with the cost. When we evaluate various alternative treatments, we can work out the benefit of each in terms of qalys. We can also work out the cost of each in terms of money. We can then calculate the qalys each produces per unit cost. This will tell us the best way of distributing our resources across different treatments: we should concentrate on those that produce the most qalys per unit cost. That is the purpose of cost-effectiveness analysis. It will not tell us whether any particular treatment is worth its cost. That would require comparing the benefit in terms of qalys with the cost in terms of money. It would require us to decide the money-value of a qaly, which health economists generally decline to do.

Health economists typically see their job as finding the right way to distribute whatever resources are given over to health, rather than judging what total resources should be given over to health. On the other hand, transport economists are more ambitious. Not only do they tell us how the resources that are to be devoted to transport should be divided between different uses, they also tell us whether each particular use is worthwhile on its own. That is the idea of cost–benefit analysis. I do not know why the two departments of economics have this different culture. In any case, the difference is small. To start doing cost–benefit analysis, health economists have only to fix a money value on a qaly. They could do this by willingness to pay or some other means. Indeed, theoretically the difference is non-existent. Theoretically, a cost is nothing more than a diminution in some people's quality of life – the quality of taxpayers' lives or the lives of whoever pays. My example of road safety in figure 12.1 shows that: the cost of safety shows up as a diminution of the people's wellbeing. In theory, then, money costs should show up in a qaly calculation, just like changes in people's state of health. They do not show up in practice because health economists deal with quality of life only in terms of health. But there is no reason in theory why they should accept that limitation.

12.4 Arguments for the two approaches

Which is the better approach to valuation: the structured or the unstructured? I shall start by mentioning some disadvantages of the unstructured approach, and mention an advantage of it later.

One disadvantage is the well-known incoherence of people's preferences in the face of uncertainty and, indeed, even not in the face of uncertainty. People's preferences suffer from framing effects, embedding effects, preference reversal, and all the other freaky effects that psychologists have discovered, to an extent that they cannot possibly be considered rational. All this is so well known by now that I do not need to spell it out.[2] I will mention one example I came across recently. In a recent survey,[3] M. W. Jones-Lee, G. Loomes, and P. R. Philips asked a sample of people how much they would be willing to pay to reduce their risk of suffering an accident on the roads that would lead to a minor permanent disability. The subjects were asked how much they would pay to reduce the risk from 24/100,000 to 20/100,000, and also how much they would pay to reduce it from 24/100,000 to 12/100,000. Thirty-seven per cent of them said they were willing to pay only the same for the larger reduction in risk as for the smaller one, and 9.4 per cent said they were willing to pay less for the larger reduction. No plausible account of rationality can be reconciled with these preferences. Discoveries like these led these three authors to adopt a structured approach to evaluating risks of injuries. They did not base their valuation directly on people's willingness to pay for changes in risk, but on a procedure that depended on expected utility theory. Evidently they did not wish to base their valuations on patently irrational preferences. This seems a reasonable attitude for them to take; I shall offer an argument for it later.

The irrationality of our preferences is a practical disadvantage of the unstructured approach. There is a more theoretical disadvantage too. I can illustrate it with the road safety example once again, though to use that example I shall have to make a supposition that may seem far-fetched. So far, I have said nothing about the probabilities of the two states of nature. Let us suppose the two people assign them different probabilities. Suppose each is confident in her own driving ability; each knows someone will be killed if there is no spending on safety, but each believes it is more likely to be the other person. Let us suppose each forms her preferences on the basis of her own expected wellbeing, calculated according to her own probabilities. Provided each is optimistic enough about her own chances of survival, each will prefer the unsafe option. An unstructured approach, then, based on people's preferences, will have to come down in favour of this option. But this is clearly the less good one. The two existing people get less wellbeing in total, and the wellbeing is unequally distributed between them. The future people certainly do not count against the unsafe option. There are fewer of them in that option, and we have perhaps grown accustomed to thinking it is a good idea to have fewer people. But that is because we fear that having too many people will reduce the general standard of life. In this example that is not so. Therefore, we certainly have no reason to be against the existence of those people, even if we are not in favour of it either. There are really no grounds for concluding that the unsafe option is the better. Yet this is the one recommended by the unstructured approach. I have already said an evaluation that used qalys would reach the opposite conclusion. This is because it would override the differing probability judgements of the two people. It is these differing judgements that cause the problem, and most structured valuations would set them aside. Here is another reason for preferring a structured approach.

But the same example reveals simultaneously an advantage of the unstructured approach. Although it is clear that the safe option is better, there is also one thing to be said for the risky option: both people prefer it. The present population is unanimously in favour of it. So a democrat must surely be in favour of the risky option. If the structured approach is in favour of the safe option, it is undemocratic. Since the unstructured approach works straight from people's preferences, it has democracy on its side.

12.5   What is best and what ought to come about

The conflicting arguments for and against the unstructured approach show that we need to make a distinction that is often missed by welfare economists. When we are faced with a choice of options, there is the question of which is best and there is the question of which ought to come about, and the answers to these questions need not be the same. Any democrat must recognize that. When there is a choice, you may believe that one of the options on offer is the best. But on the other hand, you may believe a different option is supported by most people. If so, and if you are a democrat, you may therefore believe this second option is the one that should come about. So the option you believe should come about is not the one you believe is best. That may also be the situation of a democrat faced by the example of safety on the roads. Because both people prefer the risky option, the democrat may believe the risky option should come about. Nevertheless, for the good reasons I gave, she ought to believe the safe option is the best.[4]

Since there is sometimes a difference between what should come about and what is best, which should cost–benefit analysis aim at? I think it should aim at what is best. Democracy is a matter of having a satisfactory democratic process. If the process works as it should, it will ensure that what comes about is democratic. It is the process that should bring about what should be brought about. Essential input into the democratic process, without which it will not work properly, are discussion and judgement about what is best. People who participate in the democratic process at all levels make their decisions and place their votes partly on the basis of what they believe is for the best. If they are to be well informed, they need to be informed by difficult and careful analysis of the relative goodness of the choices. This is just what good cost–benefit analysis should provide.

Is there any case on the other side, for aiming cost–benefit analysis at what should come about? The case would have to be that cost–benefit analysis is itself part of the democratic process. Democracy is a mechanism whereby the actions of individual people together determine what happens. When economists do their cost–benefit calculations, they would have to see themselves as part of this mechanism. This seems quite implausible to me; it is the economists and not the public who produce the result of the analysis. At best, economists might work out what conclusion a truly democratic process would arrive at if it was allowed to operate; they cannot see their work as a truly democratic process in its own right. So at best they could short-circuit democracy. But if they try to do this, they will subvert democracy. Suppose a decision is made on the basis of an analysis, which concludes that democracy would have led to this decision had it been allowed to operate. This is not a democratic decision. If welfare economists want to support democracy, they should concentrate on providing information about the relative goodness of the alternatives available, and leave the democratic institutions to maintain democracy.

The appeal of unstructured valuations can only be to democracy. They are based on raw preferences unfiltered by theory imposed from outside. People's raw preferences amongst options are unlikely to be good indicators of what is best. They will certainly not be if they are irrational. That is why I said in section 12.4 that the well-established irrationality of people's preferences gives good grounds for adopting the structured approach. But even if a person's preferences were rational, they might not be good indicators of what is best, for several reasons. One is disagreement about probabilities. I showed why in section 12.4. In the example of figure 12.1, I showed that both people might prefer the risky option because of their differing judgements of probability, and yet the safe option is the better. There may be no irrationality of lack of information embedded in the preferences; the people might have reached their different judgements by setting out from different, optimistic prior probabilities. So if cost–benefit analysis aims at what is best, as I think it should, the structured approach is the right one.

What makes it right is that it can be aimed at what is best. This gives us some guidance about the sort of structure a cost–benefit analyst should impose: it should be structure that aims at what is best. The analyst needs a theory of good, therefore. She needs, for instance, a theory about what is the best action to take in the face of uncertainty. She needs a theory about what makes a life good, a theory about how the wellbeing that comes in a life should be aggregated together to determine the overall goodness of a life. She needs a theory about how the length of a life contributes to determining the goodness of that life, and so on.

12.6   Valuing existence

One final note. In the example of figure 12.1, there are people who exist in one of the options being compared but not in the other. How are these people to be taken into account in a cost–benefit analysis? So far I have simply ignored them, but I want to mention them now.

It is within the spirit of the unstructured approach to count only the preferences of people who exist at present. These people are the only ones who have a vote in a democracy; people who do not yet exist do not vote. Stephen Marglin expresses the idea: 'I want the government's social welfare function to reflect only the preferences of present individuals. Whatever else democratic theory may or may not imply, I consider it axiomatic that a democratic government reflects only the preferences of the individuals who are presently members of the body politic.'[5] Marglin gives no direct weight to the wellbeing of people who do not yet exist. Their interests may be represented indirectly in the preferences of existing people, if the existing people happen to care about them. Since the special appeal of the unstructured approach is its effort to satisfy democracy, it is natural for it not to count future people.

There is a second reason why those who adopt the unstructured approach generally do not count future people.[6] Commonly, these people use willingness to pay as their measure of people's preferences. People not yet born have no purchasing power and consequently no willingness to pay for anything, so naturally they do not get counted. But this is a weak reason for not counting them. Conceivably, willingness to pay might be a useful money measure of utility for weighing up benefits to one person against another. But the arguments for willingness to pay – whatever they may be – do not say anything about which people should be counted in the first place. Should we count people not yet alive? That must be a separate question. The fact that we have settled on a particular measure for comparisons cannot preempt that question.

I have argued in favour of the structured approach because it can be directed at what is best. If we are concerned with what is best, people not yet born should certainly be counted. Compare two options that are equally good for everyone now alive, and for everyone who will ever live, bar one. Suppose one option is better than the other for one person who is not yet born but who certainly will be born whichever option is chosen. Then the one that is better for this person is plainly better. Plainly, this person who is not yet born should be counted.

If a person is definitely going to exist, there is no doubt we should count her wellbeing in evaluating the options. But in figure 12.1 the very existence of particular people is in question; the different options have different populations. What we have to evaluate is not making a future person better or worse off, but bringing a future person into existence. This is a tremendously difficult problem that needs to be faced before cost–benefit analysis of life-and-death problems can be done properly. But I am not going to try and deal with it in this chapter.

13   Qalys

13.1   Introduction

In medicine, decisions have to be made between alternative courses of action: how to treat a particular patient, say, or how to allocate resources nationally between different specialities. Qalys (quality-adjusted life years) are intended to help in this sort of decision making.

Specifically, they are intended to measure the *benefit* – or the *good,* as I shall say – that will result from each of the alternatives. The idea is that the benefit of a course of action is the extra years of life it gives people, adjusted for quality; better years count more than worse ones. In medical decisions, benefit is obviously an important consideration, but it is often not the only one. Another is fairness: when treatment is to be given to some patients and denied to others, to treat those whose treatment would do the most good is not necessarily the fairest thing to do. Other things being equal, for instance, treating a younger person is likely to do more good in total than treating an older one, because the younger has longer to enjoy the benefits. But if resources are concentrated on the young for this reason, that may be unfair to the old. So benefit and fairness may conflict.

Qalys are concerned only with benefit. Consequently, they cannot entirely determine which decision is the right one. The friends of qalys have not always acknowledged this limitation,[1] and this has exposed qalys unnecessarily to attacks from their enemies. The main objection raised against them is that their use is unfair.[2] Qalys certainly do not take account of fairness; they cannot be expected to. Fairness must be considered separately.[3] Nevertheless, benefit is plainly important, so qalys have an important role open to them. This chapter examines how well they can fill it. How well does the total of qalys produced by an action measure its benefit?

I shall not consider how to accommodate uncertainty in a valuation. I

From *Journal of Public Economics*, 50 (1993), pp. 149–67. Reprinted by permission of Elsevier Press, © 1993. I enjoyed several very helpful conversations with Michael Lockwood on the subject of this chapter. I also received useful comments from Roger Crisp. A part of my work on this chapter was supported by ESRC grant number R000233334.

think an action whose results are uncertain should be valued by first fixing a value on each of its possible results, and then following the recommendations of expected utility theory. But when it comes to 'social' valuations, involving the good of more than one person, expected utility theory is controversial. In particular, it prevents one from giving value to equality in the distribution of risk between people, and on the face of it that seems unreasonable.[4] But the issues about risk are deep and complex, and I have tried to deal with them elsewhere.[5] So here I shall concentrate on valuing outcomes without uncertainty. I take this to be a necessary first step towards valuing risky actions. Expected utility theory will come into my analysis nevertheless, because lotteries are commonly thought to be a useful device for *measuring* qalys.

My conclusion will be cautiously favourable towards qalys. I shall set qalys within a well-accepted theoretical context. I shall show that their use relies on several major assumptions, some of which are at best very broad approximations, but perhaps these assumptions are acceptable as a first approach to the problem. However, qalys do run up against one large difficulty, described in section 13.8, which at present I can see no way around.

13.2   Individual preferences

Start with the simplest case. Take a choice that affects only one person: a choice between alternative treatments for a single patient. Suppose no one else is affected by the results – no relative or dependant or anyone else. This implies that, if the treatments differ in cost, the difference will be paid by the patient. The benefit of each treatment is then simply a matter of how good it is for the one person, taking into account the cost to her.

Economists generally assume that if a person prefers one of two alternatives to the other, then that one is better for her. I call this 'the preference-satisfaction theory of good'. I shall raise a question about it later. But for the time being let us take it for granted, and see how far it can carry us. It tells us that, if we know our subject's preferences, we know what is better for her. If, say, the question is whether it is better for her to be given a treatment that relieves her pain but shortens her life, we need to know only whether she prefers a longer life with pain or a shorter life without.

If we knew the subject's preferences between alternative treatments, therefore, there would be no need to calculate qalys. But often we do not know these preferences. The subject may be too ill to express them. She may be too young to have any. Or we may be making a decision at a general level, so we do not know which particular people will be affected; we might, for instance, be wondering which sort of treatment for a disease to concentrate resources on. In these cases, we will have to make a judgement about which of the alternatives the person prefers or would prefer. Qalys could be useful here. So this gives us a reason for analysing the structure of preferences, and its connection with qalys. The analysis will also be useful when we come to consider choices that affect the good of more than one person. The most thorough analysis I know is in 'Utility functions for life years and health status' by Joseph Pliskin, Donald Shepard, and Milton Weinstein. But I do not find it perfectly satisfactory, for reasons given in the appendix to this chapter. So my own simple analysis follows in section 13.3.

13.3   Quality adjustment factors in the representation of preferences

Suppose our subject is faced with a range of alternative lives. In each she lives for a number y of years beyond those she has already lived. (The number y varies between the alternatives.) In the first of these years the quality of her life is q_1, in the second q_2, and so on. Each life can be described by a vector of variable length $(q_1, q_2, \ldots q_y)$. By a 'quality of life' I mean something like: confined to a wheelchair and in slight pain. A description like this could be filled out to any degree of detail. But since we are concerned with health, I mean particularly a description of the person's state of health. Imagine that other aspects of the quality of her life, such as her wealth, are held constant throughout this exercise.

Suppose our subject has preferences amongst these alternatives. I shall call her a *discounted-qaly maximizer* if and only if her preferences can be represented by a utility function of the form

$$V(q_1, q_2, \ldots q_y) = v(q_1) + r_2 v(q_2) + \ldots + r_y v(q_y). \tag{1}$$

The constants $r_2, r_3, \ldots$ are her discount factors, and the subutility function v gives her quality adjustment factors $v(q)$ for each quality q. (The rs may all be one; my term 'discounted-qaly maximizer' includes people who discount at a zero rate.) Throughout this chapter, I shall assume that people are discounted-qaly maximizers. This is a big assumption: one of those I suggested may be acceptable as a first approach to the problem. The appendix to this chapter derives it from more primitive conditions. This derivation does not justify the assumption, but it does show what it depends on. The most dubious condition is that, in the person's preferences, qualities of life at different times are *strongly separable*. This is actually a necessary condition if the person is to be a discounted-qaly maximizer; a utility function has an additively separable form, as (1) has, if and only if the preferences are strongly separable.[6] Strong separability means that a person's preferences about the qualities of her life in any particular group of years are independent of the qualities of her life in other years.

For a discounted-qaly maximizer, representing her preferences in the form (1) determines both V and v uniquely up to positive multiples. (They are 'ratio scales', that is to say.) The additively separable form of (1) determines V and v uniquely up to increasing linear transformations.[7] And the zero on the scale of adjustment factors is not arbitrary. It is assigned to the quality of life (if there is one) that the person would just as soon not live at all: that is, to the quality q^0 such that $(q_1, q_2, \ldots q_y, q^0)$ is indifferent to $(q_1, q_2, \ldots q_y)$ for all values of y and $q_1, q_2, \ldots q_y$.

It is traditional to assign a factor of one to healthy life: $v(h) = 1$ where h is good health. This is arbitrary and simply sets the scale of factors. This scale makes no difference till we come to decisions that involve the good of more than one person, in section 13.7.

If we knew the discount factors and the function v for a person, we should be able to predict her preferences, and this would give us a basis for assessing the benefits of different treatments. I shall concentrate on the quality adjustment factors given by v. How can they be determined? In principle, a utility function of the form (1) could be fitted econometrically to a person's preferences. But this would require more data than are generally available in practice.[8] So in practice more primitive methods are generally used.[9] In this section I shall mention two. Each requires a heroic assumption to make it work.

One possible heroic assumption is that the person does not discount her future qalys: all her discount factors r_i are one. Let us call a person a *qaly maximizer* if she does not discount. Suppose a qaly maximizer is indifferent between living some number t of years in good health and living ten years at some quality q. Then equation (1) tells us that $10v(q) = tv(h) = t$, if we adopt the convention that $v(h) = 1$. So $t/10$ gives us a measure of the quality adjustment factor $v(q)$. Here, then, is a method of estimating the adjustment factor $v(q)$: find out what value of t makes the person indifferent between t years of good health and ten years at quality q. Call this the 'time method'. Plainly it will give the right answer only if the person does not discount.

An alternative heroic assumption is that the person is *risk-neutral* about discounted qalys. To state this assumption properly, we must first suppose our subject is not only a discounted-qaly maximizer, but also conforms to expected utility theory. If she does, her preferences amongst gambles can be represented by the expected utility function

$$E(u(V(q_1, q_2, \ldots q_y))) = E(u(v(q_1) + r_2v(q_2) + \ldots + r_yv(q_y))), \qquad (2)$$

where E is the expectation operator and u is some increasing transformation of discounted qalys. The person is risk-neutral if and only if u is linear. In that case she is an *expected-discounted-qaly maximizer*: between gambles, she always prefers the one that offers a greater expectation of discounted qalys.

Suppose a person is indifferent between, on the one hand, living ten years of life at quality q and, on the other, a gamble offering a chance p of living ten years in good health and a chance $(1-p)$ of dying immediately. Then equation (2) tells us that

$$u(Rv(q)) = pu(Rv(h)) + (1-p)u(0) = pu(R) + (1-p)u(0), \tag{3}$$

where R is $(1 + r_2 + \ldots + r_{10})$. If the person is risk-neutral, so u is linear, it follows that $p = v(q)$. This gives us a second method for estimating the adjustment factor $v(q)$: find out what value of p makes the person indifferent in this choice. I call this the 'probability method'. It will give the right answer *only* if the person is risk-neutral about discounted qalys.

A simple example will illustrate the danger of error here. Amanda is a qaly maximizer – she does not discount. For her V in (1) is simply her total qalys. But suppose she is risk-averse about her total qalys. In choosing amongst gambles, she maximizes $E(u(V))$, where u is an increasing strictly concave transformation. For simplicity, let us concern ourselves only with lives whose quality is constant at q. For these lives, $V = yv(q)$. So Amanda maximizes $E(u(yv(q)))$. Let q' have an adjustment factor $v(q')$ of .5. Since Amanda does not discount, this means that Amanda is indifferent between ten years of life at q' and five years of healthy life (both lived for sure). But suppose she is indifferent between ten years at q' and a gamble giving a .71 chance of ten years in good health and .29 chance of death. (This will be so if u happens to be the square-root function.) The probability method would say the quality adjustment factor of q' is .71. But that would be wrong; the factor is .5. A quantity of qalys is obtained by multiplying a number of life years by a quality adjustment factor. But for Amanda, multiplying the number of her life years by .71, or in general by any factor obtained from the probability method, would not give the quantity of anything.

Writers on medical decision making seem attached to the probability method, at least in principle. (It is said to be difficult to put into practice.) Weinstein, for instance, says it has high 'theoretical merit'.[10] But this method will work only if people are risk-neutral about their discounted qalys, and on the face of it that seems an implausible assumption. It seems about as implausible as the assumption that people do not discount, which would make the time method valid. There is some empirical evidence that people are on average risk-neutral,[11] but it is too slight to place much trust in. I think we have little reason to trust the probability method.

13.4   A cardinal measure of good?

When a decision affects only one person, it matters only which alternatives are better or worse for the person, not how much better or worse. Only the *order* of good matters, not *amounts* of good. But we shall also need to think about decisions that affect several people. For that, we shall need to know about amounts of good for each person. (We shall also need to know how to weigh one person's good against another's, but I shall leave that question aside till section 13.7.) We shall need a *cardinal* scale of good. How can we find one? In particular, do a person's qalys measure her good cardinally? If one treatment produces more qalys for a given cost than another, it is often said to be better to direct resources towards the former rather than the latter, even though these treatments are for different diseases and different people.[12] But this conclusion – in which different people's qalys are added and compared to assess overall good – is valid only if each person's qalys measure her good cardinally. Is this a justifiable assumption? More generally, to allow for discounting, let us ask whether the discounted quantity of qalys, V in equation (1), measures good cardinally.

The term 'cardinal' can be confusing. A utility function is often called cardinal if it is defined uniquely up to increasing linear transformations. Any additively separable utility function has this property, so the function V in (1) is cardinal in this sense. But whether V constitutes a cardinal measure of the person's good is another matter. To say V is a cardinal measure of good means it is an increasing linear transform of good. Is it?

Conventional wisdom is that this question cannot be answered by examining the structure of people's preferences. The preference-satisfaction theory of good says that a person's preferences will tell us the order of her good, but nothing about the amount of her good: they tell us when one alternative is better for the person than another, but not how much better.

For instance, think again about Amanda, who does not discount her qalys. For her, V in equation (1) is simply a total of qalys. She is indifferent between ten years at quality q' and five years in good health, and the time method, which works for Amanda because she does not discount, tells us that her adjustment factor $v(q')$ is .5. Given that, it is tempting to assume that good health is twice as good for Amanda as q': that, say, ten years in good health are twice as good for her as ten years at q'. After all, ten years in good health give her ten qalys, and ten years at q' give her five. But nothing in the preferences licenses this assumption. We cannot even assume that ten years in good health are twice as good for Amanda as five years in good health. Even though Amanda does not discount, we are not entitled to assume her good is proportional to the number of years she lives. We are not entitled to assume ten qalys are twice as good for her as five.

Or take Basil, who is an expected-discounted-qaly maximizer: he is risk-neutral about qalys. Suppose Basil is indifferent between ten years at q'', and a gamble giving him equal chances of ten years in good health and dying immediately. Then the probability method, which works for Basil because he is risk-neutral, tells us that his adjustment factor $v(q'')$ is .5. Once again, we are not entitled to conclude from the preferences that ten years in good health are twice as good for Basil as ten years at q''.

All that is conventional wisdom. But some authors have taken a different view. They have thought that, although other preferences give no information about the amounts of a person's good, preferences about gambles do, at least for people who are rational. The basis of this idea is the supposition that, when faced with a choice of gambles, a rational person will always choose the alternative that has the greater expectation of good for her. Daniel Bernoulli took this view and John Harsanyi takes a similar one.[13] I call it 'Bernoulli's hypothesis'. Now apply it to Basil. Basil is indifferent between ten years at q'' and an equal gamble on either ten years in good health or death. According to Bernoulli's hypothesis, if Basil is rational, these two alternatives must give him the same expectation of good. Therefore, ten years at q'' must lie halfway on his scale of good between death and ten years in good health. If we take the goodness of death to be zero, then ten years in good health are twice as good for Basil as ten years at q''.

In general, if Bernoulli's hypothesis is correct, quality adjustment factors properly derived by the probability method would provide a cardinal measure of the person's good. This thought may help to explain why medical decision theorists are attracted to the probability method. If qalys are to determine whether one use of resources is better or worse than another, they must provide a cardinal scale of good. Bernoulli's hypothesis promises to derive a cardinal scale from people's preferences alone, and it seems to imply that the right scale is to be found by the probability method.

Now, it is actually a mistake to think that Bernoulli's hypothesis supports the probability method. Whether or not this method is valid depends only the form of a person's preferences, and Bernoulli's hypothesis has nothing to do with it. The probability method is valid if and only if the person is risk-neutral about discounted qalys. If she is not, the method does not correctly give a quality adjustment factor at all, let alone one that indicates good cardinally.

Nevertheless, Bernoulli's hypothesis can come into the argument a different way. In equation (2), the transform u of discounted qalys V is defined as that which the person maximizes the expectation of. According to Bernoulli's hypothesis, the person maximizes the expectation of her good. Therefore, according to the hypothesis, u will measure her good cardinally: it will be an increasing linear transform of her good. Bernoulli's hypothesis implies, then, that the right cardinal measure of good is not discounted qalys V, but the transform $u(V)$. Pliskin, Shepard, and Weinstein explicitly use this transform in their work.[14] These authors are concerned only with choosing between alternative treatments for a single patient, and do not make comparisons between people. This means they themselves are not committed to the view that the transform measures good cardinally. But other authors do use the transform in comparisons between people.[15] They thereby imply that it measures good cardinally.

However, Bernoulli's hypothesis is not very plausible, and qalys supply a good example of why not. Take Amanda once more, who maximizes

$$E(u(V(q))) = E(u(yv(q))).$$

Does u measure Amanda's good cardinally? Amanda is indifferent between ten years of life at q' and five years of healthy life. And she is also indifferent between ten years at q' and a gamble giving a .71 chance of ten years in good health and .29 chance of death. Bernoulli's hypothesis says that ten years at q' are .71 times as good for Amanda as ten years in good health. Is this plausible? Surely not. Surely it is more plausible to think that ten years at q' are half as good for her as ten years in good health, since ten years at q' are equally as good as five years in good health, and since Amanda does not discount her qalys. Surely the most plausible explanation of why she requires a chance as high as .71, rather than .5, to accept the gamble I described is that she is risk-averse about her good, and inclined to avoid gambles. This conclusion is not forced on us by the form of Amanda's preferences, but it simply seems more plausible for her than Bernoulli's hypothesis does. It is much less plausible to suggest that ten years at q' are .71 times as good as ten years in good health. It is much more plausible that V measures Amanda's good cardinally than that u does.

I do not think, therefore, that we should rely on Bernoulli's hypothesis to determine a cardinal scale for good.[16] I think we should stick to the conventional wisdom that preferences alone cannot give us a cardinal scale. Consequently, to find one, we shall need to give some independent consideration to the structure of a person's good. This is a matter for ethics and not decision theory.

13.5   Qalys as a measure of good

I have examined in detail the structure of a person's good elsewhere.[17] In this chapter, I shall not try to offer a sophisticated analysis, but simply mention two assumptions that could serve to support the use of qalys as a cardinal measure of good. I do not insist on the truth of these assumptions, but I hope, once again, that they may be acceptable as a first approach to the question. At least they indicate the type of assumptions that are needed. They are ethical assumptions, not assumptions about the form of preferences.

Let us assume, first, that the goodness of a life for a person is the total of the good it brings her at each of the times in her life. One good reason to doubt this assumption is that, because it counts the *total* of good only, it gives no value to evenness in the distribution of good through life. It might reasonably be thought that a uniformly good life is better (or perhaps worse) than a life with ups and downs but the same total. On the other hand, one feature of the assumption is surely indubitable: in some way or other, the good that comes to a person at each of the different times in her life will enter into determining her overall good. Her overall good, that is, is a *function* of her good at different times (and perhaps of other things too). A second feature is more controversial: this function is *symmetrical*. But this I am willing to defend. We are concerned with the goodness of the person's life as a whole, and from the standpoint of a life as a whole all times must count equally. The good at one time must count in exactly the same way as the good at another. Both are equally much the person's good. For instance, in determining the overall goodness of a life, good that comes later in the life cannot count differently from good that comes earlier.[18]

And let us assume, secondly, that the goodness of a person's life at any particular time depends only on the quality of her life at that time. In section 13.3, I explained the notion of a quality of life by means of an example: confined to a wheelchair and in slight pain. A description like this could be filled out to any degree. Presumably if it was filled out enough, it would encompass all aspects of the person's good, so it could not fail to determine how good her life is at the time. But I deliberately restricted the notion of quality to states of the person's health, and a description of her health alone will leave out many aspects of her good. I said that other aspects, such as her wealth perhaps, are supposed to be held constant. Given that they are, the quality of her life, even though it is defined in terms of health only, will determine how good her life is.

However, some other aspects of the person's good cannot be held constant, because of the nature of the question we are considering. One is the person's age. And perhaps a given quality of life (in terms of health) is better for a person at one age than at another. Perhaps good health enables you to enjoy life more when you are young than when you are old. Another aspect that cannot be held constant is length of life. And perhaps some qualities are better for a person if her life is going to be short, and others if it is going to be long. Perhaps the chance of being active is more important in a short life, and absence of pain in a long one. A third aspect that cannot in practice be held constant is the person's wealth. Treatments have costs, which are often borne by people other than the patient, by taxpayers let us say. Paying the costs is bad for these people, and it diminishes the true quality of their lives. But it does not affect their health, and it will not show up in a notion of quality that is restricted to states of health. To deal with this problem, in theory we need a broader notion of quality, and in practice we need a way of comparing the value of wealth against the value of health. But in the meantime we can set the problem aside by confining ourselves to 'cost-effectiveness analysis': we can compare the improvements to people's health that can be achieved by different methods at a given cost. In this way we can hold the costs to the taxpayer constant and allow ourselves to compare states of health only. This will not help us to decide how much money should be spent on the health service, but it will help us to decide the best allocation of whatever money is spent.

Granted the two assumptions I have made, it follows immediately that the goodness of an outcome for a person is the number of life years it brings her, adjusted for quality. The quality of a particular year of life determines how good that year is for her. Adding up these amounts gives us the total of good in her life, and I have assumed that is equivalent to how good the outcome is for her. The appropriate quality adjustment in this calculation is given by how good the quality is for the person. Future years are not discounted.

13.6   Quality adjustment factors in the measure of good

Given the assumptions of section 13.5, we have found that quality-adjusted life years are the correct measure of a person's good. There remains, however, the problem of making the right adjustment for quality. The factor $v(q)$ I introduced in section 13.3 was defined in the course of representing a person's preferences by a utility function. Now we need something different: a measure of how good a particular quality of life is for a person.

Nevertheless, we can hope that the right adjustment factors might be derivable from preferences all the same. It depends on how a person's preferences are related to her good. We shall have to make an assumption about that. And I now want to disagree with the preference-satisfaction theory. What a person prefers does not necessarily coincide with what is good for her. This is a commonly accepted proposition. It is commonly accepted that people discount their future good in forming their preferences. They sacrifice a greater amount of good coming in the further future for the sake of gaining a smaller amount in the nearer future. Derek Parfit argues that this may be rational.[19] A. C. Pigou thought it was not.[20] But, rational or not, a person who discounts her good is not maximizing her good. Good that comes to her later cannot count less in her overall good than good that comes to her earlier. So, of two alternatives, she sometimes prefers the one that is less good for her.

However, though I doubt the full-blooded preference-satisfaction theory, one part of it may be a good enough approximation for our purposes. A person's preferences may not coincide with her good across time, but at a single time they may be close enough. It may be that, when a person forms her preferences amongst alternative lives of various qualities, she maximizes a discounted total of her good. Her good in any year is determined by the quality of her life in that year. So, in the notation of section 13.3, she maximizes

$$D(q_1, q_2, \ldots q_y) = g(q_1) + \rho_1 g(q_1) + \ldots + \rho_y g(q_y),$$

where the ρs are discount factors, and $g(q)$ is the goodness for the person of quality q. But this is a representation of the person's preferences in the same additively separable form as equation (1). Under this form, the subutilities v are determined uniquely up to a positive multiple. So v must be a multiple of g. This is the conclusion we have been looking for since section 13.4. The quality adjustment factor $v(q)$, which can be determined from the person's preferences, is a positive multiple of the person's good. It is therefore an increasing linear transform of her good. That is to say, it supplies a cardinal representation of her good.

On the other hand, even this may be assuming too close a connection between preferences and good. I am impressed by a point made by A. J. Culyer,[21] that using qalys does not commit one to a narrow – he calls it 'welfarist' – conception of good. Qaly analysis assigns values to states of health, and leaves it open whether these values are determined by how people feel when they are in these states, by their preferences about them, or perhaps by some objective principles. All of these possibilities are consistent with the general idea I started with: that qalys are aimed at assessing good or benefit. We must simply allow for alternative conceptions of good.

If the adjustment factors are to be severed from preferences, then neither the time method nor the probability method can determine them. One other method is popular. It is simply to ask people how good the alternatives are. Call this the 'direct method'. Here is an example of the sort of question that may be asked, from a study by George Torrance, Michael Boyle, and Sargent Horwood:

The subject was asked to imagine being in these situations for a lifetime with everything else normal, or average. S/he was asked to place the most desirable level . . . at 100, the least desirable . . . at 0, and the others in between in order of desirability, with ties allowed, and spaced such that the relative distance between the levels corresponds to her/his feelings about the relative differences in desirability.[22]

If questions like this elicit sensible answers, they will do so whether or not the subject discounts or is risk-neutral. In some ways, therefore, this could be a more reliable way of estimating the adjustment factors than either the time method or the probability method. (Oddly enough, Torrance, Boyle, and Horwood, having obtained a scale of adjustment factors by the direct method, then choose to convert it by a formula to a different scale: one that, they believe, would have been obtained by the probability method. Such is the magnetism of the probability method.) However, the direct method is quite different from the others in that it asks for a judgement about goodness, rather than a preference. How much trust we can put in the method depends on the subject's qualifications for making the judgement.

13.7   Comparisons between people

Now I come to the question of aggregating and comparing the good of different people. Once more for the sake of a first approach to the problem, let us adopt the utilitarian principle that the goodness of an action (the choice of a particular treatment programme, say, or a particular allocation of resources) is the total resulting good of the people. I have already identified each person's good with her qalys. So the total good of the people is the total of their qalys. One action is better than another if and only if it leads to more qalys. This is the fundamental precept that guides the practical use of qalys. We have by now found some basis for it. However, there are still some things to worry about.

The first is a doubt about the utilitarian principle I assumed. This principle is only one part of utilitarianism, and it does not commit us to the rest. For one thing, it permits the broad conception of good I mentioned at the end of section 13.6, and it does not insist that quality adjustment factors should be derived from preferences. But it does rule out the egalitarian view that, for a given total of good, it is better to have this total more, rather than less, equally distributed. My own view is that the value of equality is best understood differently, in a way that is consistent with the utilitarian principle.[23] It is certainly true that qalys do not give value to equality, but they should not be expected to. Equality is an aspect of fairness, and I said in section 13.1 that fairness needs to be considered separately.

A second reason to be careful is that we are now putting different people's qalys together: we are making interpersonal comparisons of good. So far, I have argued that for a single person a qaly always represents the same amount of good; that is what is meant by saying that qalys measure good cardinally. Now we are assuming that a qaly to one person represents the same amount of good as a qaly to another. To put it differently: the same distance on different people's scales of quality adjustment factors always represents the same amount of good. The nought on each person's scale is the quality that makes life just not worth living. The one is good health. The assumption is that the distance between these two represents the same amount of good for each person.

This is quite implausible. The nought represents the same level of good for everyone, because it is the level that is just not good at all. But good health is plainly not equally good for everyone. Good health is only a state of good *health,* and nothing else in one healthy person's life may be good, whereas everything else in another's may be. Qalys to one person will represent more good than qalys to another. Prolonging the life of, say, a happy person will do more good than prolonging the life of an unhappy one.

This point has disturbing implications, and I sympathize with Torrance when he recommends qalys because they are 'egalitarian within the health domain'. Qalys treat the gap between nought and one as the same for everyone, and this, Torrance says, means that 'each individual's health is counted equally'.[24] However, looked at one way, what Torrance says is incorrect. Restoring an old person to health produces fewer qalys than restoring a young person to health, because the old person has fewer years to live. So, in a way, qalys count the health of old people for less than the health of young people. Torrance hopes to achieve fairness by using a particular scale for estimating benefit, but actually the scale he recommends, which values a year of healthy life equally for everyone, can defensibly be claimed to be unfair to the old. I think it is better to separate the question of good from the question of fairness, rather than try and adjust the scale of good to take account of fairness.[25] The assumption that healthy life is equally good for everybody is just false.

13.8   Problems of existence

Now I am going to mention what I think is the most serious difficulty over using qalys to measure the goodness of alternative actions. I can do no more than mention it; it is examined in detail in my paper 'The economic value of life'.

There are two ways of bringing it about that years of good life are lived – of producing qalys, that is. One is to prolong a person's life or make it better. The other is to bring into existence a new life. A decision made in medicine will often do both. For instance, if a child is saved she will probably later have children herself, who will enjoy good lives. What is to be done about this? Should one give equal value to qalys brought about by either method? Should they have a different value? Or what?

Traditionally, qalys brought about by creating a new life are not counted at all. This traditional procedure seems intuitively natural, but it encounters two problems, one practical and the other theoretical. The practical problem is that it leads to an anomaly at the borderline between creating life and prolonging life. A study by Michael Boyle, George Torrance, J. C. Sinclair, and Sargent Horwood attaches a high value to saving the life of a prematurely born baby, because if the baby survives she will gain a whole lifetime of qalys.[26] It seems a little odd that saving a baby should be valued so much higher than, say, saving a twenty-year-old. Helga Kuhse and Peter Singer, commenting on this study, point out how particularly odd it would be unless a similar high value is attached to the life of an unborn foetus.[27] But it is not at all clear how the traditional procedure should be applied to a foetus. It matters crucially in this procedure whether an action counts as prolonging the life of an existing person, or as bringing about the existence of a new person. So it matters crucially when a person comes into existence. Once she exists, all her future qalys will count; up till then, none of them. But the beginning of a person seems inherently vague, so it seems wrong to attach great importance to the moment when it occurs.

The theoretical problem is to find a sound justification for the traditional procedure in the first place. Philosophical support for it can be drawn from an argument of Jan Narveson's.[28] Narveson argues that a benefit has to be a benefit to somebody, and that a person is not benefited by being brought into existence, even if her life is a good one. If, therefore, an action brings it about that someone exists who would otherwise not have existed, that person's wellbeing is not a benefit arising from the action. This is intuitively plausible, and it surely expresses the intuitive attraction of the traditional procedure. The qalys of new people are traditionally not counted in the calculations because they seem not to represent a benefit to anyone. Narveson's argument leads us to the following principle for evaluating two alternative actions: the better action is the one that is better for those people who will exist whichever action is done. This principle would support the traditional procedure. Unfortunately, however, it turns out to be unacceptable. I explained why in 'The economic value of life', taking my lead from Derek Parfit's *Reasons and Persons*. The most serious objection is that one can find examples of three alternatives A, B, and C where the principle says A is better than B, B better than C, and C better than A. This is a logical contradiction.[29] A principle that implies a contradiction cannot be correct.

I think it may be possible to find a philosophically defensible way around the practical problem.[30] But I suspect the theoretical problem is insoluble. I suspect the traditional procedure has no sound justification.

An alternative is to count in favour of an action all the qalys the action brings about, including those enjoyed by people it brings into existence. The value of saving a person, for instance, would include all the qalys of her descendants. This is the procedure that would be recommended by 'classical' utilitarianism, which evaluates an actions by the total of all the good enjoyed by everyone who will live if that action is done. Classical utilitarianism has plenty of problems of its own, some of which I mentioned in 'The economic value of life'. Since I have never seen it recommended for medical decision making using qalys, I shall not dwell on these problems here.

For decisions that affect which people exist, no principles of evaluation have been found that are free from problems. Consequently, we have no unproblematic way of using qalys in those medical decisions that have such effects. This is a large fraction of all medical decisions. Moreover, the difficulties may spill over into other medical decisions too. If we doubt there should be a large difference between the value of saving a premature baby and the value of saving a foetus, that may make us doubt that the value of saving a baby is really all the qalys in the rest of her life. It may cast doubt on our whole way of using qalys.

13.9   Summary

I think that qalys have an important contribution to make to medical decision making. When there is a choice to be made, qalys are in principle a measure of the benefits each of the alternatives will bring. The benefits are not everything that matters, and qalys do not take account of other considerations such as fairness. Furthermore, there are many minor and major assumptions implicit in the use of qalys to measure good. Many are implausible, and we must therefore be cautious. But qalys could be useful nonetheless.

However, there are some common misconceptions about how quality adjustment factors should be calculated. I think the popularity of what I called 'the probability method' is misplaced.

Finally, there are the intractable problems mentioned in section 13.8. These are serious and fundamental. They afflict the whole of decision making in matters of life and death, and they remain unsolved.

Appendix to Chapter 13

Derivation of the discounted-qaly maximizing equation (1)

I shall work with continuous time; I used discrete time in the text simply for the sake of a simple presentation.

Take a person, and let Y be the greatest number of years she could live. Let y be the number she actually does live. Let Q be the set of qualities of life. Let $q(t) \in Q$ be the quality of the person's life t years after her birth. So q is a function from $\{t: 0 \leq t \leq y\}$ to Q; I shall call q a 'quality function', and say it 'lasts' y years. The pair $<y, q>$ defines a life. Assume that the person has a preference relation amongst such pairs.

Call a life of Y years a 'full life'. For a moment, think only of the preference relation amongst full lives. This may be thought of as a relation amongst those functions q that last Y years. The model we have now, confined to full lives, is an exact analogy of the model of uncertainty in Leonard Savage's version of expected utility theory.[31] Times t in $\{t: 0 \leq t \leq Y\}$ are analogous to Savage's 'states'; qualities in Q to his 'consequences'; and quality functions q (lasting Y years) to his 'acts'.

Savage supposes there is a preference relation amongst acts, and he imposes seven postulates on it.[32] Analogous postulates may be imposed on the preference relation amongst full lives, and they make good sense if they are. I shall not spell them out here. But Postulate 2, the 'sure-thing principle',[33] needs mentioning because it is the most dubious. Reinterpreted, it is an assumption of strong separability between times. It says that the value the person attaches to the quality of her life during any particular period is independent of its quality at other times.

From his postulates, Savage deduces expected utility theory. The analogous postulates will imply the analogue of expected utility theory. That is: there will be a discount function r (playing the role of a probability function) defined on times, and a subutility function v defined on qualities, such that preferences are represented by:

$$\int_0^Y r(t)v(q(t))dt.$$

The function v is unique up to increasing linear transformations.

Now take a life $<y, q>$ of any length y. Consider extending this life to Y years by adding a period of life of a constant quality q^0. That is to say, consider the life $< Y, q^+>$ where q^+ is defined by $q^+(t) = q(t)$ for $0 \le t \le y$ and $q^+(t) = q^0$ for $y < t \le Y$. Now assume there is a quality q^0 such that, for all y and for all quality functions q that last y years, the person is indifferent between $<y, q>$ and the extended life $< Y, q^+>$ I have just described. I shall call q^0 the *valueless quality*. This assumption, then, is that there is a quality of life that the person would just as soon not live as live, and furthermore that this quality is the same however long she has already lived, and whatever her life has so far been like. Put briefly: there is a quality of life that is *always valueless*.

The utility of the extended life $< Y, q^+>$ is, by the formula above:

$$\int_0^y r(t)v(q(t))dt + v(q^0)\int_y^Y r(t)dt.$$

Since v is unique only up to linear transformations, we may set $v(q^0) = 0$. We already have v defined uniquely up to increasing linear transformations; this now defines it uniquely up to multiples. Then the utility of $< Y, q^+>$ is:

$$\int_0^Y r(t)v(q(t))dt.$$

And since, by our assumption, $< Y, q^+>$ is indifferent to $<y, q>$, this may be taken as the utility of $<y, q>$. This is the continuous-time version of the discounted-qaly formula, equation (1) in the text.

In summary, the following conditions are together sufficient for a person to be a discounted-qaly maximizer:

(1) The person has preferences that conform to the analogues of Savage's postulates.
(2) There is a quality of life that is always valueless for her.

Comments on Pliskin, Shepard, and Weinstein

In 'Utility functions for life years and health status', Joseph Pliskin, Donald Shepard, and Milton Weinstein consider lives described by pairs $<y, q>$, where y is the length of the life and q its quality. For them, q is not a function but a single quality, which is assumed constant throughout the life. They make two assumptions about a person's preferences over lotteries for such lives. The first is that they are 'mutually utility independent'. This means that the person's preferences about lotteries over qualities q, with y held constant, are independent of the constant value of y, and similarly that her preferences about lotteries over y are independent of q. The other assumption is that the preferences have 'constant proportional tradeoff'. This means that 'the proportion of remaining life years that one is willing to give up for an improvement in health status from any given level q_1 to any other level q_2 does not depend on the absolute number of remaining life years involved'.[34] Pliskin, Shepard, and Weinstein show that these two assumptions imply, amongst other things, that the person is an undiscounted-qaly maximizer.

I find this analysis unsatisfactory for three reasons.[35] First, it offers no analysis of preferences over lives whose quality is not constant. Secondly, the assumption of mutual utility independence is hard to judge because it requires separability between lotteries. Compare my own assumption that qualities are separable between times. An assumption that *lotteries* over qualities are separable between times would be much stronger. Indeed, by a theorem of W. M. Gorman's,[36] it would imply risk-neutrality about qalys, which is surely implausible. This suggests to me that one ought to be cautious about assuming separability of lotteries. My own assumption that qualities are separable does much the same job better. Uncertainty is a complication rather than an essential part of the problem of valuing lives, and it ought not to be introduced into the analysis earlier than it need be. My third and most important objection is that constant proportional tradeoff is a highly specific assumption, which is out of place at the level of general theory. Furthermore, it is implausible anyway. It rules out any discounting of future qalys, and discounting is commonly taken to be a fact of life.

14   The value of living

14.1   Examples

I shall start by describing some economic problems that involve the value
of living. First, some to do with the allocation of resources in medicine.
Some of the things doctors do prolong people's lives, whereas others
improve the lives people live while they are alive. One problem in the allocation of resources is to weigh against each other these two sorts of benefits.
This problem can arise even for the treatment of a single person. For
instance, when a person has terminal cancer, her doctor can choose to concentrate on relieving her pain and making her life tolerable till she dies.
Alternatively, she can take measures to prolong the patient's life, and these
measures often involve some pain and suffering. I shall immediately introduce a type of figure I shall be using throughout this chapter. The choice I
have just described is shown in figure 14.1. The figure illustrates the two
alternative treatments. For each, the horizontal axis shows time; the vertical bar marks the present. The vertical axis shows the person's degree of
wellbeing at each time. We need to know which of the two alternative treatments is better.

This particular example may seem a purely medical problem rather than
an economic one. It is an economic problem in the most general sense; it is
a question of how best to use the scarce resources of medicine for this

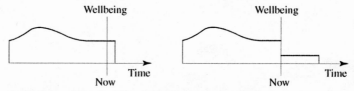

Figure 14.1 Palliative treatment versus aggressive treatment.

From *Recherches Economiques de Louvain*, 58 (1992), pp. 125–42. Reprinted by permission of
the Editor of *Recherches Economiques de Louvain*. This chapter was written with the support
of the Economic and Social Research Council, under grant number R000233334.

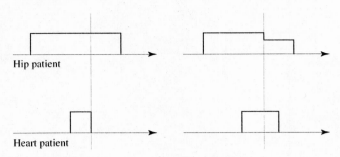

Figure 14.2 Hip replacement versus heart replacement.

person. But a slightly different example is more clearly economic. Medical resources can be directed towards life-saving techniques such as heart transplants, or towards life-enhancing techniques such as hip replacements. In this case, the people who will benefit from one use of resources are different from the people who will benefit from the other. Schematically, this problem is shown in figure 14.2. In this figure, more than one person is shown on the vertical axis.

Now think about saving the old compared with saving the young. How should we divide resources between, say, cancer treatment, which typically benefits older people, and emergency surgery for victims of road accidents, which typically benefits younger people? Figure 14.3 shows a schematic version of this choice, as one might at first conceive it. But actually figure 14.3 is not very representative. If a young person is saved after an accident, she is likely to have children later in her life – most young people do. So saving a young person is likely to have the effect that children are later born who would otherwise never have existed. The children are likely to have children of their own, and indeed they will probably start a whole line of descendants. So figure 14.4 depicts more accurately than figure 14.3 the typical choice between saving the old and saving the young.

Next I come to an example that involves the value of living on a much larger scale. Significant global warming, caused by the emission of greenhouse gases, now seems inevitable. What will be the effects of this change? How bad will they be? Indeed, will they necessarily be bad at all? The good and bad effects on human life are extremely hard to predict. But I can make one reliable prediction. Global warming will kill hundreds of thousands of people each year, mainly through the spread of tropical diseases, and also through flooding in low-lying areas. One of the major predictable harms of global warming is killing. But, more than this, there will have to be movements of population on an unprecedented scale as some parts of the world become uninhabitable and others become more habitable. It is

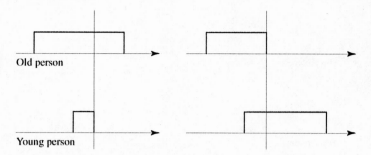

Figure 14.3 Saving the old versus saving the young.

inconceivable that these movements could occur without large effects on the size of the world's population. Global warming will make the world's population in a hundred years very different from what it would have been had the world remained cooler. I assume it will be smaller, but I am not enough of a demographer to be sure of the direction of change.

So, if we are to do any worthwhile economic evaluations of attempts to mitigate global warming – carbon taxes, sea defences, and so on – we shall certainly need to fix a value on prolonging people's lives, and also on changes in population. Very schematically, we face a choice like figure 14.5. On the left is what will happen if we do nothing much about the problem. On the right is what will happen if we try to mitigate it. People living now and in the near future will have to make sacrifices. But future people will live longer and better lives, and there may be more of them.

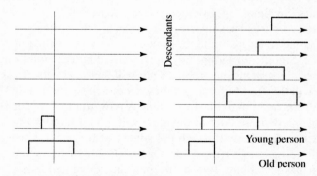

Figure 14.4 Saving the old versus saving the young, more realistically.

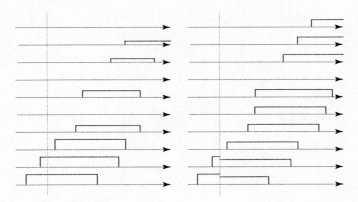

Figure 14.5 Global warming: business as usual versus respond.

14.2 The problem

The question I am going to talk about is how to make choices like the ones I have described. Each is a choice between two alternatives, and each alternative is represented in one of my figures. What I should like to do is find a way of assigning a value to the states of affairs depicted in those figures. If we could do that, then whenever we are faced with a choice, we should know that the best alternative is the one with the highest value. In general, I am interested in any choice that involves extending lives or bringing more lives into existence. Figure 14.6 shows a typical situation of the sort I am concerned with; I should like to be able to assign values to different situations like this.

If a person i exists at time t, let her wellbeing at that time be g_t^i. If no such person exists at that time, as a matter of notation let us write $g_t^i = \Omega$. Then the problem I have described is to find the form of the value function

$$g = g(g_1^1, g_1^2, \ldots g_2^1, g_2^2, \ldots g_3^1, \ldots). \tag{1}$$

I shall call the vector in the brackets a *distribution* of wellbeing; the value function g assigns a value to each possible distribution.

To ask for the form of the value function is to draw together two problems that have been treated separately up to now, with very few exceptions.[1] One is the problem of assigning a value to prolonging a person's life. This is often called the problem of 'the value of life', and is covered by a very extensive literature, chiefly in economics.[2] The other is the problem of valuing changes in population, which is also covered by an extensive literature, this time mostly in philosophy.[3] I am looking for a comprehensive

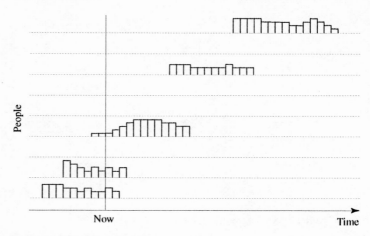

Figure 14.6 The general problem.

theory that covers both problems. Let us call it a theory of the *value of living.*

We certainly need a theory that covers both problems together. First of all, many of the practical decisions we face have effects of both sorts; I have mentioned some in my examples. And, secondly, the two must clearly be linked in principle. In one sense, prolonging a person's life and adding a new person to the world are alternative ways of doing the same thing. Both are ways of bringing it about that more years of life are lived by a person than otherwise would have been. Of course there is a crucial difference too; in one case the person exists anyway and in the other she does not. But it must be a mistake to try and deal with the problems in complete isolation from each other. I shall be saying more later about the links.

I see the problem I have described as an application and extension of the problem I tried to tackle in my book *Weighing Goods*. The good (or well-being, if you prefer that term) in the world comes distributed at different *locations,* as I put it. Good comes to different *people,* for one thing: some things are good for some people and less good for others. So people are locations of good. Times are also locations for good; good comes to people at different times. People and times each constitute a *dimension* of locations, we may say. In fact, good is distributed across a two-dimensional grid: times in one dimension, people in the other. Somehow, the good of all people at all times determines how good the world is overall. In *Weighing Goods*, I asked how good distributed across the grid is aggregated together to determine overall good. When is one distribution better or worse than another? How, for instance, is one person's good weighed against another's? But in

Weighing Goods I made the simplifying assumption that all the locations in the grid are occupied. There was no question whether or not they might be filled. I assumed, that is to say, that everyone was alive at all times. Now I want to tackle a more general and more realistic problem. I want to allow for variations in the lengths of people's lives, and for the fact that some people may or may not come into existence. This still gives us a two-dimensional grid of locations for good. My figures all show grids of this sort, and the distribution of good across them.

However, in this chapter I shall not spend much time on one question that took up a lot of space in *Weighing Goods*. People and times are two dimensions of locations, and there is a third dimension too: *states of nature*. Nothing we do has results that are certain; the results will depend on the state of nature. For instance, we do not know whether the globe will be warmed by two degrees or six degrees in the next century. Obviously the good that comes to a particular person at a particular time depends on the state of nature. So states of nature are locations of good: more good is located in some states than in others. You can imagine a third dimension added to my figures.

Though I shall spend little time on this third dimension, I do need to mention it because many people think uncertainty is essential to the whole business of setting a value on life.[4] I agree, of course, that all our decisions will always need to take uncertainty into account, because the results of anything we do are uncertain. But I have a particular view about how to approach uncertainty: I believe in expected utility theory. I believe that the value of an uncertain prospect is determined by values of its possible results, in the way expected utility theory prescribes. Suppose we are trying to set a value on some action that exposes a person to risk: heart-bypass surgery, say, which is dangerous, or building a nuclear power station, which exposes the person to a risk of leukaemia caused by leaking radiation. I think it is sensible to approach the valuation problem by first trying to evaluate the various possible consequences of the action – consequences like: the patient dies during surgery, the patient survives and is relieved from the pain of angina, the person contracts leukaemia, and so on. After that is done, we can put the values of these consequences together according to the recommendations of expected utility theory, to arrive at an overall evaluation of the risky action. That is why I am going to set uncertainty aside at the start. I want, first, to find a way of fixing a value on the various possible outcomes. Uncertainty comes in later.

Nevertheless, there is one other thing to say about uncertainty. The existence of the third dimension does in fact constrain the conclusions we can reach about the aggregation of goods in the other two. There are theorems, stemming from the work of John Harsanyi,[5] that link together aggregation in the different dimensions. Expected utility theory tells us how we should aggregate good across the dimension of states of nature. Through the theorems, this tells us something about how we should aggregate good across the other dimensions too. It tells us, for instance, how one person's good should be put together with another's. Harsanyi himself, indeed, used the theorems to argue in favour of utilitarianism, and in particular the utilitarian principle that one should simply add across people and give no value to equality. Some authors, particularly Peter Hammond[6] and Charles Blackorby and David Donaldson,[7] have used corresponding theorems in population theory too. Again, aggregation across states of nature constrains aggregation across people. So the third dimension offers the opportunity of some extra leverage in our problem. I shall return to these theorems at the end of this chapter. But till then I shall ignore uncertainty.

14.3   Two mistaken views

So there is the problem of the value of living. How should we set about solving it? Formally, it is a matter of finding the value function g in (1). One thing we might do is look for a comprehensive principle that determines the form of g at a stroke. One such principle, for instance, is *complete utilitarianism*. Complete utilitarianism says that the value of a distribution is simply the total of everybody's wellbeing at each time, summed over each person and every time the person exists. This principle is definitely wrong, as I shall be explaining. It may be too ambitious in any case to hope to find straight off a single convincing comprehensive principle. A more modest approach is to look for smaller conditions that impose plausible constraints on g, but do not determine g completely. Maybe, if we can feel secure about a few such conditions, they might determine g together. That is the traditional approach of social choice theory, and I shall try to follow it.

I shall start by mentioning two conditions that may seem plausible at first sight but that I am sure are wrong. They are assumptions that have been taken for granted by many economists. As you will see, I shall not be very successful at presenting you with correct conditions, but I can at least perform the service of warning you against some incorrect ones.

One is *separability of times*. This condition says that the value function takes the form

$$g = h(h_1(g_1^1, g_1^2, \ldots), h_2(g_2^1, g_2^2, \ldots), h_3(g_3^1, g_3^2, \ldots), \ldots). \tag{2}$$

It says that what happens at each date can be valued separately from what happens at other dates. First, wellbeing for all the people together is evaluated one date at a time: h_1 measures the value at the first date, h_2 at the second, and so on. Then wellbeing at different times is put together to arrive

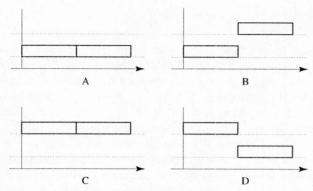

Figure 14.7 One long life versus two short lives.

at an overall assessment. I think you will recognize this as a formula that is very commonly assumed. Often people make the more specific assumption that the value function is a discounted total of wellbeing at different times. That is:

$$g = g_1(g_1^1, g_1^2, \ldots) + g_2(g_2^1, g_2^2, \ldots)/(1+r) + g_3(g_3^1, g_3^2, \ldots)/(1+r)^2 + \ldots$$

This implies separability of times.

I am sure separability of times is wrong. You can see why if you think about the following case. Imagine economic conditions change, so that people's lifetimes become longer, but their living conditions are no better nor worse while they continue. But suppose that at the same time people begin to have fewer children. The fewer births compensate for the longer lifetimes, so the total population of the world remains just as it would have been. Then at any time, there will be just as many people living as there would have been, and they will be living lives that are just as good. Consequently the separable formula, which evaluates wellbeing only at each time individually, will say the world is no better than it would have been. The change, which extends people's lives, has done no good, this formula says. But this is surely wrong; it is obviously a good thing that people are living longer. The example shows that the separable formula gives no value to the length of people's lives. But the length of people's lives is valuable.

To see this point more precisely, look at the example shown in figure 14.7. For this example, the separable formula (2) implies that

$$g(A) = h(h_1(1, \Omega), h_2(1, \Omega)),$$
$$g(B) = h(h_1(1, \Omega), h_2(\Omega, 1)),$$

$$g(C) = h(h_1(\Omega, 1), h_2(\Omega, 1)),$$
and $$g(D) = h(h_1(\Omega, 1), h_2(1, \Omega)).$$

where h is an increasing function. It follows that if $g(A)$ is greater than $g(B)$, then $g(D)$ must be greater than $g(C)$. So if A is better than B, then D is better than C. But one long life is surely better than two short ones, so A is surely better than B and C better than D. Separability must therefore be wrong.

The lesson to learn from the failure of separability is that it matters whereabouts wellbeing occurs on the vertical dimension of the grid; it matters which life it occurs in. The condition of separability makes a close parallel between the two problems I described: the value of life problem and the population problem. It says that, so long as a particular piece of wellbeing occurs at a particular time, it does not matter if it occurs within an existing life or within a new life. Prolonging life and creating life will therefore have the same value. This is plainly wrong.

This is why I said complete utilitarianism is wrong. It implies separability of times. It implies that only wellbeing matters, independently of whom it comes to.

Separability has often been assumed by economists, but other economists have often assumed a quite contrary principle. Indeed, this other principle has been taken for granted almost universally by economists interested in the value of life. It, too, is wrong. But it has a strong intuitive attraction, and I shall present it first using an example that brings out its appeal.

A couple is wondering whether to have another child, at some sacrifice to their existing child. Their problem is shown in figure 14.8. A consideration against their having the second child is that it will reduce the wellbeing of the present one. What consideration is there in favour of their having this child? The only consideration there could be is that this second child will have a worthwhile life. But a very natural view to take is that that is actually no reason in favour of their having the child. Suppose the couple decide to keep their family at its present size. There is some benefit to the existing child, but no harm is done to anyone. So how could this be a wrong decision? If a couple themselves want a second child, that is a reason for them to have one, but the good of the second child itself is no reason at all. This view has been given a philosophical backing by Jan Narveson.[8] Narveson's guiding idea is that the only consideration there can be in favour of doing anything is a benefit to someone. Now, the only way you can be benefited is by being made better off than you would otherwise have been. But being born does not make you better off than you would otherwise have been, because there is no state you would otherwise have been in, either better or worse. Therefore, being born does not benefit you. Consequently, Narveson

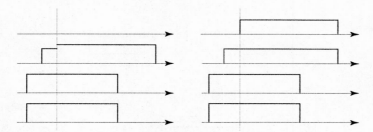

Figure 14.8 Whether to have a second child.

concludes, the wellbeing of the child is no consideration in favour of having the child.

To formalize this principle, we might say that, in comparing two alternatives, all that counts is the wellbeing of the people who exist in both. One consequence is that, if one alternative is better than another for some of the people who exist in both, and no worse for any of those people, it is better. This principle is universally taken for granted in almost all the economic literature on valuing life. So, for instance, in figure 14.5, the wellbeing of all the children and their descendants is typically totally ignored in the decision between saving an older person and saving a younger person. Only the wellbeing of existing people is taken into account.

In contrast to separability of times, this principle expresses the idea that the value-of-life problem is quite different from the population problem. Separability says it does not matter at all which life wellbeing occurs in; Narveson's principle says this is all-important. Compare the question of whether to have another child with the question of preserving the child's life once she exists. This second question is illustrated in figure 14.9. The only difference between this and figure 14.8 is that in figure 14.9 the child exists for a short time whatever is decided. According to Narveson's principle, this makes it a totally different problem.

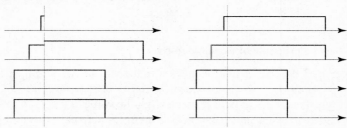

Figure 14.9 Whether to save a baby

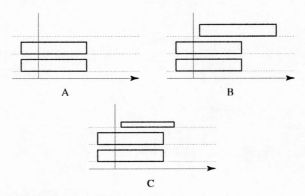

Figure 14.10 Intransitivity.

This is an intuitively attractive idea. But unfortunately, Narveson's principle turns out to be unacceptable. This is shown in figure 14.10. The principle says that alternatives *A* and *B* are equally good, because they are equally good for the two people who exist in both *A* and *B*. It also says that *A* and *C* are equally good for the same reason. It follows that *B* and *C* must be equally good. But the principle also says that *B* is better than *C*, since it is better for one of the three people who exist in both *B* and *C*, and worse for none of the people who exist in both. The principle has therefore contradicted itself.[9]

A self-contradictory principle must be wrong. Nevertheless, although Narveson's principle must be wrong, I think there must be something right about the intuition that lies behind it. I do not know what, though. I am inclined to think that the hardest problem connected with valuing life is to identify properly what is right about this intuition. When economists ignore descendants in valuing life, I do not think they are totally wrong. We need to find a justifiable principle that captures what is right about their intuition.

14.4   The principle of personal good

Section 14.3 described two principles that seem to me wrong. I am now going to mention one that I think is right. It is *separability of people*. Roughly, separability of people means that the value of a person's wellbeing – the value of having that person exist or continue to exist – is independent of which other people exist, and how well off they are. In *Weighing Goods*, I called this 'the principle of personal good', and defended it as well as I could. I think separability of times is plainly wrong, but separability of people seems to me right. I do not insist on it dogmatically. The defence in *Weighing Goods* applies only when changes in population are not in question, and I am not yet certain it can be convincingly extended to more general problems. So it may turn out in the end that the principle of personal good also has to be abandoned.

It does lead to a problem of its own. The problem arises when the principle is combined with expected utility theory. When I announced in section 14.2 that I was going to say little about uncertainty, I also announced that I favoured expected utility theory. I shall not apologize for adopting it now. I think it is the correct account of how to deal with uncertainty. Expected utility theory, like the principle of personal good, implies a condition of separability: separability of states of nature. It implies, that is to say, that what happens in one state of nature can be evaluated independently of what happens in other states. Now, it happens that separability of states of nature and separability of people – expected utility theory and the principle of personal good, in other words – are together almost enough to determine the following specific form for the value function:

$$g = \Sigma_{\{i \mid g^i \neq \Omega\}}(g^i - \alpha)$$

There are some small gaps in the derivation of this formula from the two separability conditions; some small extra assumptions are needed.[10] One of the gaps would allow us to modify the formula in a way that gives some value to equality between people. But since I am not particularly concerned with equality in this chapter, I shall ignore this option. This formula for the value function is what Blackorby and Donaldson call 'critical level utilitarianism'; they themselves derive it in a slightly different way.[11] They seem happy with it, but I am not.

According to this formula we can assess the value of a distribution as follows. For each person who exists, we calculate the difference between her lifetime wellbeing and α. Then we add up these differences, across everybody who exists. The total is the value of the distribution. This means it is a good idea to add a new person to the population if her wellbeing will be above α, but a bad idea if it will be below α. The 'critical level' α marks the boundary between lives that we should favour and those we should oppose. What level should α be? Suppose, first, it represents a low standard of living, so that people whose lifetime wellbeing is just above α have a poor life. Compare a world that has a large population, all living very good lives, with a world that has a much larger population, all living lives just above the level α. Provided the population of this second world is large enough, the formula says it is a better world. This is hard to believe. In that world, everyone's life is poor, yet just because there are so many people, it is supposed to be a better world. This is what Derek Parfit calls 'the repugnant conclusion'.[12]

On the other hand, suppose α represents a high standard of living, so that even people whose lifetime wellbeing is a bit below α live perfectly decent lives. According to the formula, it is always a bad thing that a person should exist at a level below α. The formula is in favour of preventing such people from coming to existence. Indeed, it implies it is worthwhile for existing people to sacrifice some small part of their own wellbeing to prevent them from existing. But, if the new people would live at a level only a bit below α, their lives would be perfectly decent. It is hard to believe there is anything positively wrong in their existing, so that actual sacrifices are worthwhile to prevent it.

Both a high level for α and a low level for α lead to dubious conclusions, then, and it seems to me that any intermediate level would encounter one or the other of the same problems. That is why I am not happy with critical level utilitarianism. Nevertheless, this formula follows from expected utility theory and the principle of personal good, both of which I believe. (The minor extra assumptions I mentioned offer no escape from the difficulty.) So what is to be done? Evidently some work is needed. We can hope that acceptable conclusions may emerge, and that eventually we shall come up with an acceptable value function. It may turn out, for instance, that the principle of personal good is wrong. Or we may find reasons, after all, to be convinced by critical level utilitarianism for some level of α. I do not know, but I see no reason to think we cannot make progress with the problems.

14.5   Conclusion

The questions I have examined in this chapter make a tremendous difference to the value we should assign to life. For instance, it makes a great difference to the value of saving a young person whether or not we should include the wellbeing of all her future descendants. In this particular case, most economists have up to now relied on their intuition that we should not. But intuition may not be reliable. Sometimes intuitions conflict with each other. For instance, saving a very premature baby is sometimes assumed to have a very high value, because the benefit of doing so is the whole of the wellbeing in the baby's future life.[13] On the other hand, many people feel that, when resources are scarce, they would be better used on saving, say, a twenty-year-old than a newborn baby. Certainly, the loss of an unborn foetus is commonly thought less of a tragedy than the loss of a twenty-year-old person, even if the foetus is as well developed as a viable premature baby. Helga Kuhse and Peter Singer have pointed out that the intuitions at work in these judgements are very hard to reconcile.[14] Evidently we need theoretical work to guide intuition.

In the meantime, we have no uncontentious way, in practice, of fixing a value on life. This is a difficulty for governments, which have to make decisions about the allocation of resources. But the difficulty is scarcely unique. We also have no uncontentious way of assigning value to the inequality of income in a society, or to education, or to many other things; yet governments have to act. We need research and discussion to help us move nearer to the truth. But we must not give the impression that the truth has already been discovered. It is absurd, for instance, to imagine that the techniques of economics are now able to say definitively whether resources are better used for saving premature babies or the middle-aged, on birth control or safety on the roads. On these questions economists can at the moment give hardly any guidance at all.

15 The value of a person

15.1 The basic intuition

Many people have the intuition that adding a person to the world is not valuable in itself, even if the person would enjoy a good life. If a new person will make such demands on the world's resources that her existence will do harm to people already alive, that is a reason against creating her. On the other hand, if a couple want a child, that is a reason for them to have one. But there is no reason that arises from the person's own interest. If a person could be created, and would lead a good life if she was created, the fact that her life would be good is not a reason for creating her. The existence of a person is ethically neutral in itself. I shall call this 'the basic intuition'. It must be qualified. If a person's life would be bad, were she to be created, that is a reason against creating her; a person's existence is ethically neutral only if her life would be good. Jan Narveson says, 'We are . . . neutral about making happy people.'[1] That is the basic intuition.

For instance, suppose a couple are wondering whether to have a child. Suppose there is no doubt their child's life would be good if they had one. But suppose the couple decide their own lives will be better on balance if they remain childless, and because of that they do so. Few people would think they are acting wrongly. It is not that we think the couple have a reason to have a child – her life would be good – that can justifiably be out-weighed by their own good. Instead, we think there is no positive reason at all why they should have a child. If having a child would be bad for the couple themselves, even to a small degree, that is a sufficient reason for them not to have one.

I am not going to defend the basic intuition, but I shall mention briefly two arguments that have been used to support it. Both can be found in Narveson's 'Utilitarianism and new generations'. One is this. One state of

From the *Proceedings of the Aristotelian Society*, Supplementary Volume 68 (1994), pp. 167–85. Reprinted by courtesy of the Editor of the Aristotelian Society: © 1994. This chapter was written while I was a visitor at the Research School of Social Science at the Australian National University. Valuable comments from Richard Holton and Philip Pettit had a direct impact on the chapter.

affairs is surely better than another only if it is better for someone. But a
state of affairs in which someone exists is not better for that person than
one where she does not exist. So creating a person does not in itself bring
about a better state of affairs. The second argument is this. Whatever moral
duties we have, they are surely duties owed to people as individuals. But we
cannot owe a person a duty to bring her into existence, because failing in
such a duty would not be failing anyone. So bringing a person into existence
cannot be, in itself, a moral duty.

I expressed the basic intuition by saying that a person's existence is ethically neutral. But this is unclear and imprecise, and it turns out to be very
hard to express the intuition in a precise and coherent form. This chapter
explores some of the difficulties, and some possible ways around them. The
basic intuition may be ultimately incoherent. But since it is common and
attractive, it is worth the effort of trying to put it into coherent form.

15.2   The constituency principle and counterexamples

Suppose a change leads to the existence of a new person, and also benefits
or harms existing people. If the person's existence is neutral, the value of
this change must be given by its value to the existing people; the fact that a
person is created should not count either way. So it is natural to try and
express the basic intuition by:

> *The constituency principle.* Suppose two states of affairs have the
> same population of people, except that an extra person exists in
> one who does not exist in the other. Suppose the extra person has
> a good life in the state in which she exists. Then one state is at least
> as good as the other if and only if it is at least as good for the people
> who exist in both.

The constituency principle tries to capture the basic intuition in terms of the
goodness of states of affairs, or more precisely in terms of betterness
between states of affairs. For the sake of economy, I have stated the principle in terms of the 'weak' betterness relation 'at least as good as'. As stated,
the principle implies parallel principles for the 'strict' betterness relation
'better than', and for the relation 'equally as good as'. That is to say: one
state is better than the other if and only if it is better for the people who exist
in both; and one state is equally as good as the other if and only if it is equally
as good for the people who exist in both. The people who exist in both states
form a constituency that determines the relative goodness of the states.

By the 'population' of a state of affairs, I mean all the people who live at
any time. A state of affairs is a complete history for the world, and the constituency principle compares the value of different possible histories.

Unfortunately, this principle is false. The following example shows why. Consider these three alternative states of affairs:

Example 1.   1*A*: $(w_1, w_2, \ldots, w_n, \Omega)$
               1*B*: $(w_1, w_2, \ldots, w_n, 1)$
               1*C*: $(w_1, w_2, \ldots, w_n, 2)$

In this example and others, I use the following notation. Each possible state of affairs is represented by a vector that shows its distribution of wellbeing. Each place in the vector stands for a person who lives at some time in at least one of the states we are comparing. The corresponding place in the different vectors stands for the same person. If a person exists in one of the states, I assume it is determinate whether or not she (or her counterpart) exists in each of the other states. In a state where she does not exist, her place in the vector contains an Ω. In a state where she does exist, her place contains a number that indicates her lifetime wellbeing. I assume wellbeing can be measured on a cardinal scale that is comparable between people. I take the scale to be such that a life with a positive level of wellbeing is good rather than bad. In all my examples, there are many people whose wellbeing is the same in all the options. I shall not bother to specify what these people's wellbeing is. In Example 1, they are the first n people.

The problem represented in Example 1 is whether or not to add person $n+1$ to the population, and if she is added, whether or not to make her wellbeing 1 or 2. Think of it as the question facing a couple wondering whether or not to have a child, and what arrangements to make for her wellbeing if they do. In the example, the couple themselves will be affected neither for better nor worse by their decision. They are among the first n people.

According to the constituency condition, 1*A* is equally as good as 1*B*, since it is equally as good for all the first n people, who exist in both. Likewise, 1*C* is equally as good as 1*A*. In the comparison between 1*B* and 1*C*, the constituency includes the extra person $n+1$, and 1*C* is better for that person. So the constituency principle says 1*C* is better than 1*B*. The principle implies, then, that 1*C* is equally as good as 1*A*, 1*A* is equally as good as 1*B*, but 1*C* is better than 1*B*. This is a contradiction. As a matter of logic, the relation 'equally as good as' is transitive, and the constituency principle implies it is not. Therefore the constituency principle is false.

Two more examples will be useful.

Example 2.   2*A*: $(w_1, w_2, \ldots, w_n, 5, \Omega)$
               2*B*: $(w_1, w_2, \ldots, w_n, 6, 1)$
               2*C*: $(w_1, w_2, \ldots, w_n, 4, 4)$

Think of this as a problem facing parents who already have one child $n+1$ and are wondering whether to have a second $n+2$. If they do, they can divide their resources between the children either equally or unequally. This example is a version of Derek Parfit's 'mere addition paradox'.[2]

The constituency principle implies that $2B$ is better than $2A$. In this comparison the constituency is the first $n+1$ people. $2B$ is better than $2A$ for these people together, since it is equally as good for the first n and better for person $n+1$. For a similar reason, the constituency principle implies $2A$ is better than $2C$. However, in the comparison between $2B$ and $2C$, the constituency includes person $n+2$ too. Which of the two is better for all these people? The constituency principle itself does not say, but it is very plausible to assume it is $2C$. $2C$ has more wellbeing in total, and it has it equally distributed between the two children. Given this plausible assumption, the constituency principle implies that $2C$ is better than $2B$. So altogether this principle implies that $2B$ is better than $2A$, $2C$ better than $2B$, and $2A$ better than $2C$. This is a contradiction. As a matter of logic, the strict betterness relation 'better than' is transitive. Granted the extra plausible assumption, the constituency principle implies it is not. So the constituency principle is false.

In Example 2, the constituency principle implies an intransitivity in strict betterness, which is a more serious contradiction than the one revealed by Example 1. On the other hand, the contradiction only arises because of the auxiliary assumption that $2C$ is better for the $n+2$ people than $2B$. In the next example, the constituency principle implies an intransitivity in strict betterness without any auxiliary assumption.

Example 3. $3A$: $(w_1, w_2, \ldots, w_n, 1, 3, \Omega)$
$3B$: $(w_1, w_2, \ldots, w_n, 2, \Omega, \Omega)$
$3C$: $(w_1, w_2, \ldots, w_n, 3, \Omega, 1)$
$3D$: $(w_1, w_2, \ldots, w_n, \Omega, \Omega, 2)$
$3E$: $(w_1, w_2, \ldots, w_n, \Omega, 1, 3)$
$3F$: $(w_1, w_2, \ldots, w_n, \Omega, 2, \Omega)$

The constituency principle implies that $3B$ is better than $3A$, $3C$ better than $3B$, $3D$ better than $3C$, and so on round to $3A$ better than $3F$.

Notice that options $3A$ and $3C$ must be equally good. The only difference between them is the identity of the people who exist, and which of them has a wellbeing of 1 and which 3. This difference shows in the different orders of the elements in the vectors $3A$ and $3C$. But there is nothing special about the order in which the people appear in the vectors. By putting them in a different order, I could represent the state of affairs $3C$ by the same vector as, with my present ordering of people, represents $3A$. So $3A$ and $3C$ must be equally good. Yet in only two steps, the constituency principle implies $3C$ is better than $3A$. This is enough to show the principle is false.

How should we respond to the conclusion that the constituency principle is false?[3] One possible response is to give up the constituency principle along with the basic intuition that led to it. This is the response of population theories that are sometimes called 'impersonal'.[4] Since the basic intuition remains attractive, this response pays a penalty in abandoning it, and it has some other difficulties of its own.[5] Another is to express the intuition in a deontic form that does not involve betterness. For instance, in Example 2 we could understand it to say the parents ought to choose $2B$ if faced with a choice between $2A$ and $2B$, and they ought to choose $2C$ if faced with a choice between $2B$ and $2C$, and they ought to choose $2A$ if faced with a choice between $2C$ and $2A$. There is no contradiction in this. There is still some explaining to do, however. Why should the parents make these choices, if they are not choosing the better option in each case? Indeed, what is the relative goodness of these options, and what stops the threatened intransitivity of betterness from arising? What should the parents do if faced with a choice amongst all three options, and why? Evidently, a theory is needed to develop this response.[6]

I am going to leave these two responses aside, and concentrate on others that try to preserve the intuition, and express it in terms of goodness. All of these responses adopt theories about the structure of the betterness relation that may be called 'nonstandard'. The first claims that this relation may be intransitive, the second that it may be conditional in a particular sense, the third that it may be relative to one's viewpoint, and the fourth that it may be vague. If the first of these claims is true, it invalidates the argument I have given against the constituency principle, which assumed transitivity. So this response can preserve the principle itself. The others give up the constituency principle, but give a different expression in terms of betterness to the basic intuition that underlies it. I shall discuss the first three in this chapter; I leave the fourth to Adam Morton.[7]

15.3   Intransitive betterness

In 'Intransitivity and the mere addition paradox', Larry Temkin uses examples like mine to argue not that the constituency principle is false, but conversely that the betterness relation is intransitive.

Temkin argues that, when we compare the goodness of two options, particular criteria are relevant to the comparison, and different criteria may be relevant to different comparisons. Whether or not an option A is better than B depends on how A and B measure up against the criteria that are relevant to the comparison between A and B. When we compare the pair B and C, different criteria may be relevant, and different criteria again when we compare C and A. The result may turn out to be that A is better than B, B better than C, and C better than A. Because different criteria are relevant to each comparison, nothing prevents this from happening. So the betterness relation may be intransitive.

Take Example 2, for instance. In the comparison between $2A$ and $2B$, what is relevant according to the constituency principle is the wellbeing of the first $n+1$ people. We can conclude that $2B$ is better than $2A$. For the same reason, $2A$ is better than $2C$. But in the comparison between $2B$ and $2C$, the constituency principle tells us that the wellbeing of all the first $n+2$ people is relevant. This different criterion makes $2C$ better than $2B$. So we get an intransitive betterness relation, it seems.

But despite this point, I am going to insist the betterness relation is transitive. Why? Temkin mentions one theory that would give grounds for insisting on it. He calls it 'the intrinsic aspect view'.[8] It says that the goodness of a state of affairs is an intrinsic property of that state. If this is so, we can derive the conclusion that the betterness relation is transitive. If A is at least as good as B and B at least as good as C, then, according to the intrinsic aspect view, A's intrinsic goodness must be at least as great as B's, and B's at least as great as C's. Consequently, A's intrinsic goodness must be at least as great as C's. So A must be at least as good as C.

Now, this derivation of the transitivity of betterness does not actually require the premise that goodness is an intrinsic property. If A is at least as good as B and B at least as good as C, then A's goodness is at least as great as B's, and B's at least as great as C's. Consequently, A's goodness is at least as great as C's. So A must be at least as good as C. The basis of this argument is simply that goodness is a property, and that betterness is the comparative of goodness. There is no need for goodness to be an intrinsic property. The comparative of *any* property is necessarily transitive.

Many relations are not transitive. 'To the left of' is not – think of people sitting round a table. But no intransitive relation can be the comparative of any property. There is no property of leftness, for instance. The relation 'judged by me to be at least as good as' may be intransitive, since it is not the comparative of any property. When I make judgements of betterness, different criteria may come to my mind as I make different comparisons, and the result may be intransitive judgements. My examples show how this can happen. But, because betterness is the comparative of the property of goodness, betterness must be transitive. Therefore, my judgements of betterness cannot possibly be correct unless they are transitive. So long as my judgements are intransitive, I still have work to do in sorting them out.

When I work on my intransitive judgements, the result may be that I come to change one of them, and so make them transitive. Or the judgements may refuse to change; it may seem to me that I have made the very best possible judgements, accurately taking into account all the proper ethical criteria, and yet these judgements may still be intransitive. If Temkin is right that different criteria may be relevant to different comparisons, I cannot guarantee in advance that my judgements will turn out transitive. But if they do not, they cannot be judgements of betterness, whatever I may have intended. To express them accurately, I shall have to put them in other – perhaps deontic – terms.

In any case, even if betterness could be intransitive, Temkin's argument cannot be used to support the constituency principle. Example 3 shows why not. When the constituency principle compares $3A$ and $3B$, the criterion it uses is the wellbeing of person $n+1$. When it compares $3B$ and $3C$, the criterion it uses is the same: the wellbeing of $n+1$. Temkin suggests betterness might not be transitive because the criteria might be different in different comparisons, but in these two comparisons the criteria are the same. So Temkin has given us no reason to doubt transitivity in this case. Given transitivity, the constituency principle implies $3C$ is better than $3A$. But I explained earlier that $3C$ and $3A$ must be equally good. So the constituency principle is false.

15.4   Conditional betterness

Look again at Example 1. I think most people who share the basic intuition will know what to think about this example. Since no existing person would be affected for better or worse, the basic intuition says it does not matter whether or not the parents have a child. However, intuition also says that, if they do have a child, they should make sure she is as well off as possible. Put generally, it does not matter morally whether we add a new person to the population (provided her life will be good), but, if we do add one, we must do our best for her. This idea makes good sense, and in cases like Example 1 it provides a satisfactory guide to action. If a couple have a choice between $1A$ and $1B$ only, it says it does not matter which they choose. Likewise, it does not matter which they choose if they have a choice between $1A$ and $1C$ only. If they have a choice between $1B$ and $1C$, they should choose $1C$. If they have a choice between all three options, they should not choose $1B$, but it does not matter whether they choose $1A$ or $1C$.

So the intuition works as a guide to action in these cases, and on the face of it, it seems possible to express it in terms of goodness. We may say that creating a person is equally as good as not creating her, but, if she is created, it is better that her life should go well rather than less well. This formula uses an idea of conditional betterness: it is better that her life should go well, conditional on her existence. I shall develop this idea by applying it first in the different context of continuing an existing life rather than creating a new one.

In his paper 'The Makropulos case', Bernard Williams considers what reason we have to continue our lives, if we have the choice, rather than to die. Most of us, he says, want all sorts of things and many of them are things we cannot get unless we continue to live. Death would prevent the satisfaction of these wants. That is a bad thing about death, and a reason to prefer living. Williams then considers this rejoinder: 'Many of the things I want, I want only on the assumption that I am going to be alive . . . It might be suggested that not just these special cases, but really all wants, were conditional on being alive.'[9] A want that is conditional on my being alive would give me no reason to avoid death. But Williams insists that many of us have wants that are *categorical,* by which he means they are not conditional on being alive. Categorical wants give us reasons for remaining alive.

What does it mean for a want to be conditional on being alive? If I want P conditional on Q, one thing that must mean is that I prefer $Q\&P$ to $Q\&\neg P$, whereas I am indifferent between $\neg Q\&P$ and $\neg Q\&\neg P$. Suppose I want the sea to be smooth next week conditional on my crossing the Channel next week. This means I prefer crossing a smooth sea to crossing a rough one, but if I am not going to cross, I do not care how rough the sea is. Notice that this conditional preference has implications for my preferences between crossing the Channel and not crossing it; it cannot leave me perfectly indifferent between the two. Because crossing a smooth sea comes higher in my preference ordering than crossing a rough sea, this implies the two cannot both stand level in the ordering with not crossing at all. If, say, I am indifferent between crossing a rough sea and not crossing at all, I must prefer crossing a smooth sea to not crossing at all. So, although my desire for a smooth sea is only conditional on my crossing, it implies I have a reason to cross in particular circumstances (if the sea will be smooth), or else not to cross in particular circumstances (if the sea will be rough). It may be puzzling how a want that comes into play only when a certain condition is satisfied can imply anything about my reasons for bringing about this condition itself. But the puzzle arises only from the habit of thinking that reasons are given by wants or preferences taken one by one. If instead, you think that reasons derive from the whole structure of a person's preference ordering, the puzzle will disappear.

But when Williams mentions wants that are conditional on being alive, he is evidently not thinking of conditional wants that work in quite the way I have just described. Suppose I want a warm autumn this year conditional on being alive during the autumn. This implies I prefer living through a warm autumn to living through a cold one, and I do not care what the autumn will be like if I am dead by then. That much carries over from what I said in the previous paragraph. However, Williams does not intend it to follow that I am not indifferent between living through the autumn and dying before then. For instance, he does not intend it to follow that, if I am indifferent between dying and living through a cold autumn, then I prefer living through a warm autumn to dying. If this followed, then conditional wants by themselves would be enough to ensure that most of us have a reason to continue living, and Williams would have no need to invoke categorical wants. Evidently, he intends wants that are conditional on living to leave me indifferent between dying and living in any circumstances. From now on, I shall restrict the term 'conditional want' to wants that are conditional in this stronger sense, so a want that is conditional on some condition leaves me indifferent about the condition itself. Intuitively, conditional wants like this seem to make sense. It seems we could make sense of a person who says she is perfectly indifferent about whether she lives or dies, but if she lives she wants to be in good health.

Williams assumes that all reasons derive from wants, so the only reasons one could have for remaining alive are to satisfy one's wants. But let me now generalize his idea to allow for the possibility that there are other good things in life apart from the satisfaction of wants. I shall introduce the more general idea of conditional *goods*.[10] To say something is a good means it is better pro tanto that this thing should exist rather than not. To say something is a good conditional on *P*, means that, if *P*, it is better pro tanto that this thing should exist than not. I mean 'conditional' to have the strong sense I just described for wants. So a good that is conditional on my remaining alive does not contribute to making it better that I remain alive rather than die, whether or not I shall get the good if I remain alive. Only, if I do remain alive, it is better that I should get the good rather than not. A conditional good does not generate a reason why I should remain alive. If all my goods are conditional on remaining alive, there is no reason why I should remain alive.

Are there any goods that are conditional in this sense on remaining alive? It seems plausible there are. If satisfying a person's want is good, then satisfying a conditional want will be a conditional good. So if there are wants that are conditional on remaining alive there will be goods that are conditional on remaining alive. In any case, I find it independently plausible there are such goods: that some things, though good, do not generate a reason for living in order to get them. To take one example, the Epicureans believed that *pleasure* is the only good, and that it is conditional on remaining alive. They believed it is good to have pleasure while you are alive, but it gives you no reason to remain alive. Since they believed the only sort of good there is is conditional on living, they believed death does no harm.[11] When Williams insists in 'The Makropulos case' that some wants are categorical, he is explicitly directing his argument against the Epicureans. He denies the Epicurean view that all goods are conditional, but he accepts that some are.

Are there really, as Williams thinks, any goods that are *not* conditional on remaining alive, so they give us a reason why we should remain alive? Plausibly, one sort of good that is not conditional in this way is furthering or completing a task we have embarked on: a career, perhaps, or bringing up children. I find it plausible that the good of finishing this chapter is a reason for staying alive till I finish it, so this good does not seem conditional on my staying alive. On the other hand, the good of furthering or completing a task is perhaps conditional on living to start the task. I may have a reason for living to complete my next paper, which I have not started yet. But if I do have a reason, perhaps it is not to get the good of completing the paper. Perhaps it is to get the good of furthering my career, which I *have* started.

This is only barefaced speculation, but I am going to carry it a bit further. Suppose that furthering or completing a task is the only sort of good that is not conditional on continuing to live, and suppose that all goods of this sort are conditional on living to start the task. That is to say, suppose the reasons why we should move forward through life are always to further or complete the tasks we have embarked on; we are propelled by a sequence of overlapping tasks. As we go, we pick up other sorts of goods such as pleasure, but these are all conditional on living and do not themselves give us a reason for living. If this is so, it meshes with the basic intuition that motivates this chapter, that the existence of a person is morally neutral.

What is the value of creating a person? It is not necessarily all the good her life will contain, but all the good that is not conditional on her existence. It is only this unconditional good that generates a reason why she should exist. My speculative suggestion is that, once a person is alive, the only goods that are not conditional on her remaining alive are completing or furthering tasks she has embarked on. Even these goods are conditional on her being alive up to the time of embarking on the task. So they are all conditional on the person's existing in the first place. If my suggestion is right, therefore, there is no value in creating a person. To accept this conclusion, you do not have to be convinced by my speculation that all the goods in a person's life are the specific sort I described. So long as you agree that all the goods in a person's life are conditional on the person's existence, that is enough.

This amounts to an argument in support of the basic intuition that a person's existence is morally neutral, but as an argument it is so speculative that I put no weight on it. Its importance for my purposes is that it offers us the idea of conditional good as a resource for trying to shape the basic intuition into a coherent form. Conditional good is conditional in a stronger sense than my desire for a smooth sea is conditional. When it comes to evaluating the condition itself, conditional good is neutral. If a person's wellbeing is good conditional on the person's existence, her wellbeing makes no difference to the value of her existence. Therefore, even though a life with more wellbeing is conditionally better than a life with less, both may be equally as good as no life at all. This expresses the intuition that began this section.

However, though it is attractive and though it may express an intuition, I think we have to conclude that the idea of conditional good is incoherent. It implies a structure for the betterness relation that it cannot have. In Example 1, if we say $1C$ is conditionally better than $1B$, and both are equally as good as $1A$, there is no disguising the fact that really we are simply saying $1C$ is better than $1B$, and both are equally as good as $1A$. This is a contradiction. It might be tolerable in practice in cases like Example 1, because in those cases it contradicts only the transitivity of the relation 'equally as good as'. This makes betterness a 'quasi-transitive relation',[12] and it can lead to sensible recommendations about how to act; I laid them out for Example 1 at the beginning of this section. If the idea of conditional good always led to sensible recommendations, I would work on it some more, to try and find some way of giving it formal coherence. But in more complicated examples, it does not even do that. In Example 2, if we think a person's good is conditional on her existence, we shall think $2B$ is better than $2A$, $2C$ better than $2B$, and $2A$ better than $2C$. This will give us no sensible prescriptions for action. In this case, conditional betterness leads to intransitivity in the strict betterness relation, and that is intolerable. I think the idea has to be abandoned.

15.5   Relative betterness

A relativist response to the failure of the constituency principle has been worked out by Partha Dasgupta.[13] Up to now, I have assumed there is a single betterness relation, but Dasgupta thinks there are many. He thinks betterness is relative to a population, so that each population has its own betterness relation. One option may be better than another from the point of view of one population and worse from the point of view of a different population. Specifically, Dasgupta suggests that the goodness of an option relative to a particular population is a weighted sum of people's wellbeing, giving more weight to the members of the population in question. For example, let us evaluate the options in Example 2 relative to the population consisting of the first $n+1$ people. Since person $n+2$ is not in this population, she gets a lower weight. If her weight is less than a quarter, $2A$ will be better than $2C$ from the point of view of the first $n+1$ people. The four units that $n+2$ gets in $2C$ is outweighed by the extra one unit that $n+1$ gets in $2A$ compared with $2C$.

How does relative betterness determine what ought to be done? If an existing population has to make a choice between a number of available options, what should it do? One might assume it ought to do what is best according to its own betterness relation, but that is not Dasgupta's view. Dasgupta recommends a two-stage procedure for deciding. Stage one goes like this. For each possible population, compare together all the options that contain just that population, and select the one that is best according to the betterness relation of that population. Since none of the options being compared contains any people outside this population, this means selecting the option that has the greatest unweighted total of wellbeing. For instance, in Example 2, we compare $2B$ and $2C$ because they share the same population, and select $2C$ because it has the greater total of wellbeing. We select $2A$ because no other available option has the same population. By the end of stage one, we have selected one option for each possible population.

In stage two, the population that has to make the choice compares together all the options that have been selected at stage one. Dasgupta says it should choose the one that is best according to its own betterness relation. This means, in stage two, giving more weight to its own wellbeing. In Example 2, suppose the choice is in the hands of the first $n+1$ people, including the parents and the first child. They compare $2A$ and $2C$, which are the two options selected by stage one. If they ought to give other people's wellbeing less than a quarter the weight they give their own, they should choose $2A$. If the weight is more than a quarter, they should choose $2C$. In Example 1, suppose the choice is in the hands of the first n people. They compare $1A$ and $1C$, which are the two options selected at stage one. They should choose $1C$ if the weight they should give other people is more than zero. If the weight is zero, $1A$ and $1C$ have the same weighted total, so it does not matter which they choose.

How do these conclusions about the examples square with intuition? Dasgupta does not discuss cases like Example 3, where more than one option has the same number of people, but where the identities of those people are different, so I shall leave those cases aside. In Example 1, I suggested most people's intuitions are clear: it would be wrong to choose $1B$ if $1C$ is available, but the choice between $1A$ and $1C$ does not matter ethically. Dasgupta's theory reproduces this conclusion if and only if a population should give a zero weight to people who do not belong to it. In any case, it is obvious that Dasgupta's theory can hope to capture the basic intuition that a person's existence is neutral only if it makes this weight zero. Given that, in Example 2 the theory favours option $2A$. I think many people's intuitions might not be clear in this example. Still, $2A$ is a plausible choice. So Dasgupta's theory may not only represent our intuitions adequately; in some cases it may take us beyond them, as an ethical theory should, and deliver an answer where intuition fails.

So Dasgupta offers us a coherent theory that could perhaps capture the basic intuition, at least in these cases. However, the theory needs to be justified. We need a justification for the idea of relative betterness, and for the two-stage procedure. I shall consider each in turn.

Why does Dasgupta think betterness is relative to the population, and why does he think betterness relative to a population gives more weight to the population's own wellbeing than to other people's? The answer is that he treats population-relativity as a type of community-relativity. He thinks members of a community have special claims on each other that outsiders do not have. A population forms a community, and from its point of view people not yet born are outsiders. Dasgupta particularly has in mind the community of the family. 'Family members', he says, 'have a special claim upon one another. Potential persons don't have this claim. "They" are not members of the community.'[14]

So Dasgupta treats a person whose existence is in question as an outsider, and gives less weight to her interests on that account. In Example 2, for instance, he would take it to be in the interests of the second child $n+2$ to have $2C$ come about, where she is created, rather than $2A$, where she is not. But he would say her interest may be outweighed by the more heavily weighted interest of the first child $n+1$. I said Dasgupta's theory can reproduce the conclusions of our basic intuition only by giving a zero weight to outsiders. But it is most implausible that any community could be justified in giving a zero weight to outsiders. It might be justified in giving outsiders a lower weight than it gives its own members, but not in ignoring their interests entirely. So the theory can get the appropriate answer only by taking up an implausible extreme position.

The reason it is in this bind is that it thoroughly misrepresents our basic intuition from the start. Our intuition is that a child has no interest in being created, not that she has an interest that may be outweighed or ignored. It is not in a person's interest to be created, because being created does not make a person better off than she would otherwise have been. This intuition is not relativist; anyone can recognize it, including the person herself if she is created. Indeed, it is a classic mistake to treat a person who might or might not be created as an outsider who has an interest in being created, as though she is a person-in-waiting, who might or might not be granted the privilege of existence. I conclude that, if we are to have a relativist theory of population, it cannot be founded on community-relativity.

Now to the justification of Dasgupta's two-stage procedure. Let us now accept that each population has its own relative betterness relation. How should an existing population act? According to the theory, it ought not simply do the best it can according to its own betterness relation. Through the two-stage procedure, betterness relative to other populations helps to determine what a particular population ought to do. Why? Each population is constrained by the acts of its successors. If it chooses to bring a particular successor population into existence, what happens after that will be determined by the successor. The acts of the successor population will no doubt partly depend on its own relative betterness. So the betterness relation of one population will help determine the constraints faced by its predecessors. This is one way betterness of one population could affect what another ought to do. Is this what Dasgupta has in mind?

It may be, but I think not entirely, for two reasons. First, one population constrains another by what it will do or would do if it existed, but Dasgupta gives us no account of what a population will or would do. He considers only what a population ought to do, and it would be naive to assume that every population will do what it ought.

The second reason is brought out by Example 2. If the parents decide to have a second child, the result will be either $2B$ or $2C$. The parents might well be able to determine the choice between these options before the second child is even conceived. Dasgupta assumes they could not determine this choice, but at one point he does raise the question of which they should choose if they could.[15] He does not answer explicitly, but he gives the impression he likes the answer '$2C$'. This is certainly a plausible answer. In the example, if the final result of the decision-making process was either $2B$ or $2C$, the population in existence would be the later expanded population that includes the second child. Surely, therefore, the right choice between $2B$ and $2C$ is determined by what is better from the point of view of the expanded population. If the parents were able to choose between $2B$ and $2C$ before the second child was conceived, then plausibly they ought to choose $2C$. I think Dasgupta would agree. Yet, according to the relative betterness relation of the population existing before the second child is conceived, $2B$ is better than $2C$. So what the predecessor population ought to do here seems to be determined directly by the successor population's betterness relation, and not by its own. It is not simply that the successor's acts constrain the predecessor's options. The successor's betterness has direct moral force over the predecessor.

This is puzzling. If the predecessor population ought to choose $2C$ rather than $2B$, were it to have the choice, what does it mean to say $2B$ is better than $2C$ relative to this population? To be sure, $2B$ is more in this population's interest than $2C$, but its own interest is not in question. Dasgupta's relative betterness relations are not meant to express the interests of particular populations; they are meant to express moral betterness from each population's point of view. Yet we have just seen that they do not tell us what a population ought morally to do. So I do not know what Dasgupta's idea of relative betterness really amounts to. It would make good sense if each population ought to do the best it can relative to its own betterness. But the two-stage procedure implies that is not so.

In summary, Dasgupta's relativist theory is a worthwhile attempt to capture the basic intuition. But I have two different doubts about its foundations. So I am still not convinced that the basic intuition can be coherently expressed in terms of goodness.

Notes

1 INTRODUCTION: ETHICS OUT OF ECONOMICS

1. For instance, see Leonard Savage, *The Foundations of Statistics*, p. 17, and Kenneth Arrow, *Social Choice and Justice*, p. 47.
2. This argument is dealt with more thoroughly in my *Weighing Goods*, chap. 7.
3. There is a fuller discussion of this example in my 'Goodness is reducible to betterness', chap. 10 in this volume.
4. Epicurus, 'Letter to Menoeceus', p. 85.
5. The same point is made by Fred Feldman in 'Some puzzles about the evil of death'.
6. See 'Fairness', chap. 7 in this volume.
7. See 'Qalys', chap. 13 in this volume.
8. See my *Weighing Goods*, chap. 4, and the appendix to 'Qalys', chap. 13 in this volume.
9. For instance, see J. A. Mirrlees, 'The economic uses of utilitarianism', and Thomas Schelling, 'Self-command in practice, in policy, and in a theory of rational choice'.
10. The argument is developed in my *Weighing Goods*.

2 'UTILITY'

1. Bentham, Principles of Morals and Legislation, p. 2.
2. Mill, *Utilitarianism*, p. 213. Mill is not using 'Utility' as a synonym for 'Happiness'. The initial capitals and the expression 'directive rule of human conduct' make this clear. Mill never identifies utility with happiness or pleasure, though there are some loosely worded remarks in *Utilitarianism* that may suggest he does.
3. Jevons, *The Theory of Political Economy*, p. 46.
4. Marshall, *Principles of Economics*, p. 64.
5. *Ibid.*, p. 93.
6. Edgeworth, *Mathematical Psychics*, p. 45.
7. Sidgwick, *The Methods of Ethics*, pp. 423-4.
8. *Ibid.*, p. 424.
9. It was fully formed in John Hicks and R. G. D. Allen, 'A reconsideration of the theory of value'.
10. Derek Parfit pointed this out to me.
11. Edgeworth, *Mathematical Psychics*, p. 16.

12. Robbins, *An Essay on the Scope and Nature of Economic Science*, p. 95.
13. For instance, see Amos Tversky and Daniel Kahneman, 'Rational choice and the framing of decisions'.
14. My own argument for this point is in my *Weighing Goods*, chap. 5.
15. More precisely, for it to be properly defined which of two alternatives has the greater expectation of good, good needs to be defined uniquely up to an increasing linear transformation.
16. See Bernoulli, 'Exposition of a new theory on the measurement of risk'.
17. Some appear in my *Weighing Goods*, chaps. 10 and 11.
18. Ellsberg, 'Classic and current notions of "measurable utility"', p. 528.
19. Von Neumann–Morgenstern utility function. This is Harsanyi's term for a utility function that has the expected utility form.
20. Harsanyi, 'Can the maximin principle serve as a basis for morality?', p. 600.
21. For instance, see Sen, *On Ethics and Economics*, pp. 14–15.
22. Pigou does not use 'utility' at all in *The Economics of Welfare*.
23. Sen, *The Standard of Living*, pp. 5–14.
24. Sen has replied to this comment in his 'Utility'.
25. For instance, Gerard Debreu, *Theory of Value*, p. 56.
26. For instance, Angus Deaton and John Muellbauer, *Economics and Consumer Behavior*, p. 28.
27. I use 'utility' this way myself in *Weighing Goods*.
28. See the quotation in section 2.3, p. 00.

3 EXTENDED PREFERENCES

1. For instance, by Kenneth Arrow in 'Extended sympathy and the possibility of social choice', and John Harsanyi in *Rational Behaviour and Bargaining Equilibrium*, pp. 57–60.
2. See the references in n. 4.
3. Harsanyi, *Rational Behaviour and Bargaining Equilibrium*, pp. 57–60.
4. The argument appears in rudimentary form in Harsanyi's 'Cardinal welfare, individualistic ethics, and interpersonal comparisons of utility', pp. 17–18 in the reprinted version, and independently in Jan Tinbergen's 'Welfare economics and income distribution', p. 501. It also appears in Serge-Christophe Kolm's *Justice et équité*, pp. 79–80.
5. Harsanyi, *Rational Behavior and Bargaining Equilibrium*, pp. 58–9.
6. *Ibid.*, pp. 31–2.
7. Kolm, *Justice et équité*, pp. 79–80. I take this translation from John Rawls, 'Social unity and primary goods', p. 174.
8. See my 'Utility', chap. 2 in this volume.
9. Arrow, 'Extended sympathy and the possibility of social choice', p. 159.
10. Susan Hurley impressed this point on me.

4 DISCOUNTING THE FUTURE

1. Ramsey, 'A mathematical theory of saving', p. 261 in the reprinted version.
2. One economist who comes down firmly against pure discounting is Robert Solow in 'The economics of resources or the resources of economics'. On the other hand, there is a sustained argument in favour of pure discounting in

Partha Dasgupta and Geoffrey Heal, *Economic Theory and Exhaustible Resources*, pp. 255–82.

3. Stephen Marglin is one exception. See the quotation in section 4.7, p. 64.
4. Stiglitz, 'The rate of discount for benefit–cost analysis and the theory of second best', p. 156.
5. I shall ignore several complications. In particular, I shall ignore the difference between the interest rates faced by consumers and producers, which is caused by taxation. There is a more detailed treatment in my *Counting the Cost of Global Warming*, chap. 3.
6. A smaller complication is this. I argued that the relative prices of commodities will measure their relative values to a person, at the margin. But the argument works only if the person buys or sells some amount of each commodity. If she chooses not to buy any of some commodity (and if she has none to sell), that commodity's price does not indicate its value to her. Evidently, its value to her is not more than its price, or she would buy some, but it may be less than its price. Like the complication of nonmarketed commodities, this complication can also be dealt with by using the person's willingness to pay for the commodity, in place of its price.
7. There is a fuller account of technological fertility in my *Microeconomics of Capitalism*, particularly pp. 36–7.
8. See my *Microeconomics of Capitalism*.
9. Cowen and Parfit, 'Against the social discount rate', particularly p. 151.
10. Cowen and Parfit do not suggest market rates will be zero. But they do claim interest rates will be zero at the 'optimum', when savings in the society are at the level they should be. This is because they do not believe in discounting future commodities; they take present and future commodities to have the same value. So long as future commodities are cheaper than present commodities, they think savings are not as high as they should be. Savings should be increased, which means that more future commodities should be consumed instead of present ones. They think that increasing savings should eventually bring the price of future commodities up to the level of present ones. That is to say, interest rates should be brought down to zero. But this is mistaken. Under present environmental conditions, interest rates cannot generally be zero at the optimum. Suppose we grant that savings are at present too low. If they are increased, this will increase the rate of growth of the world economy. Long before interest rates are driven down to zero, the increased savings will bring about a positive rate of growth in per capita income: people will be getting richer as time passes. (Indeed, that may well be so already, even with savings at their present low level.) Consequently, the marginal value of commodities to people will be declining; as people get richer, they attach less value to extra commodities. Future commodities will be less valuable than present ones, then. Commodities ought to be discounted, that is to say, even at the optimum. Cowen and Parfit cannot legitimately take it for granted that they should not be.
11. Parfit, *Reasons and Persons*, pp. 480–6.
12. *Ibid.*, p. 484.
13. *Ibid.*
14. There is a fuller catalogue in my *Counting the Cost of Global Warming*, pp. 60–92.

15. This is known amongst economists as the 'Hotelling rule', because it appears in H. Hotelling's 'The economics of exhaustible resources'.
16. *Reasons and Persons*, p. 483.
17. Parfit makes a concession he ought not to make. He points out that we can compensate for some deformities by providing the victim with commodities as compensation. We must compensate for present deformities with present commodities. But we can compensate for future deformities by setting up a fund now to buy future commodities. The fund will grow over time with interest. Since the fund will grow, it will be cheaper to compensate for future deformities than present ones. Provided we set up the fund, says Parfit, this is a reason for valuing future deformities less than present ones. But there is a mistake in his reasoning. The fund earns interest because future commodities, in general, are cheaper in the present than present ones. That is what interest is: it is the fact that future commodities are cheaper in the present than present commodities. In equilibrium, they are therefore less *valuable* than present ones; they bring less benefit as the margin. A present deformity will require some quantity of present commodities as compensation. A future deformity will require a greater quantity of future commodities, because the future deformity is just as bad as the present one, but the future commodities are less valuable. The fund earns interest just as quickly as commodities decline in value, so it will just be able to provide compensation to the same value whenever it is spent. Consequently, future deformities can only be compensated for at exactly the same present cost as present deformities.
18. Pigou, *The Economics of Welfare*, pp. 29–30.
19. Marglin, 'The social rate of discount and the optimal rate of investment', p. 97. I would be misrepresenting Marglin if I did not make one point. Marglin thinks the government should base its decisions on the preferences of the present generation, but he does not think it should use market interest rates in its calculations. Because of something called the 'isolation paradox', he thinks the market rate does not properly measure what the present generation would like to leave to its successors. I cannot go into the details of the isolation paradox here.
20. The point is developed in more detail in my *Weighing Goods*, chap. 7. Parfit makes a similar point in *Reasons and Persons*, pp. 480–1.
21. In their 'Positive time preference', Mancur Olson and Martin Bailey claim to have evidence that people are imprudent, but their argument is seriously flawed. See my *Counting the Cost of Global Warming*, p. 110, n. 21.
22. My own tentative views about it are given in *Counting the Cost of Global Warming*, pp. 94–108.

5 CAN A HUMEAN BE MODERATE?

1. Actually, not all the axioms of decision theory are conditions of consistency. For instance, one axiom is *completeness*: for any pair of alternatives A and B, either A is preferred to B, or B to A, or the two are indifferent. This is not required by consistency.
2. There is a careful survey of money pump and Dutch book arguments by Mark Machina in 'Dynamic consistency and non-expected utility models of choice under uncertainty'.

3. Jeffrey, 'On interpersonal utility theory', p. 656.
4. There are weaker consistency axioms, but not defined on preferences. See Amartya Sen, *Collective Choice and Social Welfare*, p. 17.
5. They are not 'context-free', to use Edward McClennen's terminology in *Rationality and Dynamic Choice*, p. 29.
6. In commenting on a previous discussion of mine (in 'Rationality and the sure-thing principle') about the same example, McClennen (*Rationality and Dynamic Choice*, p. 67) suggests I simply took it for granted that a preference ordering must be context-free. This criticism is not perfectly just. The whole point of the example is that Maurice's preferences *do* depend on what McClennen calls the 'context': on what choice is on offer. Nevertheless, by the device of individuating alternatives finely, Maurice is able to arrange all his preferences in a coherent, constant order. He is able to make them satisfy both transitivity and McClennen's condition of context-freeness. I did not *assume* Maurice's preferences were context-free; I showed how context-dependent preferences can be converted into context-free ones by fine individuation.
7. Provided her preferences are *complete*, that is: for any pair of alternatives, either she prefers one to the other or she is indifferent between them. Then, if she does not prefer B_c to B_a, either she prefers B_a to B_c, or she is indifferent between them. Consequently, since she prefers A_b to B_a, she prefers A_b to B_c. Similarly, if she does not prefer C_a to C_b, she prefers B_c to C_a, and if she does not prefer A_b to A_c, she prefers C_a to A_b. So she prefers A_b to B_c, B_c to C_a, and C_a to A_b. This is an intransitivity.
8. Savage, *The Foundations of Statistics*.
9. First by Maurice Allais in 'The foundations of a positive theory of choice involving risk'. See also, for example, Edward McClennen, 'Sure-thing doubts'.
10. See Paul Samuelson, 'Probability, utility and the independence axiom'.
11. I have gone into them in my *Weighing Goods*, chap. 5.
12. The following alternative, tighter principle seems implausible: that it is not rational to have a preference between two alternatives that are equally good. Suppose one alternative is better for one person, and the other for someone else. These two considerations might exactly balance, so that the alternatives are equally good. Even so, it seems rational for one of these people to prefer the alternative that is better for herself.
13. I am not concerned with the question of 'radical interpretation' discussed by Donald Davidson in *Inquiries into Truth and Interpretation* and David Lewis in 'Radical interpretation', amongst others. This question is about how a person's preferences can come to be understood by an observer from the outside. My question is about how rationality can guide a person from the inside. The answers to the two questions have many points of contact, and the questions are treated together by Susan Hurley in *Natural Reasons*, especially chap. 5. But the answers also diverge at many points. For one thing, intelligibility, which is the aim of interpretation, differs from rationality; a person may be intelligible without being rational. For instance, a person (indeed everyone) might regularly attach too much importance in decision making to small probabilities of loss. This is intelligible but irrational. No doubt, as Davidson would point out, it is intelligible only against an extensive background of rationality. But it means that the axioms of conventional decision theory, which represent the requirements of rationality, do not represent the requirements of intelligibility.

Conventional decision theory is therefore not the right instrument for the task of interpretation.

14. I take this version of functionalism from Lewis, 'An argument for the identity theory'.

15. The test is not infallible, because we have to allow for the possibility that offering the person a choice between *A* and *B* may alter her preference between *A* and *B*. A particular preference, that is to say, may be 'finkish'. (See Lewis, 'Dispositional theories of value', p. 117, n. 6.) A finkish preference is not context-free. As n. 6 above explains, under fine individuation Maurice's preferences are context-free, and so not finkish.

16. Perhaps one might make sense of the counterfactual 'if the person were, *per impossibile*, to have a choice between *A* and *B*, . . .', and define a functional role in these terms. But doing that would give us no help with the epistemology of nonpractical preferences. There would be no canonical test of the sort I have described. Knowledge of nonpractical preferences would have to be acquired in one of the ways I am about to consider.

17. Some arguments for this point (at least, for the point that a desire cannot be a feeling) are to be found in Michael Smith, 'The Humean theory of motivation'. Smith's main argument is that a desire has 'propositional content' and a feeling does not. As it stands, I think this argument is inadequate. A desire might be an attitude *to* a proposition, just as fear is an attitude *to* a bull. The fear does not contain the bull, and the desire need not contain the proposition. As the fear is a feeling, so might the desire be. But Philip Pettit has pointed out to me (see Frank Jackson and Philip Pettit, 'Functionalism and broad content') that if a desire for *P* is *necessarily* a desire for *P* rather than for some other proposition (and this seems plausible) then Smith is right. No feeling could be necessarily directed towards *P* rather than towards some other proposition.

18. David Hume, *A Treatise of Human Nature*, Book 2, Part 3, Section 3.

19. By Smith, for instance, in 'The Humean theory of motivation'.

20. Hume, *A Treatise of Human Nature*.

21. *Ibid.*

22. Lewis, 'Desire as belief'.

23. 'Desire, belief, and expectation'.

24. Lewis, 'Dispositional theories of value', p. 121.

6 BOLKER–JEFFREY EXPECTED UTILITY THEORY AND AXIOMATIC UTILITARIANISM

1. Harsanyi, 'Cardinal welfare, individualistic ethics, and interpersonal comparisons of utility'.

2. For instance, Peter Hammond, 'On reconciling Arrow's theory of social choice with Harsanyi's fundamental utilitarianism'; Richard Jeffrey, 'On interpersonal utility theory'; and Amartya Sen, 'Welfare inequalities and Rawlsian axiomatics'.

3. For instance, see his *Rational Behaviour and Bargaining Equilibrium*.

4. See his 'Cardinal utility in welfare economics and in the theory of risk-taking' and 'Cardinal welfare, individualistic ethics, and interpersonal comparisons of utility'.

5. For instance, in K. C. Border, 'More on Harsanyi's cardinal welfare theorem'; Peter Fishburn, 'On Harsanyi's utilitarian cardinal welfare theorem', and Peter Hammond, 'Ex-ante and ex-post welfare optimality under uncertainty'; and 'Ex-post optimality as a dynamically consistent objective'.
6. Savage, *The Foundations of Statistics*.
7. For instance, the proofs by Hammond cited in note 5.
8. Savage, *The Foundations of Statistics*.
9. See my *Weighing Goods*, chap. 10.
10. See Hammond, 'Ex-post optimality as a dynamically consistent objective', and my 'Uncertainty in welfare economics'.
11. *The Foundations of Statistics*, p. 25.
12. Jeffrey, *The Logic of Decision*; Bolker, 'Functions resembling quotients of measures' and 'A simultaneous axiomatization of utility and subjective probability'.
13. *The Logic of Decision*, p. 157.
14. For an account of Boolean algebras, see Roman Sikorski, *Boolean Algebras*.
15. See *ibid.*, p. 58.
16. *The Foundations of Statistics*, p. 31.
17. Bolker, 'A simultaneous axiomatization of utility and subjective probability', p. 337.
18. Bolker, *ibid.* and 'Remarks on "subjective expected utility for conditional primitives"'; Jeffrey, *The Logic of Decision*, p. 161.
19. See Jeffrey, *The Logic of Decision*, pp. 150–5.
20. See *ibid.*, p. 106.
21. *Ibid.*, p. 142.
22. See David Lewis, 'Prisoners' dilemma is a Newcomb problem'.
23. An exception is Terence Horgan in 'Counterfactuals and Newcomb's problem'.
24. See Allan Gibbard and William Harper, 'Counterfactuals and two kinds of expected utility'; David Lewis, 'Causal decision theory'; and Brian Skyrms, 'Causal decision theory'.
25. For instance, R. J. Barro and D. B. Gordon in 'Rules, discretion and reputation'.
26. See Robert Nozick, 'Newcomb's problem'.
27. The connection between the time-inconsistency problem and the Newcomb problem was noticed by Roman Frydman, Gerald O'Driscoll, and Andrew Schotter in 'Rational expectations of government policy'.
28. See Ellery Eells, *Rational Decision and Causality*, and Richard Jeffrey, 'How to probabilize a Newcomb problem'.
29. See Jeffrey, *The Logic of Decision*, pp. 82–3.
30. This distinction is more thoroughly examined in chap. 6 of my *Weighing Goods*.
31. *Review of Economic Studies*, 57 (1990), pp. 477–502.
32. This is proved in the Appendices, not reprinted here.
33. This is proved in the Appendices, not reprinted here.
34. The original edition of the chapter contains a full discussion of this claim.
35. Fishburn, 'On Harsanyi's utilitarian cardinal welfare theorem'.
36. Hammond, 'Ex-post optimality as a dynamically consistent objective'.
37. Hammond, 'Ex-ante and ex-post welfare optimality under uncertainty'.
38. *Weighing Goods*, chap. 7.

7 FAIRNESS

1. Elsewhere, I have applied the theory to the distribution of divisible goods such as income. See my 'What's the good of equality?' and *Weighing Goods*, chap. 9.
2. There are non-maximizing versions of teleology (for instance, Michael Slote's in 'Satisficing consequentialism'), but for simplicity I shall ignore them here.
3. Godwin, *Political Justice*, p. 703.
4. Sidgwick, *The Methods of Ethics*, pp. 414–16.
5. Narveson, 'Utilitarianism and new generations'.
6. The locus classicus for this view is John Rawls, *A Theory of Justice*, pp. 22–7.
7. See, for instance, Anthony Atkinson and Joseph Stiglitz, *Lectures on Public Economics*, pp. 353–5.
8. Nozick, *Anarchy, State and Utopia*, p. 29, n.
9. In 'Taming chance', Jon Elster mentions two examples where weighted lotteries have been used in practice.
10. The arguments of Lewis Kornhauser and Lawrence Sager in 'Just lotteries' are closely parallel to mine in many ways. The main difference is that their arguments permit these authors to recommend a lottery only when claims are exactly equal.
11. An argument like this is used by Jonathan Glover in *Causing Death and Saving Lives*, and by Nicholas Rescher in 'The allocation of exotic life saving therapy'.

8 IS INCOMMENSURABILITY VAGUENESS?

1. This corresponds to condition C2 of Adam Morton's 'Hypercomparatives'.
2. See Morton, 'Comparatives and degrees'.
3. 'Hypercomparatives'. Morton himself deals with the degrees to which predicates are satisfied, but not with degrees of *truth*.
4. Morton assumes we shall eventually reach a level where the indeterminacy is hard, but I am not convinced by his arguments. I think we may reach a level where there is no indeterminacy, however.
5. See Michael Dummett, 'Wang's paradox', and Kit Fine, 'Vagueness, truth and logic'.
6. See Fine, 'Vagueness, truth and logic', pp. 284–5.
7. But see Timothy Williamson, *Vagueness*, pp. 154–6, and the references there.
8. 'Are vague predicates incoherent?', p. 135.
9. Value incommensurability', p. 119.
10. *Weighing Goods*, pp. 136–7.
11. Another example is Charles Blackorby, 'Degrees of cardinality and aggregate partial orderings'.
12. *On Economic Inequality*, chap. 3.
13. *Collective Choice and Social Welfare*, chaps. 7 and 7*.
14. This argument is from *Collective Choice and Social Welfare*.

9 INCOMMENSURABLE VALUES

1. See his 'Are there incommensurable values', his *Well-Being*, chap. 5, and his 'Incommensurability: what's the problem?' The latter is Griffin's most recent piece on the subject, and my main source for the views I attribute to him.

2. Actually, he only doubts the incommensurability of what he calls 'prudential values'. He thinks moral values may be well be incommensurable. (See 'Incommensurability: what's the problem?') But Griffin's 'moral values' are more strictly moral rules such as: 'Do not deliberately kill the innocent.' I take value to be synonymous with goodness, and since these rules are not about goodness, I do not count them as values at all.

3. Griffin, *Well-Being*, p. 80.

4. See my 'Is incommensurability vagueness?', chap. 8 in this volume, for more details.

5. Raz, *The Morality of Freedom*, p. 326.

6. One way it can arise is if one value lexically dominates another. This means that any increase in one value, however small, is better than any increase in the other, however big. Suppose water and whisky are both good, but any increase in the amount of whisky is better than any increase in the amount of water. Suppose the standard is one litre of whisky, and the chain is composed of various amounts of whisky together with one litre of water. Then any option in the chain with less than a litre of whisky is worse than the standard. Any option in the chain with a litre or more of whisky is better than the standard. The chain contains no options in between.

7. Joseph Raz (*The Morality of Freedom*, p. 326) takes the existence of an intermediate zone as a central feature of incommensurability, though not its definition. (I did the same in my 'Choice and value in economics'.) My account of incommensurability agrees with Raz's in many ways.

8. See Timothy Williamson, *Vagueness*.

9. *Well-Being*, pp. 96–8.

10. *Ibid.*, p. 96.

11. *The Morality of Freedom*, p. 324.

12. They are set out in my 'Is incommensurability vagueness?', chap. 8 in this volume.

13. *The Morality of Freedom*, p. 324.

14. Raz develops this argument and responds to it in 'Incommensurability and agency'.

15. The same point is made by Ruth Chang in 'Incommensurability, incomparability and value'.

16. This point is made in my 'Choice and value in economics', and by Raz in *The Morality of Freedom*, pp. 338–40.

17. For instance, see Edward McClennen, *Rationality and Dynamic Choice*.

10 GOODNESS IS REDUCIBLE TO BETTERNESS: THE EVIL OF DEATH IS THE VALUE OF LIFE

1. For accuracy, I should explain this more formally. Many one-place properties can be possessed by objects to a greater or lesser extent. These properties can be treated formally as two-place relations. For instance: _ is wet to extent _, where the first place is for an object and the second for an extent. Similarly, many two-place relations can be satisfied by pairs of objects to a greater or lesser extent. Cardinal comparatives are in this class of relations. They can be treated formally as three-place relations. For instance: _ is taller than _ to extent _, where the first two places are for objects and the third for an extent.

2. *The Logic of Decision*, p. 82. The zero turns out to be the goodness of the necessarily true proposition.
3. Parfit, *Reasons and Persons*, p. 433.
4. *Ibid.*
5. *Ibid.*, pp. 395 and 489.
6. *Ibid.*, p. 489.
7. *Ibid.*, p. 487.
8. *Ibid.*, p. 388.
9. *Principia Ethica*, p. 10.
10. *Ibid.*, pp. 15–16.
11. Francis Kamm accepts this as a plausible answer, in *Creation and Abortion*, pp. 130–1.
12. Nagel, 'Death', p. 9.
13. *Ibid.*, p. 10.
14. Epicurus, 'Letter to Menoeceus', p. 85.
15. Nagel, 'Death', p. 4.
16. *Ibid.*, pp. 4–7. My views on Nagel's response are in complete agreement with Fred Feldman's expressed in 'Some puzzles about the evil of death'.
17. Nagel, 'Death', p. 6.
18. *Ibid.*, p. 3.

11 TRYING TO VALUE A LIFE

1. I have since learnt that this remark is incorrect. See R. Boadway, 'The welfare foundations of cost–benefit analysis'.
2. Mishan, *Cost–Benefit Analysis*, chaps. 22 and 23. See also Jacques Dréze, 'L'utilité sociale d'une vie humaine'.
3. This remark is retracted on pp. 170–1 of my *Weighing Goods*.
4. *Cost–Benefit Analysis*, p. 172.

12 STRUCTURED AND UNSTRUCTURED VALUATION

1. See, for instance, A. Mehrez and A. Gafni, 'Quality-adjusted life years'.
2. See, for instance, Amos Tversky and Daniel Kahneman, 'Rational choice and the framing of decisions'.
3. Jones-Lee, Loomes, and Philips, 'Valuing the prevention of non-fatal road injuries'.
4. There is fuller discussion in my *Weighing Goods*, chap. 7.
5. 'The social rate of discount and the optimal rate of investment', p. 97.
6. See Jacques Drèze, 'From the "value of life" to the economics and ethics of population' and my 'Reply to Blackorby and Donaldson, and Drèze'.

13 QALYS

1. For instance, see Alan Williams, 'The value of qalys'.
2. For instance, see John Harris, 'QALYfying the value of life'.
3. See Michael Lockwood, 'Quality of life and resource allocation' and my 'Good, fairness and qalys'.

4. See, for instance, Graham Loomes and Lynda McKenzie's useful example in 'The scope and limitations of qaly measures', p. 97.
5. In my *Weighing Goods*, chaps. 5, 7, and 10.
6. For instance, see, Angus Deaton and John Muellbauer, *Economics and Consumer Behavior*, pp. 137–42.
7. For instance, see my *Weighing Goods*, p. 74.
8. See the informal exercise in Pliskin, Shepard, and Weinstein, 'Utility functions for life years and health status'.
9. See Weinstein, 'Risky choices in medical decision making'.
10. *Ibid.*, p. 205.
11. John Miyamoto and Stephen Eraker, 'Parameter estimates for a qaly utility model'.
12. For instance, by Claire Gudex in 'The qaly'.
13. Bernoulli in 'Exposition of a new theory on the measurement of risk' and Harsanyi in, for instance, 'Can the maximin principle serve as a basis for morality?', p. 600.
14. 'Utility functions for life years and health status'.
15. For instance, George Torrance, Michael Boyle, and Sargent Horwood in 'Application of multi-attribute utility theory'.
16. There is a discussion of this hypothesis in my *Weighing Goods*, pp. 142–8 and 213–22.
17. In my *Weighing Goods*.
18. This no longer (in 1998) seems correct to me.
19. *Reasons and Persons*, chap. 14.
20. *The Economics of Welfare*, pp. 24–6.
21. 'Commodities, characteristics of commodities, characteristics of people, utilities, and the quality of life'.
22. Torrance, Boyle, and Horwood, 'Application of multi-attribute utility theory', p. 1051.
23. See my *Weighing Goods*, chap. 9.
24. Torrance, 'Measurement of health state utilities for economic appraisal', p. 17.
25. See my 'Good, fairness and qalys'.
26. Boyle, Torrance, Sinclair, and Horwood, 'Economic evaluation of neonatal intensive care of very-low-birth-weight infants'.
27. Kuhse and Singer, 'Age and the allocation of medical resources'.
28. Narveson, 'Utilitarianism and new generations'.
29. See my *Weighing Goods*, pp. 11–12.
30. See my 'The economic value of life'.
31. *The Foundations of Statistics*.
32. See the endpapers *ibid.*
33. *Ibid.*, p. 23.
34. Pliskin, Shepard, and Weinstein, 'Utility functions for life years and health status', pp. 210–11.
35. There is another good critique by Loomes and McKenzie in 'The scope and limitations of qaly measures'.
36. Gorman, 'The structure of utility functions'.

14 THE VALUE OF LIVING

1. One exception is W. B. Arthur, 'The economics of risk to life'.
2. For instance, M. W. Jones-Lee, *The Economics of Safety and Physical Risk*.
3. For instance, Derek Parfit, *Reasons and Persons*, Part IV.
4. See the discussion in my 'Trying to value a life', chap. 11 in this volume.
5. First in Harsanyi's 'Cardinal welfare, individualistic ethics, and interpersonal comparisons of utility'.
6. Hammond, 'Consequentialist demographic norms and parenting rights'.
7. Blackorby and Donaldson, 'Social criteria for evaluating population change'.
8. Narveson, 'Utilitarianism and new generations'.
9. There is a very extensive discussion of the idea in Parfit's *Reasons and Persons*, Part IV, and a further discussion in my 'The value of a person', chap. 15 in this volume.
10. For more details see my *Counting the Cost of Global Warming*, chap. 4.
11. Blackorby and Donaldson, 'Social criteria for evaluating population change'.
12. Parfit, *Reasons and Persons*, chap. 17.
13. See Michael Boyle, George Torrance, J. C. Sinclair, and Sargent Horwood, 'Economic evaluation of neonatal intensive care of very-low-birth-weight infants'.
14. Kuhse and Singer, 'Age and the allocation of medical resources'.

15 THE VALUE OF A PERSON

1. Narveson, 'Moral problems of population', p. 73 in the reprinted version.
2. Parfit, *Reasons and Persons*, pp. 419–41.
3. This chapter only adds to the large existing literature on the intransitivity that seems to be generated by the basic intuition. The seminal discussion is Parfit's, in *Reasons and Persons*, pp. 419–41. An important recent contribution is Peter Singer's in 'Possible preferences'.
4. One of the best worked-out theories of this type is in Charles Blackorby and David Donaldson, 'Social criteria for evaluating population change', and Charles Blackorby, Walter Bossert and David Donaldson, 'Intertemporal population ethics'. The term 'impersonal' is not a good one. None of these theories suggests there is a sort of good that does not belong to a person.
5. There is a critique of the work of Blackorby, Donaldson, and Bossert in my 'The welfare economics of population'.
6. Many of Narveson's arguments are expressed in terms of what we ought to do, rather than what is better. There is a persuasive argument on deontic lines in Paul Seabright, 'Creating persons'.
7. See his 'Two places good, four places better', which is a symposium-partner of this chapter's.
8. 'Intransitivity and the mere addition paradox', p. 159.
9. 'The Makropulos case', p. 85.
10. I first suggested this idea in 'Some principles of population'. It was adopted by Partha Dasgupta in 'Lives and well-being'.
11. See Epicurus, 'Letters to Menoeceus', particularly p. 85. In 'The Makropulos case', Bernard Williams comments particularly on a different Epicurean work: Lucretius' *On the Nature of the Universe*.

12. Amartya Sen, 'Quasi-transitivity, rational choice and collective decisions'.
13. I shall describe the most recent version of Dasgupta's theory, which appears in his *An Inquiry into Well-Being and Destitution*, pp. 377–95. An earlier version appeared in his 'Lives and well-being'. David Heyd supports a similar relativism in *Genethics*.
14. *Inquiry into Well-Being and Destitution*, p. 386.
15. 'Lives and well-being', p. 120.

Bibliography

Allais, Maurice, 'The foundations of a positive theory of choice involving risk and a criticism of the postulates and axioms of the American School', in *Expected Utility Hypothesis and the Allais Paradox*, edited by Maurice Allais and Ole Hagen, Reidel, 1979, pp. 27–145.

Arrow, Kenneth J., *Collected Papers*, vol. 1, *Social Choice and Justice*, Blackwell, 1984.

'Extended sympathy and the possibility of social choice', *American Economic Review: Papers and Proceedings*, 67 (1977), pp. 219–25, reprinted in his *Social Choice and Justice*, pp. 147–61.

Arthur, W. B., 'The economics of risk to life', *American Economic Review*, 71 (1981), pp. 54–64.

Atkinson, Anthony B., and Joseph E. Stiglitz, *Lectures on Public Economics*, McGraw-Hill, 1980.

Barro, R. J., and D. B. Gordon, 'Rules, discretion and reputation in a model of monetary policy', *Journal of Monetary Economics*, 12 (1983), pp. 101–21.

Bentham, Jeremy, *An Introduction to the Principles of Morals and Legislation*, Pickering (London), 1823.

Bernoulli, Daniel, 'Specimen theoriae novae de mensura sortis', *Commentarii Academiae Scientiarum Imperialis Petropolitanae*, 5 (1738), translated by Louise Sommer as 'Exposition of a new theory on the measurement of risk', *Econometrica*, 22 (1954), pp. 23–36.

Blackorby, Charles, 'Degrees of cardinality and aggregate partial orderings', *Econometrica*, 43 (1975), pp. 845–52.

Blackorby, Charles, Walter Bossert, and David Donaldson, 'Intertemporal population ethics: a welfarist approach', *Econometrica*, 65 (1995), pp. 1303–20.

Blackorby, Charles, and David Donaldson, 'Social criteria for evaluating population change', *Journal of Public Economics*, 25 (1984), pp. 13–33.

Boadway, R., 'The welfare foundations of cost–benefit analysis', *Economic Journal*, 84 (1982), pp. 926–39.

Bolker, Ethan D., 'Functions resembling quotients of measures', *Transactions of the American Mathematical Society*, 124 (1966), pp. 292–312.

'Remarks on "subjective expected utility for conditional primitives"', in *Essays on Economic Behavior Under Uncertainty*, edited by M. Balch, D. McFadden, and S. Wu, North-Holland, 1974, pp. 79–82.

'A simultaneous axiomatization of utility and subjective probability', *Philosophy of Science*, 34 (1967), pp. 333–40.

Border, K. C., 'More on Harsanyi's cardinal welfare theorem', *Social Choice and Welfare*, 2 (1985), pp. 279–81.

Boyle, Michael H., George H. Torrance, J. C. Sinclair, and Sargent P. Horwood, 'Economic evaluation of neonatal intensive care of very-low-birth-weight infants', *New England Journal of Medicine*, 308 (1983), pp. 1330–7.

Broome, John, 'Choice and value in economics', *Oxford Economic Papers*, 30 (1978), pp. 313–33.

Counting the Cost of Global Warming, White Horse Press, 1992.

'Desire, belief, and expectation', *Mind*, 100 (1991), pp. 265–7.

'The economic value of life', *Economica*, 52 (1985), pp. 281–94.

'Good, fairness and qalys', in *Philosophy and Medical Welfare*, edited by J. M. Bell and S. Mendus, Cambridge University Press, 1988, pp. 57–73.

The Microeconomics of Capitalism, Academic Press, 1983.

'Rationality and the sure-thing principle', in *Thoughtful Economic Man*, edited by Gay Meeks, Cambridge University Press, 1991, pp. 74–102.

'Reply to Blackorby and Donaldson, and Drèze', *Recherches Economiques de Louvain*, 58 (1992), pp. 167–71.

'Some principles of population', in *Economics, Growth and Sustainable Environments*, edited by David Collard, David Pearce, and David Ulph, Macmillan, 1988, pp. 85–96.

'Uncertainty in welfare economics, and the value of life', in *The Value of Life and Safety*, edited by Michael W. Jones-Lee, North-Holland, 1982, pp. 201–16.

Weighing Goods: Equality, Uncertainty and Time, Blackwell, 1991.

'The welfare economics of population', *Oxford Economic Papers*, 48 (1996), pp. 177–93.

'What's the good of equality?', in *Current Issues in Microeconomics*, edited by John Hey, Macmillan, 1989, pp. 236–62.

Burns, Linda Claire, *Vagueness: An Investigation into Natural Languages and the Sorites Paradox*, Kluwer, 1991.

Chang, Ruth, 'Introduction', in *Incommensurability, Incomparability and Practical Reason*, edited by Ruth Chang, Harvard University Press, 1998, pp. 1–34.

Cowen, Tyler, and Derek Parfit, 'Against the social discount rate', in *Justice Between Age Groups and Generations*, edited by Peter Laslett and James S. Fishkin, Yale University Press, 1992, pp. 144–61.

Culyer, A. J., 'Commodities, characteristics of commodities, characteristics of people, utilities, and the quality of life', in *Quality of Life: Perspectives and Policy*, edited by Sally Baldwin, Christine Godfrey, and Carol Propper, Routledge, 1990, pp. 9–27.

Dasgupta, Partha, *An Inquiry into Well-Being and Destitution*, Oxford University Press, 1993.

'Lives and well-being', *Social Choice and Welfare*, 5 (1988), pp. 103–26, reprinted as 'Population size and the quality of life', *Proceedings of the Aristotelian Society*, Supplementary Volume 63 (1989), pp. 23–40.

Dasgupta, Partha, and Geoffrey Heal, *Economic Theory and Exhaustible Resources*, Cambridge University Press, 1979.

Davidson, Donald, *Inquiries into Truth and Interpretation*, Oxford University Press, 1984.

Deaton, Angus, and John Muellbauer, *Economics and Consumer Behavior*, Cambridge University Press, 1980.

Debreu, Gerard, *Theory of Value*, Wiley, 1959.

Drèze, Jacques, 'From the "value of life" to the economics and ethics of population: the path is purely methodological', *Recherches Economiques de Louvain*, 58 (1992), pp. 147–66.

 'L'utilité sociale d'une vie humaine', *Revue Française de Recherche Opérationelle*, 22 (1962), pp. 93–118.

Dummett, Michael, 'Wang's paradox', *Synthese*, 30 (1975), pp. 301–24.

Edgeworth, F. Y., *Mathematical Psychics*, Kegan Paul, 1881.

Eells, Ellery, *Rational Decision and Causality*, Cambridge University Press, 1982.

Ellsberg, Daniel, 'Classic and current notions of "measurable utility"', *Economic Journal*, 64 (1954), pp. 528–56.

Elster, Jon, 'Taming chance: randomization in individual and social decisions', *Tanner Lectures on Human Values*, 9 (1988).

Epicurus, 'Letter to Menoeceus', in *Epicurus: The Extant Remains*, translated and edited by Cyril Bailey, Oxford University Press, 1926, pp. 83–93.

Feldman, Fred, 'Some puzzles about the evil of death', *Philosophical Review*, 100 (1991), pp. 205–27.

Fine, Kit, 'Vagueness, truth and logic', *Synthese*, 30 (1975), pp. 265–300.

Fishburn, Peter C., 'On Harsanyi's utilitarian cardinal welfare theorem', *Theory and Decision*, 17 (1984), pp. 21–8.

Frydman, Roman, Gerald P. O'Driscoll, and Andrew Schotter, 'Rational expectations of government policy: an application of Newcomb's problem', *Southern Economic Journal*, 49 (1982), pp. 311–19.

Gibbard, Allan, and William L. Harper, 'Counterfactuals and two kinds of expected utility', in *Foundations and Applications of Decision Theory*, vol. I, edited by C. A. Hooker, J. J. Leach, and Edward F. McClennen, Reidel, 1978, pp. 125–62.

Glover, Jonathan, *Causing Death and Saving Lives*, Penguin, 1977.

Godwin, William, *Political Justice*, Penguin Edition, 1976.

Gorman, W. M., 'The structure of utility functions', *Review of Economic Studies*, 35 (1968), pp. 367–90.

Griffin, James, 'Are there incommensurable values?', *Philosophy and Public Affairs*, 7 (1977), pp. 39–59.

 'Incommensurability: what's the problem?', in *Incommensurability, Incomparability and Practical Reason*, edited by Ruth Chang, Harvard University Press, 1998, pp. 35–51.

 Well-Being: Its Meaning, Measurement and Moral Importance, Oxford University Press, 1986.

Gudex, Claire, 'The qaly: how can it be used?', in *Quality of Life: Perspectives and Policy*, edited by Sally Baldwin, Christine Godfrey, and Carol Propper, Routledge, 1990, pp. 218–30.

Hammond, Peter. J., 'Consequentialist demographic norms and parenting rights', *Social Choice and Welfare*, 5 (1988), pp. 127–45.

 'Ex-ante and ex-post welfare optimality under uncertainty', *Economica*, 48 (1981), pp. 235–50.

 'Ex-post optimality as a dynamically consistent objective for collective choice under uncertainty', in *Social Choice and Welfare*, edited by Prasanta K. Pattanaik and Maurice Salles, North-Holland, 1983, pp. 175–206.

'On reconciling Arrow's theory of social choice with Harsanyi's fundamental utilitarianism', in *Arrow and the Foundations of the Theory of Economic Policy*, edited by George R. Feiwel, Macmillan, 1987, pp. 179–221.

Harris, John, 'QALYfying the value of life', *Journal of Medical Ethics*, 13 (1987), pp. 117–23.

Harsanyi, John C., 'Can the maximin principle serve as a basis for morality? A critique of John Rawls's theory', *American Political Science Review*, 69 (1975), pp. 594–606.

'Cardinal utility in welfare economics and in the theory of risk-taking', *Journal of Political Economy*, 61 (1953), pp. 434–5, reprinted in *Essays on Ethics, Social Behavior, and Scientific Explanation*, Reidel, 1976, pp. 3–5.

'Cardinal welfare, individualistic ethics, and interpersonal comparisons of utility', *Journal of Political Economy*, 63 (1955), pp. 309–21, reprinted in his *Essays on Ethics, Social Behavior, and Scientific Explanation*, Reidel, 1976, pp. 6–23.

Rational Behaviour and Bargaining Equilibrium in Games and Social Situations, Cambridge University Press, 1977.

Heyd, David, Genethics: *Moral Issues in the Creation of People*, University of California Press, 1992.

Hicks, John, and R. G. D. Allen, 'A reconsideration of the theory of value', *Economica*, 1 (1934), pp. 52–76, 196–219.

Horgan, Terence, 'Counterfactuals and Newcomb's problem', *Journal of Philosophy*, 78 (1981), pp. 331–56.

Hotelling, H., 'The economics of exhaustible resources', *Journal of Political Economy*, 39 (1931), pp. 137–75.

Hume, David, *A Treatise of Human Nature*, edited by L. A. Selby-Bigge and P. H. Nidditch, Oxford University Press, 1978.

Hurley, Susan, *Natural Reasons*, Oxford University Press, 1989.

Jackson, Frank, and Philip Pettit, 'Functionalism and broad content', *Mind*, 97 (1988), pp. 381–400.

Jeffrey, Richard C., 'How to probabilize a Newcomb problem', in *Probability and Causality*, edited by James H. Fenton, Reidel, 1988, pp. 241–51.

The Logic of Decision, 2nd edn, University of Chicago Press, 1983.

'On interpersonal utility theory', *Journal of Philosophy*, 68 (1971), pp. 647–56.

Jevons, W. Stanley, *The Theory of Political Economy*, Macmillan, 1871.

Johnston, Mark, 'Dispositional theories of value', *Proceedings of the Aristotelian Society*, Supplementary Volume 63 (1989), pp. 139–74.

Jones-Lee, M. W., *The Economics of Safety and Physical Risk*, Blackwell, 1989.

Jones-Lee, M. W., G. Loomes, and P. R. Philips, 'Valuing the prevention of non-fatal road injuries: contingent valuation vs standard gambles', *Oxford Economic Papers*, 47 (1995), pp. 676–95.

Kamm, F. M., *Creation and Abortion: An Essay in Moral and Legal Philosophy*, Oxford University Press, 1992.

Kolm, Serge-Christophe, *Justice et équité*, Centre National de la Recherche Scientifique, 1972.

Kornhauser, Lewis A., and Lawrence G. Sager, 'Just lotteries', *Social Science Information*, 27 (1988), pp. 483–516.

Kuhse, Helga, and Peter Singer, 'Age and the allocation of medical resources', *Journal of Medicine and Philosophy*, 13 (1988), pp. 101–16.

Lewis, David, 'An argument for the identity theory', *Journal of Philosophy*, 63 (1966), pp. 17–25, reprinted with additions in his *Philosophical Papers*, vol. I, Oxford University Press, 1983, pp. 99–107.

  'Causal decision theory', *Australasian Journal of Philosophy*, 59 (1981), pp. 5–30.

  'Desire as belief', *Mind*, 97 (1988), pp. 323–32.

  'Dispositional theories of value', *Proceedings of the Aristotelian Society*, Supplementary Volume 63 (1989), pp. 113–37.

  'Prisoners' dilemma is a Newcomb problem', *Philosophy and Public Affairs*, 8 (1979), pp. 235–40.

  'Radical interpretation', *Synthese*, 23 (1974), pp. 331–44.

Lockwood, Michael, 'Quality of life and resource allocation', in *Philosophy and Medical Welfare*, edited by J. M. Bell and S. Mendus, Cambridge University Press, 1988, pp. 33–56.

Loomes, Graham, and Lynda McKenzie, 'The scope and limitations of qaly measures', in *Quality of Life: Perspectives and Policy*, edited by Sally Baldwin, Christine Godfrey, and Carol Propper, Routledge, 1990, pp. 84–102.

Lucretius, *On the Nature of the Universe*, Penguin, 1951.

McClennen, Edward C., *Rationality and Dynamic Choice*, Cambridge University Press, 1990.

  'Sure-thing doubts', in *Foundations of Utility and Risk Theory with Applications*, edited by B. P. Stigum and F. Wenstop, Reidel, 1983, pp. 117–36.

Machina, Mark J., 'Dynamic consistency and non-expected utility models of choice under uncertainty', in *Essays in the Foundations of Decision Theory*, edited by Michael Bacharach and Susan Hurley, Blackwell, 1990, pp. 000–00.

McMahan, Jeff, 'Death and the value of life', *Ethics*, 99 (1988), pp. 32–61.

Marglin, Stephen A., 'The social rate of discount and the optimal rate of investment', *Quarterly Journal of Economics*, 77 (1963), pp. 95–111.

Marshall, Alfred, *Principles of Economics*, 8th edn, Macmillan, 1920.

Mehrez, A., and A. Gafni, 'Quality-adjusted life years, utility theory and healthy-years equivalents', *Medical Decision Making*, 9 (1989), pp. 142–9.

Mill, John Stuart, *Utilitarianism*, in his *Collected Works*, vol. X, Toronto University Press, 1969, pp. 203–59.

Mirrlees, J. A., 'The economic uses of utilitarianism', in *Utilitarianism and Beyond*, edited by Amartya K. Sen and Bernard Williams, Cambridge University Press, 1982, pp. 219–38.

Mishan, E. J., *Cost–Benefit Analysis*, North-Holland, 1969.

Miyamoto, John M., and Stephen A. Eraker, 'Parameter estimates for a qaly utility model', *Medical Decision Making*, 5 (1985), pp. 191–213.

Moore, G. E., *Principia Ethica*, Cambridge University Press, 1903.

Morton, Adam, 'Comparatives and degrees', *Analysis*, 44 (1984), pp. 16–20.

  'Hypercomparatives', *Synthese*, 111 (1997), pp. 97–114.

  'Two places good, four places better', *Proceedings of the Aristotelian Society*, Supplementary Volume 68 (1994), pp. 187–98.

Nagel, Thomas, 'Death', in his *Mortal Questions*, Cambridge University Press, 1979, pp. 1–10.

Narveson, Jan, 'Moral problems of population', *Monist*, 57 (1973), pp. 000–00, reprinted in *Ethics and Population*, edited by Michael D. Bayles, Schenkman, 1976, pp. 59–80.

'Utilitarianism and new generations', *Mind*, 76 (1967), pp. 62–72.

Nozick, Robert, *Anarchy, State and Utopia*, Basic Books, 1974.

'Newcomb's problem and two principles of choice', in *Essays in Honor of Carl G. Hempel*, edited by Nicholas Rescher, Reidel, 1969, pp. 114–46.

Olson, Mancur, and Martin Bailey, 'Positive time preference', *Journal of Political Economy*, 89 (1981), pp. 1–25.

Parfit, Derek, *Reasons and Persons*, Oxford University Press, 1984.

Peacocke, Christopher, 'Are vague predicates incoherent?', *Synthese*, 46 (1981), pp. 121–41.

Pigou, A. C., *The Economics of Welfare*, 4th edn, Macmillan, 1932.

Pliskin, Joseph S., Donald S. Shepard, and Milton C. Weinstein, 'Utility functions for life years and health status', *Operations Research*, 28 (1980), pp. 206–24.

Ramsey, Frank, 'A mathematical theory of saving', *Economic Journal*, 38 (1928), pp. 543–9, reprinted in his *Foundations: Essays in Philosophy, Logic, Mathematics and Economics*, edited by D. H. Mellor, London: Routledge and Kegan Paul, 1978, pp. 261–81.

Rawls, John, 'Social unity and primary goods', in *Utilitarianism and Beyond*, edited by Amartya Sen and Bernard Williams, Cambridge University Press, 1982, pp. 159–86.

A Theory of Justice, Oxford University Press, 1972.

Raz, Joseph, 'Incommensurability and agency', in *Incommensurability, Incomparability and Practical Reason*, edited by Ruth Chang, Harvard University Press, 1998, pp. 110–28.

The Morality of Freedom, Oxford University Press, 1986.

'Value incommensurability: some preliminaries', *Proceedings of the Aristotelian Society*, 86 (1985–6), pp. 117–34.

Rescher, Nicholas, 'The allocation of exotic life saving therapy', *Ethics*, 79 (1969), pp. 173–86.

Robbins, Lionel, *An Essay on the Scope and Nature of Economic Science*, 2nd edn, Macmillan, 1935.

Samuelson, Paul A., 'Probability, utility and the independence axiom', *Econometrica*, 20 (1952), pp. 670–8.

Savage, Leonard J., *The Foundations of Statistics*, 2nd edn, Dover, 1972.

Schelling, Thomas C., 'Self-command in practice, in policy, and in a theory of rational choice', *American Economic Review Papers and Proceedings*, 74 (1984), pp. 1–11.

Seabright, Paul, 'Creating persons', *Proceedings of the Aristotelian Society*, Supplementary Volume 63 (1989), pp. 41–54.

Sen, Amartya K., *Collective Choice and Social Welfare*, Holden-Day and Oliver and Boyd, 1970.

On Economic Inequality, Oxford University Press, 1973.

On Ethics and Economics, Blackwell, 1987.

'Quasi-transitivity, rational choice and collective decisions', *Review of Economic Studies*, 36 (1969), pp. 381–93, reprinted in his *Choice, Welfare and Measurement*, Blackwell and MIT Press, 1982, pp. 118–34.

The Standard of Living, edited by Geoffrey Hawthorne, Cambridge University Press, 1987.

'Utility: ideas and terminology', *Economics and Philosophy*, 7 (1991), pp. 277–83.

'Welfare inequalities and Rawlsian axiomatics', *Theory and Decision*, 7 (1976), pp. 243–62, reprinted in *Foundational Problems in the Special Sciences*, edited by R. Butts and J. Hintikka, Reidel, 1977, pp. 271–92.

Sidgwick, Henry, *The Methods of Ethics*, 7th edn, Macmillan, 1907.

Sikorski, Roman, *Boolean Algebras*, Springer-Verlag, 1960.

Singer, Peter, 'Possible preferences', in *Preferences*, edited by Christoph Fehige and Ulla Wessels, de Gruyter, 1998, pp. 000–00.

Skyrms, Brian, 'Causal decision theory', *Journal of Philosophy*, 79 (1982), pp. 695–711.

Slote, Michael, 'Satisficing consequentialism', *Proceedings of the Aristotelian Society*, Supplementary Volume 58 (1984), pp. 139–63.

Smith, Michael, 'The Humean theory of motivation', *Mind*, 96 (1987), pp. 36–61.

Solow, Robert, 'The economics of resources or the resources of economics', *American Economic Review: Papers and Proceedings*, 64 (1974), pp. 1–14.

Stiglitz, Joseph, 'The rate of discount for benefit–cost analysis and the theory of second best', in *Discounting for Time and Risk in Energy Policy*, by Robert Lind et al., Resources for the Future, 1982, pp. 151–204.

Temkin, Larry S., 'Intransitivity and the mere addition paradox', *Philosophy and Public Affairs*, 16 (1987), pp. 138–87.

Tinbergen, Jan, 'Welfare economics and income distribution', *American Economic Review: Papers and Proceedings*, 47 (1957), pp. 490–503.

Torrance, George W., 'Measurement of health state utilities for economic appraisal', *Journal of Health Economics*, 5 (1985), pp. 1–30.

Torrance, George W., Michael H. Boyle, and Sargent P. Horwood, 'Application of multi-attribute utility theory to measure social preferences for health states', *Operations Research*, 30 (1982), pp. 1043–69.

Tversky, Amos, and Daniel Kahneman, 'Rational choice and the framing of decisions', *Journal of Business*, 59 (1986), pp. 250–78.

Weinstein, Milton C., 'Risky choices in medical decision making: a survey', *Geneva Papers on Risk and Insurance*, 11 (1986), pp. 197–216.

Wiggins, David, 'Claims of need', in *Morality and Objectivity*, edited by Ted Honderich, Routledge and Kegan Paul, 1985, pp. 149–202, reprinted in his *Needs, Values, Truth*, Blackwell, 1987, pp. 1–57.

Williams, Alan, 'The value of qalys', *Health and Social Service Journal* (18 July 1985), pp. 3–5.

Williams, Bernard, 'The Makropulos case: reflections on the tedium of immortality', in his *Problems of the Self*, Cambridge University Press, 1973, pp. 82–100.

Williamson, Timothy, *Vagueness*, Routledge, 1994.

Index

Printed in the United Kingdom
by Lightning Source UK Ltd.
105181UKS00002B/4